PRAISE FOR
The Crystal Bluep

"There are dozens of books about the use of crystals for healing and personal exploration. Beatriz Singer's *The Crystal Blueprint* is unique because it dives deep into the history, folklore, science, and speculation about why crystals have fascinated us for millennia. For a broad-ranging survey about one particular type of crystal (quartz), and what it might do for you, this is the book to get."

— **Dean Radin**, Ph.D., chief scientist, Institute of Noetic Sciences, and author of *Real Magic*

"*The Crystal Blueprint* is required reading for any lover of crystals—and anyone who believes in transformation from the inside out."

— **Heather Askinosie and Timmi Jandro**, founders and creators of Energy Muse and authors of *Crystal Muse*

"*The Crystal Blueprint* refocuses and broadens our investigation of the wondrously interconnected relationship between the human and mineral kingdoms."

— **Lawrence Stoller**, founder of Crystalworks, award-winning artist, and author of *Primal Beauty*

The Crystal
Blueprint

Hay House Titles of Related Interest

YOU CAN HEAL YOUR LIFE: The Movie, starring Louise Hay & Friends
(available as a 1-DVD program, an expanded 2-DVD set,
and an online streaming video)
Learn more at www.hayhouse.com/louise-movie

THE SHIFT, starring Dr. Wayne W. Dyer
(available as a 1-DVD program, an expanded 2-DVD set,
and an online streaming video)
Learn more at www.hayhouse.com/the-shift-movie

Breaking the Habit of Being Yourself: How to Lose Your
Mind and Create a New One, by Dr. Joe Dispenza

Crystal Muse: Everyday Rituals to Tune in to the Real You,
by Heather Askinosie and Timmi Jandro

Crystals: How to Use Crystals and Their Energy to Enhance
Your Life (Hay House Basics), by Judy Hall

Energy Strands: The Ultimate Guide to Clearing the Cords
That Are Constricting Your Life, by Denise Linn

Resilience from the Heart: The Power to Thrive in Life's Extremes,
by Gregg Braden

All of the above are available at your local bookstore,
or may be ordered by visiting:

Hay House USA: www.hayhouse.com®
Hay House Australia: www.hayhouse.com.au
Hay House UK: www.hayhouse.co.uk
Hay House India: www.hayhouse.co.in

The Crystal Blueprint

RECONNECT WITH YOUR AUTHENTIC SELF
THROUGH THE ANCIENT WISDOM AND
MODERN SCIENCE OF QUARTZ CRYSTALS

BEATRIZ SINGER

HAY HOUSE, INC.
Carlsbad, California • New York City
London • Sydney • New Delhi

Published in the United States by: Hay House, Inc.: www.hayhouse.com®
Published in Australia by: Hay House Australia Pty. Ltd.: www.hayhouse.com.au
Published in the United Kingdom by: Hay House UK, Ltd.: www.hayhouse.co.uk
Published in India by: Hay House Publishers India: www.hayhouse.co.in

Cover design:: Barbara Levan Fisher • *Interior design:* Bryn Starr Best
Images on pages 19, 81, 99, 118, 122, 123, 125, 127, 133, 134, 135, 136, 147, 148, 150, 152, 153, 155, 157, 163, 211, 218, 229, 230, and 253 courtesy of Diseño Natural Armónico.

Excerpts from *The Dhammapada,* by Gil Fronsdal, ©2005 by Egil Fronsdal. Reprinted by arrangement with The Permissions Company, Inc., on behalf of Shambhala Publications, Inc., Boulder, Colorado, www.shambhala.com

Permission to reprint excerpt from *Upanishads* granted from Gnosophia Publishers. Credit: "Oneness / Unity / Wholeness," *Wisdom for the Soul: Five Millennia of Prescriptions for Spiritual Healing,* Larry Chang, ed., 2006.

Excerpt from *The Magic of Jewels & Charms* by George Frederick Kunz, © 1971. Reprinted by permission of Dover Publications, Inc.

Library of Congress Cataloging-in-Publication Data

Names: Singer, Beatriz.
Title: The crystal blueprint : reconnect with your authentic self through the
  ancient wisdom and modern science of quartz crystals / Beatriz Singer.
Description: 1st edition. | Carlsbad, California : Hay House, Inc., 2019. |
  Includes bibliographical references.
Identifiers: LCCN 2018034240| ISBN 9781401954857 (tradepaper : alk. paper) |
  ISBN 9781401954864 (ebook)
Subjects: LCSH: Quartz crystals--Therapeutic use.
Classification: LCC RZ415 .S56 2019 | DDC 615.8/52--dc23 LC record available at
https://lccn.loc.gov/2018034240

Tradepaper ISBN: 978-1-4019-5485-7
e-book ISBN: 978-1-4019-5486-4

10 9 8 7 6 5 4 3 2 1
1st edition, February 2019

Printed in the United States of America

. . . .

May the crystalline light that starts to shine today

within you illuminate and bring blessings to others . . .

May this light take root and spread seeds to the

very darkest corners of the mind of humanity . . .

May it grow so intensely that separation

no longer resonates with us.

May all be the creators and perpetuators

of a new paradigm that prioritizes a crystalline self.

Through our interconnectedness, may we develop authentic

pathways so that we can begin to live now the crystalline world we

owe to ourselves and future generations.

. . . .

CONTENTS

INTRODUCTION

A New Crystal Paradigm

"Crystals hold the key to unlocking a vast new technology based upon the manipulation of etheric energies for healing as well as other applications. Because of their special geometric patterning, crystals are able to tap into universal energy patterns and frequencies that science is only beginning to discover."

— RICHARD GERBER[1]

It is estimated that ten billion quartz crystals are used every year in electronic devices.[2] They are found in smartphones, wireless applications, computers, credit cards, wristwatches, digital cameras, TVs, automobiles, stoves, medical devices, and much more. As quartz crystals are one of the main drivers behind the Digital Revolution, it's almost impossible to imagine modern life without them.

Moreover, these same crystals we see in so much of our technology have been used over the course of many centuries and by many different cultures around the world for *healing*. Crystal healing is alive and well today, with modern-day healers harnessing the energy of quartz crystals to help alleviate all manner of contemporary suffering.

What is it that has drawn scientists and engineers around the world to crystal technology? What is it that has drawn so many intuitive and indigenous healers, past and present? And what are the similarities between the ways these two groups have used the stones? What, in short, is the mystery of crystals? And what do we make of these interesting connections? How can we, in today's world, draw from these insights to reduce our own suffering and reconnect with our authentic selves?

The answers to these questions, and more, are in this book.

The Crystal Blueprint is the story of a six-faceted, natural, transparent stone known as quartz, which comes in many shapes and colors. Most of us are not familiar with its particular story. Many people today associate this mineral with modern technology. However, quartz crystals have been with us since the beginning of time. There are even some theories that relate quartz to the origin of life. Quartz crystals are part of the earth's core, which is also linked to our planet's electromagnetic field—without which life would be impossible. Indeed, our own bodies possess innumerable crystalline structures related to vital functions. Crystals are more connected to us than we know. Humanity has a special resonance with quartz, making it an excellent healing tool.

What I refer to as the crystal blueprint is the intrinsic ability of crystals to concentrate, balance, and amplify electromagnetic energy; this is true for not only the quartz crystals we know so well but also for the crystalline structures in our bodies. The crystal blueprint was present in ancient sites known for their healing and regenerative power and is now inside the technology we use every day. The crystal blueprint is the model behind ancient wisdom, aboriginal healing rituals, our electronic devices, and modern crystal healing. As you will discover in this book, the crystal blueprint also has another purpose and value that will allow us to resonate and reconnect with our authentic selves—the transparent part of us that is connected to the universe and exists beyond human suffering.

Quartz crystal has been used for various purposes since ancient times by cultures around the world, and its relevance has been such that it is repeatedly referenced by most of our world's religions. Where our ancestors used crystals to protect themselves from their enemies, or to ensure a safe passage to the afterlife, we use them to protect against negative energies, thoughts, and emotions, as well as modern diseases and misfortunes of all kinds—especially suffering.

As the dominant mineral of mountaintops and the primary constituent of beach, river, and desert sand, quartz is ubiquitous, plentiful, and durable. Quartz is often found in pockets in the bedrock, as well as the veins that cut through rocks, which comprise sheet-like bodies of crystallized minerals. Veins usually require immense pressure to form, and quartz crystals are developed deep in the earth's crust over the course of billions of years, withstanding all sorts of adversities—including high temperatures, compaction, and lithification (the process whereby sediments form into solid rock). Quartz crystals are also exposed to a great deal of processing and manipulation due to lengthy manufacturing operations. First, they are mined, which can include the use of hammers and chisels, compressed air, and, sometimes, explosives and bulldozers. Then, they are sold to buyers, transported across great distances, and cut and polished into new forms.

Nevertheless, they are unbroken; they shine and share their light—their authentic crystalline nature—with us.

The journey to this world is not an easy one, nor is the journey of crystals to the surface to be part of our lives.

Disconnection from Your Crystal Blueprint

Do you remember the moment of your birth? That moment when you emerged from your mother's womb and came into contact with the surrounding world for the first time? Those who were born in a hospital might have experienced the feel of the unwelcoming hands of a stranger or unfamiliar voices and sounds in the delivery room. This doesn't even include the experiences of those born by caesarean section or into other unfortunate circumstances such as wars, physical disabilities, etc. Aside from all this, there were the sensations and information that we might have absorbed as we developed within the womb.

From the moment of our conception, we are constantly bombarded by information from our parents, culture, society, philosophy, religion, teachers, and peers. When we come into the world, we are fragile and vulnerable; unlike some animal species, we lack the basic mechanisms to protect ourselves from our immediate environment. We lack the power to choose consciously. We are born without instructions; the sad thing is that we discover them only through the dilemmas of life.

Unfortunately, the information we absorb early in life becomes the database and program that commands all our experiences. We act and react according to this hidden information. The database accepts and recognizes only the information that matches what we've learned and rejects the new or unknown. That means that if the information I receive is the same as the information in my unconscious, it is approved; and if not, it is discarded. This is the root of all belief systems—not only individual but social, educational, religious, political, etc. This is also the principle that holds us together and yet has separated so many, leading to disagreements, wars, and many conflicts in our world.

Going back to the time of our conception, imagine all the information we have received since then without the possibility of choice. We are not given the alternative to choose or to be our real selves. Instead, most of the time, information is imposed on us. We follow old models, without questioning, because we do not know better. Our predetermined information does not allow us to open ourselves to new perspectives and explore other possibilities. And so too often we follow the same paths our ancestors walked, stumbling through patterns handed down for hundreds of years—unless we're both willing to recognize the cycles and able to create new beliefs and experiences based on our authentic truth.

Interestingly, like us, the wisdom and knowledge of crystals have been influenced by societies and civilizations throughout history. Sadly, crystals have lost their real significance and meaning, as various mind-sets and paradigms have obscured their profound wisdom and transformative power.

The transformative power I experienced with crystals during difficult periods of my life, in addition to my curiosity as a journalist, sparked my fascination for this ancient tool and my need to know everything about it.

Like all of you, I have been a victim of suffering. I was born to Romanian parents in a Latin American society, and I spent most of my life in great dissatisfaction. I didn't identify with the beliefs of those around me. At the same time, I knew that there was something greater than the life I felt obligated to live back then.

At age 25 I experienced cancer, and later I went through two painful divorces, the forced separation of my two children, and economic insecurity. It was a path of many difficulties that led me to a process of deep inner searching.

I went on a quest to find solutions to expel suffering from my life. It was the beginning of a spiritual journey.

I was exposed to different truths and points of view from cultures and philosophies around the world. I also discovered ancestral techniques and disciplines that helped me to rediscover my true nature, heal myself, and gain a greater understanding of the life that I wanted to live from now on. All of these experiences ultimately led to my calling as a crystal healer.

I could see that the cancer had come to transform the old structures of my mind, thus giving me the chance to see other points of view—among them, the power of choice.

I would have loved to have experienced the possibility of choosing paradigms that were truly mine from the moment of my conception in my mother's womb. I would have filtered my parents' and environment's information. This would have allowed me to be my authentic self from the moment I was born, avoiding many wounds and so much inherited suffering. I would have chosen better alternatives that allowed me to expand rather than restrict myself. I would have known who I really was from my first connections with the world, and I would have taken the steps necessary to develop my true potential.

Crystals helped me to reconnect with my transparency, my authentic self. When I began working with crystals, I experienced rapid changes and a new sense of completeness. They catalyzed processes and accelerated learning that I had pending so I could free myself from information and situations that no longer fit the authentic story I wanted for my life. And when I say *authentic*, I mean the story I wanted to create and live, not the story that others made me believe was mine. But I will talk about this in further detail later.

The crystals captured my attention for three reasons. The first is their silent but forceful presence, which has been consistent during our human existence on the face of the earth. If these objects really lack importance, as many believe, why have they accompanied us throughout our history?

Crystals are mentioned in both the Old and New Testament. They have been used as jewels, ornaments, and important parts of temples and rituals in a variety of cultures and civilizations of the world, including those of the ancient Sumerians, Egyptians, Greeks, Babylonians, Romans, Arabs, and Mayans, to name a few. They are also linked with sacred sites such as Machu Picchu and Stonehenge. Crystals are one of the primary components of Egypt's pyramids. As I mentioned earlier, they continue to be an important part of our lives—not only as part of our cultural legacy but as a vital part of our current technology.

The second reason crystals caught my attention is the way they work. Their functioning resembles that of our unconscious minds. Quartz crystals record and store information indiscriminately, 24 hours a day, but unlike our minds, they are easy to deprogram and reprogram—and this feature makes them wonderful tools for healing.

The third reason is the copious scientific research that has been carried out with crystals through their application in modern technology. This research has demonstrated the impressive properties of crystals and helped us to better understand their use in ancient and contemporary healing processes.

If we compare the results obtained through ancient techniques such as meditation, mindfulness, and yoga to appease the mind and transcend suffering, we can perceive that crystals not only support these processes but also amplify and catalyze them.

Through the symbolic and energetic language inherited from ancients and modern times—of colors, shapes, geometric configurations, and vibrational frequencies—crystals transform our minds and bodies, reconnecting us with who we really are.

In this book, I do not intend to give magic formulas. The texts are supported, for the most part, by ancient traditions, science, and my 19 years of practice with crystals.

Crystal energy has always been present on our planet and continues to behave in the same way it always has. This book is not about proving crystals' infinite benefits; it's about opening your mind.

It is also about recognizing that the story of quartz crystals is your own story.

We cease to shine when we resonate with stories that are not authentic to us, in the same way that crystals' wisdom has ceased to shine in our present lives due to the prevailing limited paradigms we have picked up from other people and institutions—including the distorted history and hidden agendas of small groups in power, the beliefs picked up through the dark ages of religion, Cartesian concepts of duality and the split between body and mind, and false ideas about crystals that are disclosed with the primary intent of selling.

The story of crystals collides with the story of humanity to remind us that we are more than our individual and collective learned beliefs.

I am a witness to the fact that crystals are tools that help restore our whole well-being. They helped me realize the true role of suffering in my life, the places where it originated, and its wounds so that I could work to transcend them and to become the best version of myself. I share these tools with you throughout this book. I invite you to experience the ancient ancestral art of crystal healing and to enjoy its innumerable benefits—the greatest being reconnection with your authentic self.

Regardless of background, we all have the same needs. This includes the need to know who we are beyond who we *believe* we are. The need to become aware of how important it is to protect our unconscious. The need to find solutions to the problems of today's world, where people are fighting and killing each other by choosing their responses according to the beliefs stored in their learned databases. The need to transform our limiting models for more expansive and inclusive ones. The need to awaken from autopilot so we can take responsibility to build the lives we all deserve.

I wrote this book for myself while I was transiting one of the darkest places of my journey, and it is the result of my own inquiry, experiences, and self-work. It represents what I have learned and what has worked for me. All I have written in this book is not only applicable on an individual level, it can also help improve relationships, education, leadership, international relations, and more. Among its many uses, it can bring the much-desired peace we all long for in this world.

My goal in writing this book is to give you an instruction manual to explore yourself through the evolution of the crystal paradigm, from the ancient past to our present, to help you rediscover who you really are, as well as the true power of crystal energy beyond our learned beliefs.

My approach to quartz crystals is practical and based in the real world. I integrate ancient wisdom and crystal science from different schools of thought and, in the process, demystify a subject that has often been kept on the margins. I connect science with crystal healing and draw on my knowledge as a journalist, sufferer, healer, scholar, and practitioner of several South American and world ancestral traditions.

I want you to understand the physical and electrical properties of crystals and how they work—not only in your smartphones and other electronic devices but in your mind and heart, where you will learn to transcend suffering and reconnect to the authentic self. I connect the dots for you to recognize inner patterns and find inspiration to heal. I encourage you to include crystals as part of your daily practice, to expand your actual options and step into the best version of yourself.

How This Book Is Set Up

In "Part I: Crystal Healing and What It Can Do for You," I explore what crystal healing is, as well as the psychological roots and ramifications of suffering, or disconnection from the authentic self. I describe what crystal healing is for me and the way that crystals, through resonance, can become great tools for transcending suffering and reconnecting with our authentic story. I also offer a detailed description of the unconscious, its relationship to suffering, and how our learned information creates our experiences and reality.

In "Part II: A Brief History of Quartz and Crystal Healing," I bring to your awareness the use and meaning of stones from a historical point of view—from the beginning of human civilization to our present times—to understand how crystal knowledge and paradigms evolved with our beliefs. You will also be guided through the various symbols, patterns, and meanings associated with crystals over the millennia. Additionally, you will learn about contemporary approaches to quartz crystal, from the rituals and practices of indigenous and aboriginal people around the world to those of today's crystal healers—and you will see how they are connected.

In "Part III: The Science Behind Crystal Healing," I discuss energy, frequency, and resonance from a mind, body, and quartz perspective. You will learn quantum theory explanations of how energy behaves in crystal healing and understand the language of energy to see how it is expressed through crystals' electromagnetic properties. I explain how the very same qualities that make crystals so desirable in modern technology are what have drawn healers to them for millennia—and are what allow *us* to use crystals to heal our bodies and reconnect with the authentic self today. I also share a guide to finding aspects of your body that resonate with crystals to make crystal healing more effective.

The final part of the book, "Part IV: Establishing a Crystalline Body and Mind," is about the specifics of crystal healing. I describe the connection between the processes of deep Earth and the processes of the deep unconscious, making the connection between crystals and humanity. I also guide you to heal and transform by walking you step-by-step through the process of crystal healing: how to choose a crystal healer, how to use quartz in different ways to release mind patterns and illness, and much more. You will learn about the stages of healing that enable us to reconnect with the authentic self, as well as the physical and emotional experience of undergoing a crystal healing session and what happens next. Information from other parts of the book is integrated here to establish us in a crystalline mind-set so that we can experience eventual reconnection to the authentic within ourselves. Finally, I conclude by bringing crystal healing to our collective condition and revealing how our entire planet might benefit from this ancestral tool.

The Crystal Blueprint was written with the help of countless teachers, healers, scientists, authors, and philosophies. Without this wisdom and knowledge, it would have been impossible to dig in and write this book. I honor them and am grateful for those experts and healers who allowed me to share this information with you.

Although it may be difficult for you to grasp in this moment due to our collective programming, there are plenty of possibilities to change the world. One of those possibilities includes quartz crystals.

When we use our will, we have the option to align with our true path or to go against it. When we align with our true path, our will is united with a field of multiple possibilities that includes our well-being.

When we are not living our truth, we live in suffering. If we free ourselves from attachment to our unconscious learned beliefs, which we inherited from those who came before us, we can become free to be ourselves. As we free ourselves from our internal programming, inherited paradigms, and old wounds, we shine. The moment we accept and trust our unique personal path, we align with universal laws that provide us with everything we need to achieve everything we ever dreamed of. This is not a gift for the few; it is the birthright of each and every one of us.

The Crystal Blueprint is meant for your authentic self, not your mind. It is not a typical book about crystals, where crystal meanings are provided as the ultimate prescriptions for your problems. Instead, it is a journey of self-exploration to discover who you are beyond your learned beliefs. Its purpose is to open your mind so that you can see the crystalline nature in everything: yourself, crystals, and the world.

This book is not meant to do the work for you; rather, it was written to encourage you to take responsibility for your own inner work and transformation. I am not going to offer you endless lists of stones and their "meanings," which come from false filters consisting of childhood wounds and learned information that is fed by your mind rather than true resonance. Instead, I will encourage you to reconnect to the authentic part of yourself through resonance with your true energies, which are imperceptible to the mind. When you actually resonate with the stones that are chosen by the unconscious, authentic part of yourself, the energy will be directed precisely to whatever needs healing. This will emerge from what is true for you, rather than what your mind expects due to its false programming. The idea is to break the endless cycle of false information generated by the mind and start walking your unique path, whatever that might be.

This is an open invitation to join me in this crystal journey through psychology, ancient traditions, science, and crystal healing. You will expand your limited learned beliefs and recognize and apply the power of quartz so that you can become aware of what you need to heal within yourself to reconnect with your crystalline nature, with what you may have forgotten dwells in each and every one of us—our authentic selves.

After all, we are all crystals remembering our original crystal blueprint.

CRYSTAL LOVE!

BEATRIZ

PART I

CRYSTAL HEALING AND WHAT IT CAN DO FOR YOU

CHAPTER 1

What Is Crystal Healing?

"A crystal can be a tool as well as a companion in our continual journey of changing and growing."

— LAWRENCE STOLLER[1]

WHO COULD EVER IMAGINE that a crystal, a transparent and apparently inanimate object that originates within the depths of the earth, could have so much power and impact over our lives?

Whether or not we are aware of it, crystals have left an indelible mark on the past through many cultures and civilizations. Today is no different. Their presence in our lives is inevitable, as they are essential parts of most electronic devices required in our modern lifestyle. As we utilize crystals for communication and various applications in medicine and other industries, we are slowly discovering what our ancestors already knew: quartz crystals have the potential to bring wellness and serve humankind.

In one way or another, crystal energy healing is a bridge between past and present. The wisdom inherited from our ancestors about the symbolic relationship between stones and the different effects they have on our unconscious—our bodies' organs and the contents of our minds—can now be wedded to modern knowledge to reconnect with our full wellness.

Science has added knowledge beyond the hidden mysteries of crystals known so well to the ancients by offering us vital information on our energetic subatomic nature and the properties of quartz. In this world of frequencies and wavelengths, suffering originates in the tension between lower and higher frequencies, between our acquired frequencies from our environment—learned information—and our original frequency, which is authentic to us. This tension prevents our evolution. Crystalline properties can transform the origin of that tension and restore balance, leading us to resonate with the higher version of ourselves. Resonance is also that unconscious power that crystals have over us and one of the main keys to understanding the real power of crystal healing.

The real gift of crystal healing is reconnecting us to our authentic frequency—to who we really are—and the new possibilities that come with this knowledge.

This is the gift that crystal healing brought into my life.

My Journey to Crystals

I was not born a crystal healer, nor did I come from an environment where holistic knowledge was promoted. But the universe has many ways to align you with your original path; in my life, my first alignment took the shape of cancer and divorce at age 25. This opened a crack in the world I was used to and led to a self-exploration process—and, eventually, to crystals.

Officially, my connection to crystals began in India. I had never experienced crystal energy until my trip to this country in the year 2000. I joined a group of friends to visit Sai Baba's ashram near Bangalore, a city in the southern region of India. We would go to the temple to pray, chant mantras, meditate, and do karma yoga, or unselfish community service. It is known that around ashrams, our energy is amplified in order to serve our self-inquiry process. During my stay, I began to experience a fascination I had never experienced before with crystals. I spent a lot of time in the shops around the ashram, observing crystals and placing them on different parts of my body. These clear stones were the perfect tools to help me reconnect with my truth; unknowingly, through resonance, they were bringing out my crystalline self.

In one of those shops, I met my Hindu masters, and this is where the story of my life would reach the point of no return. Over the next three weeks, these two men seated me on a small bench in the middle of a very tiny room, maybe the size of a bathroom, with the walls covered from floor to ceiling with shelves that were filled with the purest clear quartz crystals.

The quartz began to amplify my energy, and I started to become aware of many things I had never recognized before. I saw how the wounds and learned beliefs of my parents affected my life. I also remembered how different I felt from the people who surrounded me during my childhood and how I never identified with their stories. In a way, crystals were allowing me to view my life as an observer rather than a protagonist in my own story. The images were just coming to me, like they might on a movie screen; my life was passing in front of me without my emotions being involved in the process. Watching it, I could see, in a profound way, all the things that affected me and connected me with my fears and suffering.

That first week was all about watching my fears, my emotions, and my insecurities from this detached vantage point. The second was about making the connection as to why I felt those things, and the third week was about shedding them and empowering myself.

I clearly remember the last day with my teachers. After I had released all that didn't belong to me, a song came into my mind. The song was beautiful and had many voices, like a church choir. The voices were angelic and high-pitched. I could feel the higher vibrations moving through me. I was wondering where all the voices were coming from, and then I had a realization: they were coming from the crystals.

Later, the journalist inside me was motivated to search for the scientific answers to this experience. I discovered that sound is produced when colliding atoms or molecules bump into each other. The sound we hear is the vibration they produce in the process. The amplified frequencies of crystals and my empty unconscious allowed me to experience vibration as sound. This is an experience I still have when I meditate with crystals and during some crystal healings.

I spent most of my time in India reconnecting with my real path beyond all my learned beliefs. I was no longer the repetition of the stories I learned from others; I was my true self. Crystals had helped me to reconnect with this very real part of me.

After experiencing my true self, I knew that I wanted to devote my life to helping people awaken from their false selves and guiding them to reconnect to their real story and potential. I wanted other people to experience what I had and to open a door in their lives that would lead to peace and lasting joy.

I ended up studying with two world-renowned crystal healing teachers, Katrina Raphaell and JaneAnn Dow.

After reading *Crystal Enlightenment*, I knew Katrina Raphaell, one of the pioneers of crystal healing, was the best person to start my crystal training with. Katrina was a very reputable crystal healer at that time. She used crystals and gems methodically to heal and offered one of the few serious crystal trainings available. I believed she was a good first stepping stone to learning the basics that would allow me to open a crystal practice.

In 2001, I went to Hawaii, where Katrina's Crystal Academy of Advanced Healing Arts was located. In the next 21 days, I received my Crystal Healing Certification training. Katrina taught me how to work with crystals in a very technical way, from the perspective of the mind. Based on a preconceived protocol, the healer chooses the stones for the client's layout. In this protocol, the client has a more passive role, while the healer works with crystals according to previously acquired information. I learned the various frequencies of different stones and stone layouts and how to choose stones to place on the chakras (energetic centers) of the body. She emphasized that being a crystal healer required a great deal of integrity and responsibility, and that training was needed in order to practice crystal healing safely; after all, the stones were very powerful and required knowledge before you could hope to work effectively with them.

Following Katrina's advice, I worked with JaneAnn Dow. I began working with her one month after I finished my crystal training with

Katrina in the year 2001. She had been dedicated to her personal research and study of crystals and healing for many years. She wrote the book *Crystal Journey* and helped Katrina gather information for her book, *Crystal Enlightenment*. Her work and attunement with geometric configurations of quartz has revolutionized crystal knowledge. As I expected, she was a vast resource of crystal wisdom. She had valuable knowledge about hundreds of stones, their unique vibrations, and how they work in crystal grids. She taught me to connect with crystals intuitively, which included how to understand their language and what they were trying to communicate symbolically. She also taught me that reading patterns was a fundamental part of crystal sessions. In this model, the client chose the stones for the crystal healing session and had a more active role during the healing. Before she died, JaneAnn showed me that the ways in which stones were chosen and arranged by the client were important patterns that assisted in his or her healing.

Katrina and JaneAnn helped me to integrate two different but complementary paradigms of healing. I learned the crystal healing mind-set from Katrina, while JaneAnn revealed to me the symbolic language of stones and, drawing on my personal experience of suffering, how to recognize suffering patterns and read them in people and stones to bring healing. JaneAnn also taught me that the importance of working with crystals lies in their ability to alleviate suffering.

Today, there are some crystals that I call "masters" because they teach me in unusual ways. If you work with crystals in meditation and other practices that I teach through my workshops, you will learn to understand their language. By releasing all the bits of information that don't belong to us, we can open a space to recognize their magical guidance and healing. While many people have gurus they follow, my spiritual guides are the crystals. After all, despite the many processes that crystals undergo deep in the earth, they remain pure in their essence—and that is their wisdom. They teach me all the time that I have to remain authentic, regardless of the massive amounts of information I constantly receive from my environment. They encourage me to stick to my truth.

I can say that I have experienced crystal energy healing many times in my life . . . first in India, later in Colombia, and now throughout my life's ongoing processes. Today, I offer crystal workshops, consultancies, and sessions in California and other parts of the world—spreading the good news that people can experience long-lasting transformation and the alleviation of their suffering. If you open yourself to receive their information, crystals can help you walk long distances in a short time.

So, What *Is* Crystal Healing, Really?

I have been in the crystalline world for almost 20 years now and continue to offer professional, one-on-one crystal healing to my clients. I consider myself unique in the field; as an expert on suffering, my gift is my capacity to discern the original wounding that is the source of patterns of suffering. I help people see these things for themselves and harness crystal energy in service of their healing and eventual reconnection with their authentic selves.

Crystal healing was born from the evolution of primitive crystal mysticism. It reached its apex in the Dark Ages, when fanaticism, irrational beliefs, and inaccuracy were prevalent. For that reason, the discipline of crystal healing was neglected by science for centuries. Regardless of its origins, I believe that crystal healing can be a valid and rewarding study. Much knowledge has been gained in the last century regarding crystal properties and energy from a quantum physics and crystallography perspective. This knowledge cannot be ignored, either by science or by metaphysical circles.

Crystal healing works through patterns, both energetic and symbolic. Moreover, the reason it is so effective is its resonance.

In crystal healing, resonance can have many meanings. Energetically, it could mean that our frequency is attracting a similar frequency in the form of a crystal. When a crystal is vibrating at the same natural frequency as our bodies and minds, it can help to raise or lower our frequencies to bring transformation and balance. We can also resonate with symbols from a mind and body perspective.

To resonate with symbols from a mind perspective means we resonate with the meaning that some symbols—in the form of colors, shapes, textures, sizes, etc.—can have for our unconscious. Crystals can also resonate with different patterns related to our learned unconscious programming, from individual beliefs and wounds to collective paradigms.

From a body perspective, a crystal resonates with similar shapes in our bodies, as well as with chemical composition, pigments, and the crystalline structures that make up our bodies' energy patterns. For example, there, are pyramidal neurons in our brains that resemble the inner structure of quartz. The main component of quartz is silicon dioxide, which is present in our bones. Rhodopsin is a purple pigment in our eyes similar in color to amethyst. Our bodies are also made up of a series of crystalline structures, including oscillating solid and liquid crystals that make up our bodies' overall energy patterns.

Crystal expert Marcel Vogel has mentioned that the symmetry and structure of the human energy field reveal the same properties of crystals in their material form. Dan Willis, a research associate of Vogel's, says:

> The crystal is a quantum converter that is able to transmit energy in a form that has discrete biological effects. This is most likely a resonant effect. . . . This crystallinity [of the body] is apparent on both a subtle energetic or quantum level as well as the macro level. The bones, tissues, cells, and fluids of the body have a definite crystallinity about them. . . . The physical body is comprised of liquid crystal systems in the cell membranes, intercellular fluids, as well as larger structures such as the fatty tissues, muscular and nervous systems, lymph, blood, and so on. Through the use of an appropriately tuned crystal to which these structures are responsive, balance and coherence can be restored by delivering the necessary "information" or energetic nutrients needed.[2]

Today, we know that the heart is one of the primary crystalline structures in the human body. The HeartMath Institute has evidence that the heart contains the largest electromagnetic field within the body.[3] Placing crystals over the heart can bring well-being to the rest of the body and harmonize our surroundings, including our relationships.

Unfortunately, some crystal healers ignore the science of the very subject in which they claim expertise. Conversely, the mainstream scientific community dismisses the claims of crystal healers that mind and body can be balanced through these stones. In debating who is right or wrong, we are losing sight of valuable knowledge.

I feel that my task is to reclaim the magic and sacredness that crystals once had during ancient times. Moreover, I know that science can help us gain an understanding of crystals' occult mysteries, restore the credibility of crystal healing, and demystify an ancient practice that has been seen as a placebo rather than acknowledged for its true properties and benefits.

My training as a journalist is what has enabled me to notice and investigate connections that have been largely ignored by the crystal healing and scientific community. I offer a rigorous commitment to research and inquiry to understand, beyond metaphysics and skepticism, the true knowledge behind this ancient art. To that end, the work I present is meant to guide people who are struggling in a variety of challenging life situations, so that they can break free from unhealthy unconscious patterns of thinking and behavior.

If we think about human suffering as a kind of darkness, then crystal energy is what brings light and allows us to see all that is hidden inside. Quartz crystals help us gain awareness of the sources of our suffering and find release.

Judy Hall, an internationally renowned crystal author of more than 40 books, defines crystal healing as a noninvasive, gentle form of healing that combines well with other forms, bringing body, mind, psyche, and spirit back into balance by entraining them with a more perfect energy form—that is, the crystal.

Crystal healing can be so much more powerful than many other types of vibrational healing. I have found that people are drawn to crystal healing in search of a spiritual experience that can be accessed in a nonthreatening way. But that is not the real power of crystal healing, although it can be a side effect. After my clients come to me, they realize that crystals can actually help them transform deep imbalances and wounds. And the process is not always "gentle."

Crystals are a powerful catalyst for healing processes because they bring to the surface unconscious internal content that needs our intervention. Thus, they can be a great companion in any self-exploration task—including mindfulness, therapy, and meditation.

Working with Crystals

Today, most crystal practitioners balance the body and mind by placing gems such as quartz over the seven vibrational vortices in the body (known as chakras) and the electromagnetic field surrounding it. There are some who use crystal grids, while others use crystal essences. Still others use their crystal artwork to heal.

The context may be different, but the intention is the same. The ancients and contemporary healers alike use crystals as a tool for transformation and reconnection to the authentic self.

From a symbolic point of view, each crystal may represent an organ, belief, emotion, or disease. People who work with chakras tend to use specific crystals for each chakra. Each crystal can also represent an archetype—a symbol within your unconscious mind or energy field that has deep meaning—such as your mother, your father, light, darkness, air, fire, the sun, the moon, the universe. Altogether, crystals hail from every part of the world, so we could say there is a United Nations of crystals, where each crystal has not only the energy of the country where it was extracted but also of the entire planet.

Through crystals, you can communicate with the hidden parts of yourself that you are not aware of: your core wounds, forgotten experiences that originated destructive behaviors, and early harmful memories . . . and you can also become aware of your true gifts and path.

When I worked with Katrina, I learned that there are stones that work on the physical body, others that work on the emotional body, others on the mind, and others on the level of the spirit.

For me, crystal healing is an ancient vibrational technique that uses quartz crystals of different frequencies—in the form of different colors, sizes, and thicknesses—as valuable tools for transformation. Because of their unique symbolism and properties, which science already knows, they can interact with the energy patterns of the body and mind to help you gain awareness of the real source of your discomfort and suffering. This initiates a learning and transformation process that will lead you to reconnect with who you authentically are.

How My Crystal Practice Evolved

As humans, we must evolve from one state to the next, and my practice was no exception. Katrina and JaneAnn gave me the basis to practice crystal healing, but with current scientific knowledge and my own personal experience, my crystal technique accordingly went through its own evolution.

At the beginning, when I first learned to work with crystals, I did it by following the chakra system I'd learned from Katrina. It is natural that when you are not very familiar with any technique, you merely follow the rules. Later, as I worked with myself and others, I gained experience and knowledge that came from within.

Stones that I used to place on a particular part of the body were shifted to other parts, depending on each unique situation or circumstance, as well as on my intuition. I also encourage my clients to participate in their healing experience with questions: "Where do you feel this stone should go?" Usually, they don't know anything about crystals. They trust in my experience to guide them through their healing process, but they choose the stones. In this way, I am not controlling their energy, and the process is authentic for them—it is a two-way street where they can open themselves up to the experience of healing. Then, I place the crystals they choose over their bodies and energy field and complement these stones with others that I sense will work well. While I am a guide, the client is the one doing the true work—healing him- or herself.

I ask my clients a wide variety of questions: "What are you feeling? Is there any memory or sensation you are experiencing? Are you comfortable?" When the client is fully engaged, the results of the healing are amazing. Sometimes, the healing is so straightforward that I do not have to ask them anything. We all have our unique, nontransferable blueprint, and what generally works for one person will not necessarily work for someone else.

I want to break old paradigms rather than create more rigid systems. Thus, I want everybody to resonate with the technique they feel is authentic for them. One can work with crystal grids, mandalas, meditation, by placing stones over the heart, with a crystal healer, or by oneself. I don't want people to stick to one fixed idea, because quartz crystals are all about transformation, starting with our mind-set.

Prescriptive versus Resonant Energy

Today, most crystal healing is prescriptive. That is, when people have a specific problem, they go to their books to prescribe for themselves the crystal that is said to best solve that problem. The books might offer such advice as using a rose quartz to heal your heart, an amethyst to heal your mind, or a citrine to transform your emotions.

Many of the books we find on crystals are manuals prescribing the use of different stones for different problems and situations; their authors rely on their intuitions to confirm their veracity.

But what *is* intuition, really?

Intuition is authentic information. It is a very important part of us that requires responsibility and self-awareness to work with and access. For the most part, we are not reading the information we receive objectively, because it passes through all the filters of our worldview or experiences learned from others. The same happens when we receive other people's information.

False intuition is the sum of all our beliefs—i.e., mind information—when we are not engaged in real internal work. Real intuition is the result of committed internal work, which allows us to discern authentic information from that of the mind.

When I refer to prescriptive crystal healing, I refer not only to the prescriptive books that offer us a bunch of stones with different explanations as to what they do and how they can help us but also to those practices we learn from others that we accept without questioning or discernment. For example, if you have a thyroid problem, I will place this blue crystal that I learned works well with the thyroid over your throat chakra. That is prescription. But the practice of prescription could be limited, as our authentic selves respond to our authentic needs, and these are not considered in this option.

Our ancestors didn't have the tools we have today to understand that everything is energy. Even now, our minds don't have the capacity to perceive energy consciously. But if everything is energy, we cannot continue to solve a problem from the level of the mind, which is devoid of the conscious ability to perceive energy.

Prior to the invention of written documentation, ancients worked with *resonance*. They simply picked the stone they sensed, "without mind."

But what does this *really* mean?

In our Western society, we rely on our minds to solve our problems, but ancient philosophies believed that real balance and well-being come from transcending the mind and reconnecting to the original source of information—the authentic self.

When we choose a stone through resonance, we are connecting with the authentic part of us—surpassing any content of the mind or prescriptions that are based on information that has been handed down to us.

I strongly recommend choosing resonance over prescription. Through resonance, you are focusing on the exact frequency needed to bring you healing and the exact pattern in your mind and body that you need to work with. You are working directly with energy, not through your beliefs. The information goes directly where it needs to be, without the manipulation and filtering of the mind.

In a crystal session, this is how it works: Among many crystals, you are going to feel attracted to the exact pattern—unconscious frequency or symbol—that works best for you in that moment. You might choose an amethyst, but there are different colors, sizes, and shapes of amethyst—which will impact how you work with the stone in different ways.

The colors of the crystal are related to frequencies but also to minerals. Maybe there is a mineral that you are missing in your body that you are not aware of. By resonance, you will unconsciously choose the specific crystal that will meet all your needs, from your thought patterns to your energetic and physical patterns.

When you choose the crystals unconsciously, you are having a conversation in terms of frequency. You are communicating to the crystal your frequency, and the crystal is communicating to you its frequency; with that unconscious energetic exchange of information, the process of healing starts.

We unconsciously attract to our lives all that we resonate with—including thoughts, beliefs, experiences, relationships; accordingly, we attract crystals. Through resonance, a crystal's energetic properties can transform and bring balance and change to our personal resonance—the energy of our unconscious physical and psychological parts. In this way, what we know as crystal healing occurs. When our resonance changes, we can attract new possibilities into our lives—among them, well-being and health. Also, as our inner world changes, this is reflected in our outer world, from our relationships to our surroundings.

In crystal resonance therapist Naisha Ahsian's words, "The physical law of resonance is, to me, the key to understanding how and why crystals interact with us; it's a law of physics, so it isn't about intentions. It doesn't matter what you want, it doesn't matter what you feel, it doesn't matter what you intend. It operates whether or not you are consciously aware of it."[4]

You should think not in terms of what the crystal can give you but in terms of what you really *need*. Usually, what you really need is unknown to you. Crystals can assist you to truly heal yourself, but you have to trust in a process that is being guided invisibly, through unseen wavelengths and frequencies.

Why you are attracted to a crystal depends on so many things that are difficult to understand on the level of the mind; these factors include symbols, archetypes, patterns, and energy, all of which we will discuss throughout this book.

Moreover, while you might be attracted to one crystal today, that is likely to change tomorrow. Every day, your frequency changes according to the resonance of the electromagnetic field of the earth, or your emotions, or your level of activity (if you are tired or if you feel energized), or anything that you experienced that day.

Certainly, I can tell you, "Okay, if you have problems with your partner, work with a rose quartz." But how do I know the information I'm receiving in such a prescription is true? Everybody has a different filter and has grown in a different environment. We all have our own inner wounds to contend with and our own unique paths to the authentic self. In choosing resonance over prescription, we are thereby bypassing the mind and working directly with what is authentic and true. The real source within you is choosing the stone you need to heal yourself. You're not relying on the wounds and beliefs of others. After all, the story of others is not *your* story.

While it may seem that, through resonance, *you* are choosing a stone, this is only partially true. The stone is the one choosing you. It is choosing your personal frequency in that moment so you can gain awareness of your own process.

Once, a client came to my office and asked me which stone I worked with the least. I realized I was avoiding black stones. In stone language, the stones that have deep meaning are not merely the stones we are drawn to; they are also the stones we avoid. In avoiding black stones, I was avoiding something that I was not yet aware of. Despite all the uncomfortable feelings that dark stones generated in me, I decided to work with them. I had to learn why I was afraid of them. I wore them for almost two years . . . and in the process, I learned many things. They were closely related to abrupt changes in my life—but black stones are a topic for another book. In general, I recommend that my clients connect with the frequency they feel triggers the perfect process in order to change that rusty gear and open new channels to live their authentic story.

Just as quartz crystals are harvested from minerals deep within the earth, they have been used by healers to connect with the deepest, innermost parts of the self. And because they resonate with the deepest parts of our unconscious and can act like a magnifying glass, they will help you become aware of the roots of your suffering and of your learned unconscious patterns, as well as what you are supposed to learn from them.

As mentioned previously, crystals work through a range of different frequencies, and each crystal represents a particular frequency. Remember that healers don't see the body in the same way that allopathic doctors do. We focus on energy, frequency, and symbols—not matter.

For example, when you choose crystals through resonance while you are in a crystal healing session, you may recall an unexpected scene from your past. There, you find yourself with one of your parents, living through something that you do not even consciously remember. Crystalline energy resonated and brought to your awareness that part of your story in order for you to heal it. The vibration can come through sounds, as words, sobs, or tunes; through images, such as a vivid scene in the mind's eye; and even through experiences in the body, such as different temperatures and sensations. It's important to remain open in order to experience crystal healing. It's also important to acknowledge that hidden wounds or unconscious patterns might be made up of completely different ingredients for each of us.

According to Ahsian, crystals can assist us in recognizing how we are suffering, and why we are suffering, so that we can then shift that suffering altogether. We can become conscious of how we are creating that suffering so that we can empower ourselves to overcome it and change our patterns of creating reality. She says, "We need to not use crystals and stones as a way to escape suffering. We need to use crystals and stones as a way to evolve ourselves beyond creating suffering."[5]

Crystals usually initiate profound processes that continue in our daily lives. Each process generates changes that will help us gain more clarity and understanding along the path of finding our true selves. We will continue to repeat unhealthy patterns until we take conscious action to prevent this. No matter what our condition, struggle, or belief system, crystals can help us clear everything that is not originally ours and enable us to quit repeating the patterns that perpetuate suffering.

If you compare life to a big puzzle, crystal healing will help you light each small part of the puzzle in order to take you to the next part, and so on, until you solve the entire puzzle. In this way, you can truly recognize your complete and authentic self.

Crystals: Tools to Release Suffering

Quartz crystals have the ability to bring us into balance by addressing and repairing discordant vibrations. They have the unique capacity to stabilize, guide, and amplify different frequencies and to transform one type of energy into another. This is what makes crystals so powerful and effective, both in healing and in science.

If all is energy, as quantum physics has shown us, each of our body's organs is energy and has an associated energy field. Each emotion has a different frequency, and so does each of our thoughts. The idea is that we must keep our organs' healthy frequencies in a state of resonance with those of our thoughts and emotions. As these various energy fields are constantly interacting, any prolonged desynchronization can produce a physical imbalance.

Learning to connect with quartz crystals can be a potent part of managing any disorders or imbalances at the physical, emotional, and mental level. Crystals resonate with the healthy frequencies of the universe and help restore the flow of energy within us because they have embedded in their inner structures the universal codes that help us reconnect with our inner, universal flow of energy, thus reestablishing our well-being.

Richard Buckminster Fuller, the prominent 20th-century inventor and visionary, expounded on key concepts of unified physics that support the connection of crystals to the energetic blueprint of the universe. He theorized that the triangle is the most basic unit of all structures and the tetrahedron (also known as a triangular pyramid), the most basic system of energy dynamics. According to Fuller, the tetrahedron is the most fundamental building block of the geometry that comprises the fabric of the vacuum of space that exists on all scales everywhere in the universe. Two polarized larger tetrahedrons create a star tetrahedron composed of eight smaller tetrahedrons. Putting 8 star tetrahedrons together creates a 64-tetrahedron grid inside of which 2 octaves of cube octahedrons (that is, 512 perfectly stacked tetrahedrons) are formed to create the perfectly balanced geometry of space. Fuller referred to this as the "vector equilibrium."[6] Unsurprisingly, the inner structure of quartz is a tetrahedron.

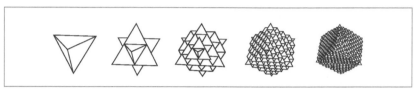

A progression of the tetrahedron pattern within the tapestry of the universe, from infinitesimal to infinite.

Nassim Haramein, Swiss physicist and Director of Research of the Resonance Science Foundation, associates the 64-tetrahedron structure with the geometry of stillness, or zero point energy field. This represents the ultimate and perfect condition wherein the movement of energy comes to a state of absolute equilibrium and, therefore, absolute stillness and nothingness. In observing space, Haramein observed that galaxies and planets accumulate matter near their center. Likewise, in our solar system, our planets orbit around the equator of the sun. Somehow, everything in the universe remains stable at its center. Matter accumulates at the center of celestial objects because there is no energy in motion here—only stillness.[7]

Haramein has spent most of his career researching the basic geometry of hyperspace, delving into subject matter ranging from theoretical physics to the knowledge of ancient civilizations. From these studies, his Unified Field Theory emerged.[8] Also known as the Haramein–Rauscher metric, this particular body of research challenges and expands our current understanding of the link between physics and consciousness. Haramein has theorized that knowing the geometry of that which produces stillness might enable us to understand the mystery beyond the vacuum of the universe.[9]

In his research, Haramein has also addressed the Platonic solids.

The ancients, including Plato, referred to the tetrahedron as the most stable geometry in the universe. Most ancient cultures used pyramidal structures in their architecture. Haramein wondered if, in their observation of the heavens, they had an understanding of nature and the cosmos that we in modern times have lost.[10]

Curiously, mystics of all eras have referred to the center in our being as the place where we can reach serenity and stability. They refer to the stillness of the mind as the place underneath all our mental noise. According to the Indian sage Nisargadatta Maharaj, "In the stillness of the mind I saw myself as I am—unbound."[11] And in the words of Eckhart Tolle, "Your innermost sense of self, of who you are, is inseparable from stillness."[12]

Stillness—being within the center—is the antidote to suffering. In a hurricane, in the midst of so much movement, the space of the center has no movement. In the same way, through tetrahedral structures such as crystals, perhaps we can reach stillness within ourselves.

The inner structure of quartz is a tetrahedron, so it follows that quartz crystal, through resonance, can similarly offer us stillness in times of chaos. Crystals very well might be able to stabilize anything that is made up of energy, including our bodies, our thoughts, and our surroundings. Our thoughts are in constant motion, so crystals can help bring stillness to the contents of our minds. They can help us cut through the noise of our learned beliefs to transcend suffering and connect with who we really are.

Our bodies mirror the amazing tetrahedral structure of quartz. In fact, the first four cells of a developing embryo form a tetrahedron. Additionally, the pyramidal structure of the tetrahedron occurs in the pyramidal neurons of the human brain.

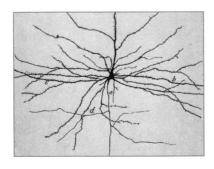

Pyramidal neurons. Courtesy of Cajal Institute, Cajal Legacy, CSIC, Madrid, Spain.

These pyramidal neurons are found in the frontal cortex, hippocampus, and amygdala. The hippocampus and amygdala are the parts of the brain associated with negative bias—which is linked to our experience of suffering. Amazingly, pyramidal neurons are also part of the frontal cortex of the brain, associated with positive emotions. These same pyramidal neurons are related to the creation of new neural pathways and habits.[13]

If crystals' inner structure resonates with the brain's inner structures, it follows that the properties of crystals can help to transform negative emotions and bring about balance. Simply put, crystals have the power to amplify positive thinking due to their amplifying properties; in other words, they work as a magnifying glass, allowing us to see in large the positive aspects, which we would otherwise not perceive due to the dominance of our negative bias.

Today, we know that up to 70 percent of our thoughts are related to our negative bias (which we will explore further in Chapter 2).[14] If crystals also resonate with the pyramidal neurons in the parts of our brains associated with negative bias, how can we use them so that they only amplify our positive rather than negative emotions? The answer is, through conscious awareness; for, where our minds go, our energy goes.

Candace Pert, neuroscientist and pharmacologist, as well as author of *Molecules of Emotion*, mentions that studies of remarkable recoveries have shown that tumor shrinkage often accompanies a patient's recognition that he or she has been harboring angry emotions.[15] When we use our minds consciously as a precision selection instrument that focuses only on positive information, crystals will amplify our efforts. With repetition and active engagement in positive thinking, crystals can help us to make lasting well-being a new habit.

As we know, we are wired to an endless field of energy. Every situation in our lives creates an energy pattern. This includes our relationships with our mothers, fathers, and those around us. All our emotions are translated within the energy field through particular frequencies. If we could compare our energies with those of the universe, we might say that the lower frequency of our inauthentic thoughts have less energy than the authentic ones. The tension between the lower frequency and our original authentic frequency creates what we know of as suffering: a condition in which energy is blocked.

A crystal can show you where there is tension—the contraction or destructive interference that might be made of our thoughts, learned beliefs, etc. Thus, when we work with crystal healing, crystals reflect to us the exact part of the story that we have to know about ourselves to become aware and take actions to reconnect to the natural flow of energy within us—as well as the source of our well-being.

Crystals can induce balance through their energetic properties, and with our committed internal focus, we can eventually release what is producing disharmony and experience transformation. Crystals give us the option to change the patterns of how we interact with the world and see our story in a new and authentic way—changing our patterns from suffering to well-being. It is our choice to consciously release that which doesn't resonate with our original nature. Becoming crystalline in this sense is a metaphor for our true essence—free of anyone else's information.

According to geologist and *New York Times*–best-selling author Gregg Braden, the crystalline nature behind many of the phenomena scientists have experienced could be a universal pattern that is both macrocosmic and microcosmic:

We are resonant beings. We are in resonance with our surroundings, with our environment, because of the internal geometry of our bones and the minerals in our bodies—and that gives us crystalline properties. The majority of the human body is water. Water is based on a tetrahedron, a crystalline-like structure. So we have crystalline-like properties, I think it's fair to say. Our Earth has water and crystals—we live on a crystalline planet. It makes sense that if we can find harmony between ourselves and our environment, to the greater degree, we can find harmony, health, healing, joy, and happiness in our lives. To me, it makes perfect sense if we can harmonize our bodies internally and then bring our bodies into harmony with our external world. That is what promotes healing, and longevity, and health.[16]

Now that I have described the principle of resonance and how it works with respect to crystal healing in this chapter, we're ready to dive into a deep exploration of the unconscious, as well as the learned information with which we resonate and create our experiences and reality. We will examine how many of the beliefs and mind-sets that filter into our unconscious awareness through family, society, and cultural influences lead to a sense of disconnection from the authentic self—a disconnection that is the very source of suffering. We will also begin to recognize why crystals are the key to understanding how we can frame the human experience of suffering and move beyond it to reconnect with our own crystal blueprint—the transparent, authentic part inside each of us.

CHAPTER 2

We Are Not Necessarily Our Unconscious Beliefs or Learned Thought Patterns

---

"We do not attract what we want, but what we are."

— JAMES LANE ALLEN[1]

HOW MANY OF US HAVE lived those moments when we were literally slammed by reality? The death of a loved one, a serious illness or injury, disease, disability, betrayal, divorce, unwanted exile, parental alienation, bankruptcy, war, and natural disaster—these are only some of the manifestations of suffering. Sometimes the crisis can wear other faces: loneliness, frustration, the feeling of disconnection from others, emptiness, uneasiness and the sense that something is missing in our lives, or the conviction that no matter how much we have, it will never be enough.

No matter our creed, philosophy, religion, social class, color, or nationality, we have all experienced suffering at one point or another. It seems as if suffering is intrinsic to our journey on this Earth. And although many of us don't express it, we fear suffering immensely and would rather avoid it than confront it.

Have you ever asked yourself why suffering has chosen you? And what the true meaning of suffering is? This chapter will dive into the many ways of looking at and experiencing suffering. We will examine a number of beliefs and behavior patterns we have inherited from our families, culture, and society—and how these relate to our suffering. Suffering can be more than a hopeless situation, as ancients realized thousands of years ago. It can be a path of transformation to reconnect with who we really are—our authentic selves.

What Is Suffering?

This is the etymology of the word *suffering*: "suffer (v.): mid–13c., "allow to occur or continue, permit, tolerate, fail to prevent or suppress," also "to be made to undergo, endure, be subjected to" (pain, death, punishment, judgment, grief), from Anglo-French *suffrir,* Old French *sofrir* "bear, endure, resist; permit, tolerate, allow" (Modern French *souffrir*), from Vulgar Latin *sufferire,* variant of Latin *sufferer* "to bear, undergo, endure, carry or put under," from *sub* "up, under" + *ferre* "to carry, bear."

These two phrases immediately caught my attention: "allow to occur" and "fail to prevent or suppress." How can two such contradictory meanings arise from that one word?

Naturally, we have a fraught and confusing relationship with suffering. We've all been exposed to pain in one form or another. We have learned to dispel suffering no matter our feelings or circumstances and to escape it at all costs. We have learned that suffering is a weakness and feel ashamed to share it openly.

Society promotes happiness at all costs, usually in the form of external things: our bodies, families, relationships, jobs, possessions, etc. We are not properly taught to deal with pain and suffering, which are important components of our *internal* reality. Society also promotes external fulfillment, but real completion might come from being connected to who we really are inside.

Ancients realized that even if suffering is inherent to existence, cessation of suffering is also possible. According to the Buddhist text *The Dhammapada*:

. . . .

All experience is preceded by mind,
Led by mind,
Made by mind.
Speak or act with a corrupted mind,
And suffering follows
As the wagon wheel follows the hoof of the ox.

All experience is preceded by mind,
Led by mind,
Made by mind.
Speak or act with a peaceful mind,
And happiness follows
Like a never-departing shadow.[2]

. . . .

What Is the Mind?

Ancients related the mind to the nature of our thoughts. According to them, the thoughts that you think every single second create the physical reality that you live and perceive around you. Neuroscientists know that thoughts originate in our brains but still don't know exactly how they are generated. Many questions remain, but we do know that electrical signals and electromagnetic energy are involved.

Our thoughts are energy and, as such, have the same properties as energy. That is, they are invisible and can be influenced and transformed by other energy forms beyond time and space. We also know, thanks to recent discoveries in quantum physics, that the mind actually influences the behavior of subatomic particles and physical matter.

Our minds and thoughts have the ability to be influenced and transformed by others, but we also have the power to influence and transform our minds with our *own* thoughts. If thoughts are actually creating our lives, it is necessary to have awareness of our thoughts, to know their source, and to exercise an analysis and review of them.

We consciously process 5 to 9 bits of information per second, and yet our nervous systems are processing 28 to 29 billion bits of information per second. We should have access to *all* those billions of bits of information, so why don't we?

The answer may lie in the unconscious part of our minds.

According to modern psychology, the mind is divided into the conscious and unconscious. The conscious mind is the one that is aware. It's the reasoning mind and the decision maker. The unconscious mind is the source of all that is conscious. It is the part of the mind that indiscriminately records all the information that the conscious mind provides. It stores the primal, instinctive thoughts that we access only involuntarily. It is formed by the many memories, experiences, and learned beliefs that we compile from early childhood (a.k.a. our mind programming), which continue to influence the people we become and the ways we interact with the world—even when we do not consciously remember those long-ago moments or when they have been suppressed. Swiss psychoanalyst Carl Jung explained that the unconscious can be divided into the personal, subjective unconscious of each individual person, and the collective unconscious, shared by all.

Most of us follow daily routines, subscribe to certain beliefs, and repeat without questioning what we have been taught by others. Our mind programming has to do with all the subliminal information we have indiscriminately received from our environment—family, society and culture—since we were in our mothers' wombs. In fact, from the time we are in the womb through the age of six years old, we are in a brain state known as a hypnagogic trance. Alongside the complex motor functions we are learning, we are indiscriminately downloading and absorbing massive amounts of information like a sponge; recording all sensory experiences that come our way. At this stage, we have not yet learned to filter out the false from the true. Regardless, this information and these impressions that we incorporate before the age of six become the foundation for our entire lives. Electroencephalogram (EEG) readings have revealed that brain frequencies in young children below the age of two are predominantly in *delta* and in children between two and six years of age are mostly in *theta*. When their brains are in delta and theta frequencies, people are most suggestible. In fact, these are the same frequencies that hypnotherapists induce to upload new behaviors into their clients.

We subjectively perceive reality according to how our minds have been programmed, filtering out all that doesn't resonate, thus processing less than one percent of reality. The unconscious mind does not distinguish between what is real and what is imagined. It simply takes in the information that it is fed, 24 hours a day—whether we are asleep, awake, or unconscious. Thus, the unconscious mind is the storehouse of all our thoughts, feelings, habits, dreams, fantasies, impulses, and deepest wounds.

Now, imagine for a moment all the false information to which we have been subjected not only by our parents but also by friends, acquaintances, the news, movies, TV, our culture, our political parties, our gender, race, religion, etc. These influences are below our conscious awareness and affect our conscious actions—determining how we respond to the world, interact in relationships, think, and relate to ourselves.

This means that, even though we may not previously have been aware, random unknown experiences and beliefs—such as an inexperienced sister's opinion, the conversation of one's rescuers on an ambulance, a random post on social media, or the lyrics of a song—have been shaping us internally, programming our unconscious and setting inner patterns. Patterns respond to what we unconsciously learned in our past. We are able to spot these because they are predictable behaviors that are generated after we receive specific stimuli. By incorporating other people's ways, we set a repeating response pattern that, with time, becomes a rigid habit that does not support different answers or points of views. These patterns regulate our choices and make up the information that is constantly creating our reality, attracting that with which we resonate and rejecting the rest. This is the same information that supports the beliefs and ideologies that define us and originate many conflicts in our world.

Neuroscience also gives us evidence of the negative bias of the brain. This refers to the idea that negative states of being (such as negative thoughts, emotions, and experiences) affect our psychology and cognitive processes much more than neutral or positive ones. Our ancestors might have benefited from this to protect themselves in the past, but in our modern times, this tendency emphasizes our focus on negative patterns rather than positive ones. These negative patterns are normally triggered and reinforced through our daily routines—for example, when we drive through traffic, hear a strange noise, argue with others, etc. They also occur when our individual needs do not feel met; in our core, there is a sense of deficit and disturbance. But when you focus on the negative, your mind's inner programming is negative, and you continue to resonate with suffering.

In the words of Dr. Joe Dispenza, "Every time you respond to your familiar reality by re-creating the same mind (that is, turning on the same nerve cells to make the brain work in the same way), you 'hard-wire' your brain to match the customary conditions in your personal reality, be they good or bad."[3]

Unconscious learned programming affects our whole being. Once we have accepted a belief or behavior, it becomes a default command in our brains, a closed information system that doesn't allow new information. This closes the possibility of expanding our unconscious information, changing our resonance, and creating new realities.

Are you aware of which part of your learned programming influences your life the most? Have you ever wondered who you are beyond your learned beliefs and experiences?

It is important to know that unconscious thought patterns are not our reality. They are simply thoughts inserted by outsiders that have been repeated so many times that they have become our autopilot response. We have identified with our learned beliefs in such a way that we become what we believe. We attract and avoid people, reject political parties, murder in the name of religious ideologies, and wage wars for beliefs we don't own.

Each person has a unique and original energetic and psychological inner structure that differs from everything we unconsciously learn and is connected to our well-being. If we wish to change our ways, we must replace negative conditioning with authentic thoughts that do not continue to bring up the past, other people's information, or old stresses whose influence we may not be aware of. When we address these and do the work to consciously change them, we pass from a stress response to a relaxation response, which is the foundation for healing.

I like to compare the unconscious to an onion and its many layers. To understand the onion metaphor, let's start with the fact that we are all human beings. Any information additional to this fact is learned and gives form to the different onion layers. In that vein, the different beliefs, wounds, and experiences we have picked up from our surroundings are the layers that separate us from the original self that resides at our core, which existed prior to our learned programming.

How can we change our repetition of other people's patterns? First, we must become aware of the references—from our parents to the information we receive from our environment—that we have picked up unconsciously. If we continue to act and react the same way, the world will be shown to us in the same way: unchanged and constantly mirroring our early false programming rather than revealing what genuinely resonates with us.

There is a Zen proverb that says: "When I was young and free, the mountains were the mountains, the river was the river, the sky was the sky. Then I lost my way, and the mountains were no longer the mountains, the river was no longer the river, the sky was no longer the sky. Then I attained *satori* [the Zen term for enlightenment], and the mountains were again the mountains, and the river was again the river, and the sky was again the sky."[4]

We all are born whole, but the unconscious information we receive fogs up our perceptual lens, not allowing us to see our true reality clearly. As I will discuss throughout this book, crystals can help us become aware of our inner programming. Their meaning to our unconscious minds and multiple properties recognized by science make them ideal tools to de-clutter our unconscious from false programming so we can restore the wholeness that was lost during our acculturation process and reconnect with who we authentically are.

The Role of Our Parents

One of the biggest challenges we are faced with is releasing learned patterns that we acquired from our parents or role models in our early development. Consciously or not, most of us feel emotionally unsafe due to learned patterns from these authority figures and the unprocessed thoughts and emotions from our foundational experiences. This is why it is so important to bring this information from the unconscious to the conscious through deep work on a consistent basis (see Chapter 9 for more details).

Many of the familiar patterns that exist in our unconscious originated in our parents or those who were close to us when we were growing up. They are the ones who most shaped us and created the beliefs that we inherited.

Beyond our genetics, we unconsciously reproduce all we've learned from those who gave us life and raised us: our parents or, in their absence, those who replaced them. Even if we are orphans, the abandonment or absence of our parents will affect us unconsciously.

If we are women, we will tend to identify with our mothers; if we are men, with our fathers. We copy their predilections, their ways of thinking and expressing themselves, and the lens through which they see the world. We take on everything, from their judgments and opinions to what they appreciate and value. We also repeat the way they relate to others; how they see and confront life; and their fears, aversions, modes of processing information and emotions, and deepest wounds.

For example, if your mother grew up without a father, the male figure is absent from her learned unconscious programming. She will have a pattern where she excludes or doesn't integrate men into her life. This can manifest in many ways: as difficulty in finding a life partner, distant relationships with men, and anger toward men, just to name a few examples of recurrent situations originating in life experiences or patterns we have unconsciously learned from others. Unfortunately, if this woman doesn't work on her wound, the pattern will be perpetuated in her daughters and the following generations.

Let's also take a man as an example. If a man is raised without a maternal presence, he will be a man devoid of love, and he will be forced to beg for love in the most precarious places. He might also develop inner rage toward this lack of love, and his relationships with women will be strained or even violent. He might be promiscuous or unfaithful and devalue female merit.

In a household, each sibling will manifest the mother/father pattern differently. These are only two examples of many external influences that shape us and are perpetuated through the generations if we don't take conscious action. Together with the education we receive from school, friends, and our surroundings, our parental influences principally mold our beliefs—which are thoughts we repeat until they have been established as a default in our unconscious minds.

Crystals are the best tool to support us in releasing harmful parental influences because they help us to translate unconscious patterns into conscious awareness. According to Carl Jung, an image is symbolic when it implies something more than its obvious and immediate meaning; that is, it has a broader "unconscious" aspect beyond the grasp of reason.[5] Crystals are carriers of such symbolic meanings, which penetrate our deeper unconscious awareness. It is believed that the earliest humans derived their symbols from an awareness of the known patterns of nature. They could understand, for example, that the sun was linked to the masculine and paternity, and the moon to the feminine and maternity, in the same way that quartz was linked to their own crystalline nature.

Crystals are some of the most basic and beautiful holders of universal patterns. Besides their different colors and shapes, they exhibit repetitive geometric patterns and have inherent vibrations to which one can become sensitive. They are important symbols that bridge the world of matter and our everyday experiences with the invisible world of energy and the unconscious. Crystals can bring our awareness from the known to the unknown, and vice versa, as well as shed light on all the processes in between.

Perhaps you absorbed the beliefs and the emotions of your surroundings as sadness, fear, anger, etc., and suppressed your own nature and who you really are. Despite all this, crystals can help you to honor the authentic within you. By their very nature, crystals are transparent. When you resonate with them, you bring transparency into your life and let go of everything that doesn't belong to you.

For example, perhaps you have been conditioned to never say no to situations with which you are uncomfortable. It is important to identify whose voice is intervening. Is it your mother's? Your father's? Someone else's? What were the situations in your childhood in which you heard the same message? What was going on at the time? What were your feelings? What limiting beliefs about yourself did you internalize?

Crystals can help you recognize the old pattern but also resonate with your own transparency—which is a requirement to create space for a new pattern and reconnect with the authentic within you. Crystals can help you recognize unconscious patterns whenever you feel triggered, when you want to make an empowered choice rather than react, when you'd rather avoid or suppress a situation, or when you find yourself being significantly impacted by an external situation. All these situations can be an impetus to shed what doesn't belong to you. Can you see the connection between what responses you were met with as a child and what comes up for you when you approach your life from a position of transparency?

The Legacy of Patriarchy

Another harmful legacy we inherit from our parents is patriarchy. This is programming inherited from patriarchal societies in which males have the privilege of dominance over females, both visibly and subliminally. This can manifest in the prevailing values, attitudes, customs, expectations, and unquestioned rules of a society. Patriarchy most likely originated in observing the biological differences between both genders. The values and implications underlying the way people interpret these differences are culturally learned as male domination and repression of feminine qualities in both men and women.

According to U.S. Department of Labor statistics, "Although women are now working in more fields than ever, they are still more likely to work in lower-paying jobs than men are, and they remain underrepresented in many occupations. Moreover, even when they work in the same occupations, many women continue to earn less than their male counterparts. Even as women have accessed more jobs in higher-paying sectors, they are still under-represented in many of the highest-paying occupations. For example, women make up less than 1 in 3 chief executives."[6]

While we might view society as the culprit for this inequality, we are introduced to the patriarchal model by both our mothers' and fathers' learned programming. Patriarchy has no gender and affects men and women alike. Some of the common attributes and patterns of patriarchy that manifest in men include: seeking to maintain control, adhering to prevailing opinions, avoiding the expression of emotions, basing relationships in anger and judgment, promoting competition and the achievement of goals, viewing women as reproductive and sexual objects, and performing only masculine roles as defined by society. In women, patriarchy can manifest as: being submissive and passive to others, denying sensitivity and intuition, having low self-esteem, exerting authoritarian control over children, supporting competitive models that are based in comparison, performing only feminine roles as defined by society, and living only through others rather than finding their own fulfillment.

In most societies, mothers have been held responsible for the welfare of their offspring, being either glorified or blamed for who and what type of person their children turn out to be. Our mothers are the gates through which we come into the world; they influence us, whether or not we are conscious of their influence. If our mothers were the people to whom we were most exposed in early childhood, they are the ones who determine how we perceive ourselves and relate to the world. Naturally, our mothers repeated what they learned from their mothers and the surrounding patriarchal society—tinted by shame, guilt, and obligation.

Our mother wounds are traumas that pass down from generation to generation and have a profound impact on our lives. These wounds consist of toxic and oppressive beliefs, ideals, perceptions, and choices.

Let's explore more closely how these patriarchal models play out in specific relationships.

The patriarchal mother relationship with a daughter forms the daughter's opinion of how she is supposed to act and how she should be treated as a woman, as well as how she should treat other women. Where I come from in Latin America, women placed their college education second to getting married—an attitude primarily reinforced by our mothers and other women.

Meanwhile, the patriarchal father relationship with his daughter forms the daughter's opinion just as strongly but with respect to men. Most fathers in my culture were authoritarian, distant figures who established relationships through fear and threats, unconsciously cursing women's future relationships with men.

For sons, the patriarchal mother relationship forms their opinions of how they are supposed to treat and be treated by women. I have a client who told me his mother never had time for him. As an adult, he perpetuated the pattern of his mother's absence by creating distance from his wife through alcoholism, infidelity, excessive work, and other activities.

And finally, the patriarchal father relationship with a son forms the son's opinion of how he should act toward other men. In most Latin American societies, *machismo* is a concept that dictates men's attitudes toward masculinity, especially with respect to their sexuality. It is considered masculine for men to indulge their sexual desires with free rein, often with several women; in contrast, women are not encouraged to indulge their appetites, and female sexuality is seen as something to restrict and control. Moreover, where machismo is prevalent, the manliness of a man is measured by the degree of his infidelity. The more unfaithful a man is, the more respect he receives from other men. Additionally, in some patriarchal religions, polygamy for men is not outlawed.

Patriarchal fathers also have a tendency to tyrannize their sons—sadly, we all repeat what we learn from authoritarian models. Jungian psychoanalyst Marion Woodman writes, "If we have been tyrannized, we can be fairly sure we're tyrannizing someone else—at least ourselves, perhaps our bodies. As we were treated, so we treat ourselves and others."[7]

Overall, patriarchy and the patterns perpetuated by our parents, their parents, and all those who came before them can imprison us in unconscious beliefs about gender and our own destinies as men and women. This prevents us from ever questioning or recognizing who we authentically are.

Unfortunately, the majority of our parents and ancestors were never aware that their parenting was unconsciously inherited from their own parents, much less that they were repeating those patterns automatically—propagating beliefs, habits, and behaviors in their children and their respective offspring. Neither did their children have the awareness or the discernment necessary to question and change this.

Reproducing the patterns of our parents makes it impossible to be self-aware, discover our authentic potential, and evolve. All that we live is re-experienced through our children and their children and their children's children. They listen to and absorb everything we pass on to them. What patterns have we learned from our parents and family that we're unconsciously transmitting to our children? Are we planting in our offspring the seeds that will help them listen to their internal wisdom, or are we imposing our beliefs—many of them unconsciously learned—onto them?

The Collective Paradigm

You have probably heard the expression "Think outside the box." The inside of the box contains our community, religion, historic era, nation, etc. Just as we learned from our parents, we tend to repeat what we have heard or learned from our environment at large. Most of us take for granted the stories we hear without stopping to question where they come from. Many of these stories have contexts that do not apply to us, but for the preprogrammed mind, this is irrelevant. They belong to the collective paradigm.

Paradigm is the Greek word for "pattern." A paradigm is a conceptual framework through which we view experience. Paradigms limit us to see the world through a specific point of view. Collective paradigms prevent us from thinking for ourselves and going beyond current models of thinking. The evolution of different paradigms throughout history has shaped our beliefs significantly as a species and has even affected how crystals are perceived by our mainstream culture.

We are so accustomed to viewing our reality as we've learned to view it that we assume collective paradigms as our own—rejecting all other options in the process, even those connected with our essence. But we can no longer continue to assume that all the stories and knowledge we've received are objective, because they were processed through the filters of the mind, prevailing ideologies, and the subjective experiences and learning of whoever came before us.

Let's take a moment to identify some of our paradigms and become aware of how they manifest in our lives.

The word *history* comes from the Greek and translates to investigation or inquiry. The Greeks gave rise to the definition of history as we know it today. They rationally explained that society functioned as a result of human actions. However, despite numerous attempts over the millennia to offer objective accounts of historical events, different versions of the same stories exist—not only because of prevailing ideology but also because of different perspectives on history's players and because of historians' varied interests and agendas in describing the world. In the words of R. G. Collingwood, "History proceeds by the interpretation of evidence."[8]

History inevitably involves an interpretation of the facts on the part of a biased observer because it captures the past from a present-day interpretation, passed through the filter of the chronicler's learned programming. Over the centuries, historians have been hired to promote specific governments; societies; and political, religious, and economic groups. These histories were told to benefit certain points of view over others and to support the causes, ideologies, or belief systems of those in power—thus ruling out the possibility of knowing the whole truth.

It's important to understand that we are *not* our history. Nor are we the history of the country where we were born or that of our culture, our religion, or our family. We are authentic beings, beyond what we've learned. Therefore, it's important to become observers of our own lives and discern the information we receive, questioning and filtering it with the purpose of stepping into our own story.

The lack of questioning on our parts begins with our internalization of systems of authority, which impose beliefs and behaviors without our awareness. The Oxford English Dictionary defines *authority* not only as "the right to command" and "the power to influence actions" but also as "power over others' opinions," "intellectual influence," "power to inspire beliefs," and "a person or institution whose expressions have the authority to be believed without question."

According to Indian spiritual philosopher Jiddu Krishnamurti, the authority "sets up a pattern, a system based on his ideation; others follow it, finding some gratification in it. Or he starts a religious mode of life which others follow blindly, or intellectually. So patterns, or ways of life, of conduct are set up, politically or psychologically, outwardly and inwardly. The mind, which is generally very lazy and indolent, finds it easy to follow what somebody else has said."[9] Achieving an authentic understanding of who we are requires that we question the ones we have attained via systems of authority.

In particular, religion is one of culture's most potent ways of exerting authority over us. Religions are born from the human desire to reestablish a connection with the divine: that unexplainable supernatural force that created the universe and that connects us with our well-being.

Despite religion's benevolent impulse, all religions have waged wars and genocides to protect and defend their doctrines. In this way, even the impulse of the authentic self—to be one with God, Spirit, the universe, or an authentic source of information—is undermined by collective paradigms based on obedience to authority.

Abraham, Jesus, and Muhammad, as well as other spiritual teachers of the world, wanted to share with everyone all the benefits of reconnecting with the authentic source of information inside each of us. Their messages were essentially the same: they wanted us to experience the source of eternal knowledge. However, although religions were born of the need to cultivate our connection with the universe, today more than ever we see that people are disconnected from their original source.

Not all those who passed on the masters' teachings, except a few disciples, did their necessary inner work or awakened to their authentic source of wisdom. They manipulated the truth through the filters of their minds' programming. But our infinite source, which some religions called *God*, goes beyond the mind and all human constructs. This is perhaps why Jesus said that if we are to enter the kingdom of Heaven, we must become like children—empty of preconceived ideas that come from our conditioning and open to learning the language of the authentic self.

However, when people visit the church, temple, or mosque, rather than connecting with the infinite source, they connect with ideology. Misconceived religion has been coated with ideas, beliefs, judgment, institutions, laws, and requirements that disconnect rather than connect us. We are not led to a direct experience of our truth; rather, we are encouraged to experience our truth through different intermediaries, blindly believing that we must follow the demands of our religious traditions. We are often taught to fear the act of questioning our religion, which we are told (according to the tradition we follow) is sinful and might lead to punishment in the afterlife.

Because of this, religion has become an obstacle to the realization of our authentic selves.

If there is one thing I have learned, it is that the path for reconnecting with who we truly are doesn't follow finite beliefs imposed by the leaders and religious institutions of the day. The path is not external; it comes from within. Crystals themselves can help us recognize the dogma we have inherited from the external world and redirect our attention to the true source and infinite power within us that surpasses all imposed thoughts and beliefs.

Media and the Internet

History, religion, and other age-old paradigms are not the only ones that continue to affect us. Contemporary media and technology also have a stranglehold on the beliefs we form.

Marshall McLuhan, one of the originators of media theory, famously said, "The medium is the message."[10] This phrase suggests that the media can influence society not just through the content that is transmitted but also through its own characteristics, which transform our connection to the world.

As I mentioned before, we receive billions of bits of information. These come through sight, sound, smell, taste, and touch. These bits, in turn, are retransmitted as information to our brains in the form of electrical waves that are filtered through our learned programming into what we know as our personal reality—a small part of the whole reality.

In our modern societies, we learn to place our attention only outside, but perfect balance requires a mix of inside and outside. The frenetic pace of our modern lives leaves little space for listening to and connecting with ourselves.

It's only been 25 years since Tim Berners-Lee created the World Wide Web (www), but in that time, the Internet has already become an integral part of everyday life for most of the world's population. It allows us to instantly access any information on the planet, at any place or time of day, through just a click. We have numerous online accounts and subscribe to dozens of websites to obtain more information. We blog, text, watch videos, and download music and movies. We find ourselves online for several hours a day, Googling, networking, purchasing, browsing social media, or reading our e-mails.

The Internet also facilitates opportunities to further our connection with ourselves. We can access the world's wisdom via the texts of masters of diverse philosophies and cultures. We can experience different practices and attend workshops that give us tools for inner work from the comfort of our own homes. All of this makes our era unique. Knowledge that has been hidden for centuries is now accessible to all.

However, the benefits don't make us any less susceptible to the drawbacks. Usually, the content we reject does not coincide with our inner data. Exposing ourselves to new points of view can expand our inner programming and widen our limited perspectives, but few of us take the time to cultivate new ways of thinking—especially when we are online.

With so many possibilities and so much information, the biggest hazard we face by exposing ourselves to the Internet is that much of its content can reprogram our minds and remove us from our authentic selves. At this rate, we can say that most of the contents of our minds, without supervision, belong to cyberspace.

There were 3.9 billion Internet users in 2018. According to Internet Live Stats, around 40 percent of the world population has an Internet connection. More than 70 percent of the youth population is online.[11] Every day, 3.5 billion Google searches are made.[12] Every 20 minutes, 55 million status updates are made; every day, 1 million links are shared and 3 million messages are sent through Facebook. Twitter's average tweets per second is in the ballpark of 6,000.[13] Instagram presently sees 4.2 billion likes daily and 95 million photos uploaded per day.[14] Given the speed at which digital connectivity is changing our lives, we might benefit from asking questions such as: Is this content true to my real self? Why is it true to me? Why is not true to me? Which learned programming is it reinforcing? Am I willing to change that programming? In which ways is this content supporting my authentic self?

The Inheritance of Suffering

My story is a testament to how the unconscious mind can inherit learned beliefs that perpetuate suffering. The main reason I became a healer was to heal my suffering and the suffering of others. I was born to a traditional Jewish family and raised in Venezuela, and I grew up in a Latin American culture that valued traditional gender roles. Exaggerated, toxic masculinity was culturally accepted. Thus, I grew up with the belief that to be a woman was to suffer and to be treated in disrespectful and nasty ways.

Because marriage was considered more important than having a career, I was married for the first time at the age of 21. I studied journalism in the midst of this and was passionate about searching for the truth behind everything. Although I worked, my career aspirations were not taken seriously. My true abilities were overshadowed by my gender and the sexist learned beliefs of the men around me. In my own community, the fact that I worked instead of taking care of my husband and the household was not accepted.

Not only was I disrespected by the men in my job, but I was also dishonored by my own husband, which led to divorce. I had known him since I was 17, and it was hard to imagine my world without him. Sadness seized me. Months later, I was diagnosed with a malignant melanoma. I had surgery, and while that part of the cancer had been removed I was told that it might return. I was 25 years old.

Everyone around me was having fun and enjoying life, and I had cancer. Why me? I had done everything that life expected from me. I was a good daughter, a good sister, a good friend, a good student . . . a good human being.

But who was I, really? Beyond being a daughter, sister, friend, Jew, Latin American, woman, journalist? The cancer had somehow awakened me from my unconsciousness and opened questions about my life and all its structures. I began a process that, later in life, would reconnect me with who I really was beyond what I had learned to believe.

Two years passed and I was married again to another Jewish man, this time in Bogotá, Colombia. We had two kids together. In Bogotá, I had the opportunity to travel and explore different cultures and philosophies. I discovered my true vocation in crystal healing. I opened my crystal practice and Centro Integración Shambalah, one of the first holistic centers in Bogotá. Soon after, fame knocked at my door. I was very busy.

But when I remarried, the pattern I'd experienced with my previous husband repeated. My second husband informed me that the most important task on my shoulders was to take care of the house and children. He allowed me to work on the condition I did it while my children were in school. He wasn't comfortable with me being a healer and sharing my time with strangers. I was often featured in the media for my work with crystals, and my husband didn't appreciate this. Later, he would use it as an argument in court to fight for the custody of my children.

Although we never had any visible fights, I didn't feel comfortable with him. In his eyes, everything I did was wrong. I wasn't a good enough mother. I wasn't a good enough housekeeper. I wasn't good enough for him. I believed all his words. My unconscious mind was filled with his negative thoughts. My self-esteem quickly diminished. I felt like I was sinking; he was clipping my wings, which were so eager to fly.

As I deepened my work with crystals, I came to recognize that *none* of this was true. I was simply absorbing his stories. Maybe he had unconsciously learned them from his father, his masculine model, who was very closed-minded. Or maybe he had a hidden agenda of which he was not even aware. Perhaps he felt that his mother's love was not enough and, thus, showed his anger in our relationship.

I didn't want to live this way anymore. I asked him to go to therapy with me, but he refused. I finally decided to part with him. We had a cordial relationship for four years until I decided to move from Colombia and take my children with me. Over the next few years, I went through a long and painful divorce process. Eventually, my ex cut off all financial support and kept my children from me. I began a legal process in Colombia to recover my children, but I quickly realized he had contaminated their minds with information against me. He made them believe that I had abandoned them and that I was not psychologically able to take care of them due to stories he invented or because I worked with crystals. All these were built in until my children were alienated from me.

The last thrust of the sword happened when my own children spoke up in court against me. It was obvious that the words of others had been placed in their minds and mouths. Those words were the ones that made me lose my last hope.

The curse of my family repeated. My kids were going to be raised without a mother. Their unconscious minds now belonged to my ex, his girlfriend, and his family. Now, my son would have to work to not repeat the story of his father, and my daughter to not repeat the story of her mother.

I moved to Santa Barbara, California, my new home . . . but by this time, I had lost my kids, my job, my income, and my friends.

My previous life was fading, and I was fading with it.

Over the next several years, I began to deconstruct the toxic programming that I had absorbed. I looked at my own conditioning, starting with the women in my family.

My earliest memories of the women in my family were that they were neither loving nor maternal. It was little wonder, given the suffering they had experienced. My great-grandmother died from the bubonic plague shortly after my grandmother was born. My grandmother then lived in a concentration camp in Europe until the end of World War II. Her husband, my grandfather, had been sent to forced labor camps, and she did not know whether he was alive or dead until the war ended. Hungry, alone, and uncertain about the future, she existed in an environment between life and death. All of this was in my grandmother's mind when she became pregnant with my mom after being reunited with my grandfather after the war.

The horrors of the war didn't end after the war. In fact, they became the main topic of conversation in my family. My father told me that when he met my grandparents, wartime was all they ever talked about. And although my mother did not live through the war physically, it was imprinted onto her mind.

Although my mother was a genius, she was deeply insecure and full of fear and mistrust of the world. She married at the age of 18, and I was born when she was 19. As a mother, she was absent. Her body was there, but she was not. She complained all the time, was hypercritical, and often cried. Instead of her taking care of me, I felt I had to take care of this fragile woman. The curse of my motherless grandmother was perpetuated through my mother's absence from my life—and now, I too could not be present for my own children.

Unconsciously, I was perpetuating a legacy that had nothing to do with me. I was living the story of suffering that is so familiar to all of us. And crystals were showing me that I did not have to continue this story.

The Real Meaning of Suffering

So, what does all this learned mind programming have to do with suffering?

As we progress through life, we realize that the false information becomes further entrenched as we are socialized and pressured to fit into our communities and cultural norms. The false programming overrides the original data we are born with. Over time, through our attachment to this false information, we come to believe that we are something other than what we are.

But through it all, the original data never fades entirely. Our true nature remains pulsating within us, even if we identify with our false information. It's this push and pull, this clash of information, that's the true source of our suffering. It can even be the source of disease. But it is also what cracks us *out* of our programming. It's what opens the space for us to clear all the accumulated data and to make room for our authentic selves to emerge and bring clarity to us.

Crystal healing works best at these clash points in life. It's precisely at these moments, when the burden of the inauthentic self becomes unbearable, that crystals have the power to transform the layers of false information and reconnect us with our original selves. As I discovered, suffering can actually bring us home to our true nature. In truth, suffering can be a great blessing and opportunity, a master in disguise knocking at our door to show us new worlds and reveal to us who we really are. Ancients knew that suffering isn't a threat, as many have come to believe, but a gateway to bring universal order into our lives. For them, crystals could decipher the inner contents of our unconscious such that we could work to free ourselves from suffering and awaken our true beings.

Crystals are such effective healing tools because they work through patterns. A pattern is a part within the whole that encodes in miniature the characteristics and functions of an entire system. By understanding this part, we can grasp a deeper understanding of the phenomenon, process, or object we are inquiring about.

Jung believed that patterns made possible the understanding of the unconscious and that by examining them, we could connect directly with those unknown places within us that impede our sustained well-being. Unfortunately, we have lost the ability to read patterns and recognize when we are out of sync with our true nature—an ability that most ancient peoples cultivated to a sophisticated degree. However, patterns are present in every aspect of our existence, from the dynamics of family life to the experiences we find within culture and society. Our conscious and unconscious mental processes and the ways we think are also patterned through our learning, beliefs, and life experiences.

A basic understanding of patterns and symbols is necessary as we shift gears to Part II of this book. Now that we have looked at the social, psychological, and familial roots and ramifications of suffering, or disconnection from the authentic self, we are ready to widen our scope. In the next part of the book, I bring to your awareness the use and meaning of stones from a historical point of view. In Chapter 3, you will learn about the evolution of the crystal blueprint from the beginning of human civilization and through the Age of Reason. I will also bring to your awareness the different symbols, patterns, and meanings of stones from ancient times to the present. Crystals' symbolic meaning can not only help us uncover our unconscious and the mysteries beyond our suffering but also reveal to us the evolutionary potential to blossom into the multifaceted, transparent beings we were designed to be.

Our unconscious must become transparent in order for us to recognize our authentic nature. Through crystals, we are given a choice. We can opt to not be victims of collective paradigms and others' stories. We can follow our own stories—transforming our patterns of suffering into well-being.

PART II

A BRIEF HISTORY OF QUARTZ AND CRYSTAL HEALING

CHAPTER 3

Crystal Healing and Protection through the Ages

"The use of quartz throughout human history is a
recurring Light-motif. From the highly advanced ancient civilizations
to the primal medicine man to the present day, crystals have been
used on many levels for a multitude of purposes."

— RANDALL N. BAER AND VICKI V. BAER[1]

IN THIS CHAPTER, you will witness the beginnings of crystal healing
and how the symbolism of stones has evolved since ancient times.
You will also be able to explore which of these meanings resonates
with you deeply so that you can begin your crystalline path of
transformation toward your own authentic self.

Crystals and stones have been sharing their wisdom with us since
time immemorial. Ancient traditions and archaeological discoveries
in India, China, Chaldea, Mesopotamia, Egypt, Greece, Great Britain,
and Central and South America, among others, indicate that crystals
have been part of our history since the emergence of humans.

In the 1920s, near Beijing, China, scientists uncovered the remains
of Peking Man, a distant ancestor of humans also known as *Homo
erectus*. Remarkably, Peking Man, who appeared between 250,000
and 400,000 years ago, collected quartz crystals. It is also around
this time that the many varieties of quartz crystals appear in the fossil

record. According to Chinese anthropologist W. C. Pei, "Of quartz crystals, about twenty pieces of different size were found together with one perfect crystal 6 centimeters in length. This crystal is smoky in color, and all the crystalline faces are complete."[2]

Moreover, quartz crystal was used by prehistoric humans as early as 75,000 B.C.E. Quartz has been found in prehistoric burial grounds, as well as the monuments of pharaohs and the ruins of Sumerian cities. Archaeologists have discovered Egyptian and Babylonian crystal scarabs, vases, and cylinders dating back to 1500 B.C.E. Egyptians were mining agate as early as 3500 B.C.E., while early inhabitants of Mesopotamia fashioned cylinder seals, signet rings, beads, and other ornamental objects from this stone.[3]

As we know from archaeological evidence, we have revered crystals as valuable objects and sacred sites since the earliest eras of known human history. From their creation to our current day, experiences of awareness and healing were well known. For the ancients, megaliths (such as stone circles, temples, and pyramids) were not common places but sites where invisible technologies were working to reconnect us to our original perfection and bring us to a state of sacred balance. According to Pierre Méreaux, a French researcher and electrical engineer, these sites are alive. Such is the case of Carnac, a megalithic site in France where 80,000 quartz-rich stones stand over an active earthquake zone that is constantly being compressed and thus is electromagnetically active.[4] It is not surprising that people routinely came to such an area in search of healing and believed that these sites possessed special powers. As mediators between humans and supernatural powers, stones held a very important place in the world of our ancestors.

Reparatio Generis Humani ("Rebirth of Mankind").

It was believed that stones had the power to co-create. A man and woman walk out onto the land, throwing stones behind them, which form babies. Reproduced with the permission of the Wellcome Library, London

History marks the beginnings of civilization somewhere between 5,000 and 5,500 years ago in ancient Sumer. From that point on, as we've been told, we've made a linear progression to becoming the most sophisticated civilization that ever existed on Earth. The idea that civilizations around the world have evolved from a primitive state toward a more advanced one is a concept that mainstream scholars have perpetuated. However, the data doesn't support that story. In fact, ancient civilizations were far more advanced than we believe. Looking at the historical references that can be found in numerous ancient civilizations around the globe, we find patterns and details that offer a different story from the one imposed by mainstream knowledge.

The Language of Symbols

According to C. G. Jung, "The whole cosmos is a potential symbol."[5] Indeed, symbols constitute a primordial language that is older than human history. Symbolic thinking has been ingrained in us from our earliest times and continues to outlast every civilization that ever was. The history of symbolism shows that everything can assume symbolic significance, from natural objects like stones to abstract forms like numbers or even geometry. Symbols are impactful, as they mirror and resonate with deep meanings that we are unconscious of. Symbols are the language of the unconscious world—the world that remains unknown and unperceived by our five senses.

In numerous ancient cultures all over the world, stones were revered as exemplars of cosmic harmony and higher spiritual truths. They were adored as sacred symbols with deep spiritual and religious significance. The earliest spiritual system known to humans is the animistic tradition, which regards all natural features as spirited, animated parts of the earth—which is regarded as the body of God, with stones and crystals being symbolic extensions of God's powers. This concept predates formal religions. When polytheistic religions emerged, the Earth Mother manifested in the shape of various gods. Sacred stones then were interpreted as the homes of gods and goddesses.

Stones were also often prized for their symbolism and the ways in which they seemed to allude to larger cosmic powers. In very early times, some stones were symbolic of certain virtues or attributes, or as symbols of deities, and were used in ceremonies. In this way, colors, deities, numbers, shapes, the elements that were represented, the animal that was related, and assigned astrological signs were transformed into symbols, as well as powerful amulets.

Amulets and Talismans of Protection

Deities and religious images carved in stone can be found from very primitive times in different sites and also throughout history—from Babylon, Egypt, Greece, and Rome to the present day. Carrying these stones, whether they were carved or natural, was a way to keep a direct connection to their special powers—especially protection, luck, and revelation.

Fetishism refers to the worship of inanimate objects for their supposed magical powers; it was especially common in ancient times. In fact, the concept of assigning life to objects is common among most early civilizations.

The animation of precious stones, since they do not move, likely originated from the symbolism and patterns that the ancients observed. Often, they would notice the unusual form of a stone or its perceived resemblance to an animal, human being, or other object, all of which resulted in an attribution of occult powers to the stone.

As their name suggests, "figured stones" are those bearing a striking image or shape, whether original to the stone or created by a man-made process. Figured stones have been with us since prehistoric times. Some were considered recipients of specific deities and myths, while others were reminders of miracles.

Animal images, in addition to body parts and carving of deities, have been used as fetishes since ancient times. The scarab, the snake, the fish, the elephant, the frog, and the owl are among the best known and most commonly used. A fetish was believed to have a power greater than the object itself naturally possessed.

The etymology of the word *amulet* comes from the Arabic word *hamalât*, meaning "to suspend something when worn." But in Latin, *amuletum* is a word that originates in the verb *amoliri*, which means "to remove" or "drive away."[6]

For the ancients, stones could be used to drive away external threats and dangers, such as illness, personality disorders, misfortune, natural disasters, or invasion, among others. When people wore these stones, they could attribute certain occurrences, such as the warding off of danger, to the stones' efficacy. This is what ultimately led to the conviction that stones were abodes for powerful spirits or even protective ancestors.

Amulets were also used for healing. For example, a popular cut for deep red jasper is a pear-shaped one. The similarity to a drop of blood is said to increase the stone's ability to stop bleeding and prevent infection. If the amulet was hung from a red ribbon, its power was believed to be magnified.[7]

The aim of the following pages is to become aware of the meaning of stones through the ages by means of their different applications and symbolism through the evolution of human thought—and to see how they reflected the cultural and psychological ideas and beliefs of ancient times. We'll gain insight into the minds and concerns of our ancestors and how they interpreted the symbols within gemstones, such as colors, numbers, astrology, and shapes.

Atlantis

Barbara Hand Clow, in her groundbreaking book *Awakening the Planetary Mind*, emphasizes not only that almost every ancient civilized society recognized to date operated at a surprisingly advanced technological level but also that such expertise and sophistication must have been acquired before the onset of the Holocene period, which is the geological epoch that began shortly after the Pleistocene, approximately 11,700 years ago. This is the context in which the story of the civilization known as Atlantis appeared for the first time, in the fabled texts *Critias* and *Timaeus*, by Greek philosopher Plato.

Plato believed that Atlantis was only one of many leading cultures in a maritime civilization. *Maps of the Ancient Sea Kings*— Charles Hapgood's classic 1966 book of early, extant maps featuring topography north and south of the equator—provides ample evidence for a global maritime civilization that was trading all over the world from 17,000 to 6,000 years ago.

Many of the texts that offer us information about Atlantis attest to the advancements of its civilization. The old legends suggest that Atlantis flourished during a period dating from at least 150,000 B.C.E. until approximately 10,000 B.C.E., when it sank into the ocean. Much of their sophisticated technology was based on the energetic applications of quartz crystals.

The technology and science of Atlantis evolved to such a degree of sophistication that it included flying devices powered by a distant energy source that transmuted the energy of the sun through crystals—similar to solar cells made of silicon crystals today. The concept of broadcasting usable energy to a distant location is an idea that was developed in the 20th century by the electrical wizard Nikola Tesla—but as history has told us, it likely had an earlier blueprint.

Atlanteans also appear to have been oriented more toward the use of vibrational medicines than drug therapies. They were famous for their knowledge of the healing powers of crystals and laid the foundation for natural and vibrational medicine. When it came to disease and illness, Atlanteans recognized that the source of disease lay not in the physical body but a "higher" spiritual body. They understood the laws of vibration and how to use them.

If someone were ill, he or she was taken to a special healing area and placed in the middle of it. The room was typically constructed of a specific crystal and in such a way that sunlight would be diffused into beams of different colored light and, therefore, different frequencies of energy. Depending on the nature of a person's illness, the person would be positioned so that a specific color of light was directed onto his or her body. Healing involved the arrangement of crystals directing vibrations to the body that were resonant with healthy energies and restored balance.

Although the physical continent of Atlantis is no more, its legacy is still alive today in some oral traditions and rituals among indigenous peoples. In fact, researchers have identified "Atlantean" megaliths throughout the world. These megaliths typically used gigantic blocks of stone, often quartz-rich granite. Such monuments can still be found around the world, from the Mycenae in the Peloponnese and the temples of Malta, to the gigantic megalithic walls of Tiwanaku in Bolivia, to Stonehenge in the United Kingdom, to the Osirion at Abydos and the Valley Temple of the Sphinx.[8]

Ancient Egypt

In 3000 B.C.E., Egyptians were already aware of the properties of crystals, which they used as protective amulets and jewelry and as remedies to improve their health. They were also used in their healing temples. In ancient times, it was a habitual practice to use an image of a specific part of the human body as a protective mechanism. This custom was especially popular in ancient Egypt, where there were amulets that represented the heart, the head, the face, or the ears, eyes, tongue, fingers, hands, arms, legs, and genitals. Egyptian amulets can still be found in the shape of body parts, animals, and other symbolic objects, as we see in these carnelian amulets:

Hand and foot amulets (2465 B.C.E.). Photo: akg-images | Metropolitan Museum of Art, New York.

Running horse amulet (200 B.C.E.–200 C.E.). Photo: akg-images | Metropolitan Museum of Art, New York.

Scarab inscription for Merytamum (1525–1504 B.C.E.). Photo: akg-images | Metropolitan Museum of Art, New York.

Reverse view of Horus stele, 4th century B.C.E. Photo: akg-images | Werner Forman.

Stones were used in steles, which were vertical rock-cut tablets made of stone-bearing inscriptions and imagery. They were particularly used in magic, deity worship, and for protection against harmful influences. Horus stele, for example, serves against attacks by harmful creatures and cures snake bites and scorpion stings.

In a passage in the *Egyptian Book of the Dead*, as translated by Sir E. A. Wallis Budge, the scribe writes: "I have taken possession of the Ureret crown; Ma'at [i.e., right and truth] is my body; its mouths are turquoise and rock crystal. My homestead is among the furrows which are [of the colour of] lapis lazuli."[9]

To the ancient Egyptians, these gems and stones symbolized all that was immortal—objects that would not lose their beauty or brilliance, even after death. A stone, especially a crystal or precious gem, symbolized the eternal. Thus, it was quite normal to allow any stone or gem that had already adorned the wearer in his or her lifetime to accompany him or her as protection and adornment on the path into the unknown.

The meaning of precious gems and crystals for the Egyptians is most strongly emphasized in this passage from the Book of the Dead, in which a deceased person is addressed: "Your breast is blue like lapis lazuli your locks are darker than the gloomy portals of the house of the dead Ra's rays illuminate your visage your dress woven with gold is decorated with lapis lazuli your limbs, bursting with vigour, covered in gold your breasts swell, like crystal eggs Horus has coloured them with lapis lazuli your shoulders are transparent as crystal."[10]

There is no doubt that crystals and gemstones were powerful symbols among the aristocracy. Archaeologists discovered 143 pieces of jewelry in the crypt of Tutankhamen, from diverse stones such as carnelian, rock crystals, and other stones. Many of the items were found in the "treasure chamber" of Tutankhamen, meaning they had been specially made for the pharaoh's passage into the afterlife.[11]

Of all the amulets found in the treasure chamber, the type most frequently encountered has the shape of a human heart. These amulets were found in carnelian, red jasper, granite, green jasper, and other materials. The heart, regarded in ancient Egypt as the seat of life, was an object of special care after death. Enclosed in a special receptacle, the amulet was buried with the pharaoh, and the belief was that only after it had been weighed in the balance of the underworld, against the symbol of law, could it regain its place in the body and spirit of the deceased.

Stephen Mehler, Egyptologist and author of *From Light into Darkness: The Evolution of Religion in Ancient Egypt*, explains that much of the information about crystals goes back further than hieroglyphics, or pictorial writing, which emerged between 6,000 and 8,000 years ago. According to the oral traditions that Mehler has studied, crystals were used in healing for many millennia.

Mehler says that the ancient predynastic Egyptians were responsible for building the pyramids and carving the Great Sphinx—and they had an incredible knowledge of stone and crystal.

Limestone and sandstone (rich in quartz) were the main building stones of ancient Egypt. The Egyptians made their ornaments, sarcophagi, statues and steles from granite, granodiorite, limestone, and sandstone.[12]

"Judging by the materials they chose, they understood the qualities of the stone," explains Mehler. "They understood the mineralogical content of the stone, and they had a specific reason for putting them in specific places at a specific time. They chose the particular stones in their monuments for their unique properties . . . for the transmission of energy, for vibration, for healing . . . which was all known by ancient people, handed down to the Greeks, handed down to the Romans, handed down to the Babylonians, and to the Western mystery schools."[13]

Mehler was told by one of his teachers that stone high in quartz content could be used for sonic resonance and also to activate and charge water in a powerful energy feedback system. Mehler also notes that glyphs featuring the placement of certain objects on a person's body for healing operations are quite common and that these objects resemble crystals. The use of quartz in energetic therapy may have been a common practice among ancient Egyptians.

"In the temple of Saqqara, crystal was used for healing, along with sound and water. There were other temples . . . where they would use the so-called alternative techniques we use today like sound, color, chanting, crystals, and herbs," says Mehler.

Ancient Egyptian priests regarded the temple as being alive. In the Egyptian desert, temples were often built where electromagnetic lines or ley lines intersected. In 1350 B.C.E., Amenhotep built "The Colossi of Memnon," quartzite singing statues at the temple of Thebes. The rising of the sun raised the frequency of the quartz's vibration, triggering a sacred and healing sound infusing peace and authentic qualities among the followers inside the temple.

New research has also surfaced an alternative theory about the Great Pyramid of Giza. Although it is believed by most to be a funerary building, as proposed by many conservative Egyptologists and mainstream researchers, others think it was devised as a wireless power plant created thousands of years ago. The pyramid may convert mechanical vibration from the earth into resonances, electricity, or magnetics from the sun's rays. The pyramid's shape works like an inverted funnel in which energy concentrates and is amplified. Given the material, geometry, and specific construction of the pyramid, the electromagnetic field that forms at the very bottom of the pyramid has been speculated by some to power numerous devices across Egypt in the same way Tesla's Wardenclyffe Tower did in the early 1900s.[14]

It is speculated that not only could the Great Pyramid be capable of generating electricity, it could also increase our vibration and frequency and in this way reconnect us with our true selves.

It is obvious that ancient Egyptians used quartz, as well as stone, as a technology to manipulate electromagnetic currents and were certainly more advanced than we give them credit for.

The Sumerians

Some historians refer to Sumer (Old Babylon) as the cradle of civilization. According to Mehler, Sumer was part of Khemit (ancient Egypt) and was known as *Sa-Mer-Ra.*

The Sumerians who settled in Mesopotamia were familiar with the art of working precious stones and gems as early as the fourth millennium B.C.E. Sumerians believed that stones were imbued with magical powers that could protect them against any mischievous or evil deeds. Besides using them in royal tombs, seals, temples, and icons of deities, they used them for protection and to cure ailments.

The oldest magical formulas that have been preserved for us are those of the ancient Sumerians. Some of them contain references to the use of precious stones as amulets:

. . . .

"Cords of light-colored wool,
Offered with a pure hand,
For jaundice of the eye,
Bind on the right side (of the patient).
A luluti ring, with sparkling stones
Brought from his own land,
For inflammation of the eye,
On the little finger
Of his left (hand), place."[15]

. . . .

Assyriologist Samuel Noah Kramer describes one of the ways Sumerians used crystal seals: "One of the favourite subjects for gem cutters in southern Mesopotamia was a scene in which a man is introduced to one god by another god; probably the owner of the seal was being introduced to his personal patron divinity."[16]

Clear quartz cylinder seal and imprint of worshiper with symbols of deities, 1595–1200 b.c.e. Photo: akg-images, Erich Lessing.

Assyria and Babylon are where we see archaeological evidence of the use of stones for amuletic purposes for the first time in the history of human civilization. Sumerian inscriptions contain numerous names of gems. Precious stones were also equated with luck and positive forces, both in the literary texts as well as in spoken language. The stars were also connected with precious stones and could influence them.

JoAnn Scurlock, internationally renowned scholar of the ancient Near East, has presented translations of texts originally written in Assyrian and Babylonian in clay tablets, some of which derive from Ashurbanipal's (685–627 B.C.E.) famous library of Nineveh. According to Scurlock, the stones could be used alone or ground up and wrapped together with other ingredients. Sometimes, finely ground stones were added to water, oil, or beer for application as a salve or healing draft.[17]

The Maya

In the middle and late 19th century, several renowned Mesoamerican scholars, starting with Charles-Étienne Brasseur de Bourbourg and later including Edward Herbert Thompson and Augustus Le

Plongeon, formally proposed that Atlantis was somehow related to the Toltecs, the South American tribe from whom the Maya, the Aztecs, and other Mesoamerican indigenous groups originated. These scholars believed that the Toltecs were the surviving population of the civilization of Atlantis.[18]

The Maya formed an advanced civilization that spread from southeastern Mexico throughout Central America. They believed that the earth was a sacred and animate entity, and thus rock crystals, or *p'uk*, were the source of universal power between humans and nature spirits.

The ancient Maya also believed that stones had souls. They had a great deal of respect and reverence for stones—as links to the past, both symbolic and actual, and as bearers of secrets.

The recovery of crystals from a number of Maya caves and archaeological sites suggests that they were an important part of daily rituals. The Maya use of crystals is associated with crystalmancy, or curing and divination through crystals. To this day, Maya families light a candle to the stones and pour alcohol over them to keep their *nahuales*, or spirits, happy.

Itzaj Maya divinatory crystals are known as *sastu'n*, which translates to stones of clarity. Nahua shamans call their large crystals *tescatl*, or mirrors. Gazing into the crystal, they are able to see patterns and communicate with the stone. The Huastec healer sees past events that caused the disease, and among the Otomi, the crystal pulls the sickness out when passed over the body.[19]

Maya priests also designated to each stone in their shrines (*encantos*) a name and a role. There was a stone that the priests referred to as their "doctor" because it was capable of healing illness; another stone was known as "savior of the world." Some were left by their ancestors, others were shown through dreams, others were found in caves, and still others came from the sites of ancient ruins. Additionally, crystals were placed with the dead in order to capture or replace the qualities of the heart or soul.[20]

According to Stephen Mehler, the Maya were especially interested in crystal skulls: "They used crystal skulls as 'computers.' Today, we actually know that a piece of quartz crystal will record the energy of anyone who ever touches it. So the skulls are like living cameras or tape recorders that are always on. This is in a metaphysical sense, not a scientific sense. There's no doubt that the ancient Maya and ancient Olmecs were using them for many, many different things: for healing, for storing energy, for storing events."

Although many scientists disparage the claims of those who have studied the crystal skulls by insisting that they were manufactured in the mid–19th century or later, according to Jaap van Etten, a Dutch biologist and crystal skull researcher and expert, "*Contemporary crystal skulls* are considered to be carved within the past hundred years. *Old crystal skulls* are those that have been carved between one hundred and fifteen hundred years ago."[21] Often, scientists determine the age of the skulls through their location or through evidence of tool marks. However, a skull could be much older than the ruins, graves, or other locations where it was discovered, or it may have been reworked to make it more aesthetically pleasing or to increase its value.

Although most of the crystal skulls found today are contemporary, there are many that are believed to be much older. According to van Etten, the most ancient crystal skulls used by the Maya were actually created in Atlantis 12,000 or more years ago. The Mitchell-Hedges crystal skull, named after the English explorer and adventurer, is one of them and was found in the Maya ruins of Lubaantun in Belize. He refers to it as a singing skull because it is believed that it emits frequencies that can be heard clairaudiently.[22]

The Inca

The Inca, or Inkakuna, was another civilization that linked its origins to Atlantis. In Quechua, the language spoken by the Inca and still in use in the high Andes, the word for "crystal" is *jespehrumi*, which translates to "sparkle of light." *Jezperizon* is the Quechua word used for the process of light beginning to shine in our hearts and minds.

The Inca consider their surrounding mountains to be *apus*, or *apukunas*, mountain spirits that connect other dimensions to this one. The Inca considered crystals the *apus'* special gifts to us, as they carry ancestral memories to remind us of our connection to our cosmic origins.

According to Julian Sasari, a *chacaruna* (Inca shaman), the Inca used crystals to make their hearts, minds, and bodies shine. Machu Picchu itself is a crystal city, as its stones contain high quantities of quartz crystal.

Jorge Luis Delgado, another *chacaruna* and author of *Andean Awakening*, says that the origin of the name Inca comes from two words: "In" from *inti*, meaning "the Andean Mountains," and "Ca" from *cana*, meaning "a ray of light." The Inca creation story underscores the notion that everything is created by light; awakening the light codes buried in human form was a requirement to become an Inca, which means "illuminated ones."

Delgado says that the Inca believed we are the children of Father Sun (Inti) and Mother Earth (Pachamama). "As children of the Earth, we come from the heart of the mother, as a filament of light. In this reality, we become like a prism, like a quartz crystal. So when we open ourselves, when we release our resistance, we let the luminosity of that light flow through our lives."

Sasari mentions that, in his community, quartz crystals are heated, and the ill person is exposed to their vapors; elders believe these vapors have healing properties and can restore balance.

Delgado has a different technique of placing stones on the body for healing. "We use three points of the body: the solar plexus, where we hold heavy energies; the heart, where we release the resistance that we have; and the third eye, which many call the first eye. We blow over a stone or crystal, program it with our intent, and put it on these three places. But the crystal doesn't do all the work; it is a support. It is when you pull out what is not comfortable inside of you, with forgiveness, that you gain power. I believe that the stone people, crystals, provide the service of helping us trust ourselves again in our power."

Crystal Applications from Greece to the Renaissance

The literature regarding precious stones has a tradition that is almost 2,000 years old. The literature on crystals that remains from the ancient period and continues through the 18th century is the source of some of the earliest studies of medicine and the physical sciences, as well as of religious traditions, beliefs, and myths about gemstones. The term often applied to these treatises is *lapidary,* a word that means "referring to precious stones or working with precious stones."

The first form of lapidary in the Western tradition consists of mineralogical studies produced in classical Greece. The second form of lapidary is the multi-volume encyclopedic works of Roman authors, who produced vast compilations of universal knowledge. The third form is the verse lapidary, which typically lists a selection of stones accompanied by physical appearance, properties, origins, and medicinal applications, usually in alphabetical order. The fourth form is the prose lapidary, which ranges from relatively concise works to comprehensive descriptions, not only of stones, but also of theories around their substance and formation, as well as the efficacy of their medical applications. The fifth type of lapidary includes texts on any subject with a separate section dedicated to giving the reader information and instructions about the medicinal use of stones. The last form of lapidary is the popular advice manual that offers information on healing techniques; this was most common in the 16th to the 18th centuries in England.[23]

The earliest lapidaries come from the ancient Greeks, who attributed a number of properties to crystals; many of the names for gems that we use today are of Greek origin. The word *crystal* comes from the Greek word *krustallos,* which was the term for ice. It was believed that clear quartz was water that had frozen so deeply that it would always remain solid.

In this period, university-trained doctors worked alongside apothecaries, midwives, clergy, and other healing practitioners, and the medical use of gemstones was accepted by most people. As a whole, the society believed that crystals could cure many illnesses: physical, mental, and spiritual. The scholarly textual tradition of ancient Greece is what later scholars and physicians looked to in exploring the healing properties of gemstones.[24]

Beginning with the mineralogical treatises of ancient Greece, ideas about the nature, origin, and therapeutic application of stones grew in number and complexity throughout the medieval and early modern periods. They would gradually evolve to adapt to social and cultural changes, as well as the development of scientific knowledge. Plato's discourses reveal the ancients' preoccupation with crystals. In his *Phaedo*, he writes: "If it could be seen from above, [the earth] is to look upon like those balls covered with twelve patches of leather, many-coloured . . . and the mountains again in like manner, and the stones have their smoothness and transparency and colours fairer in the same proportion; of which also the pebbles here, those that are so highly prized, are fragments, carnelians and jaspers and emeralds and all of that kind."[25]

The Persian Wars, which introduced the religious beliefs and spiritual customs of the Persians (the cultural heirs of ancient Sumer) to the Greeks, were determining factors in the development of the Greek art of working with gems.

The oldest surviving mineralogy book and earliest known Western work to expressly deal with the properties of stones in a medical sense is *De lapidibus* ("On Stones"), written by a successor to Plato and Aristotle, Theophrastus (372–287 B.C.E.). In this lapidary, Theophrastus builds upon theories from Plato and Aristotle on the nature of the physical world. Theophrastus states that only stones have the power to: 1) act upon other substances, 2) react to other substances, and 3) fail to react to other substances.[26]

Theophrastus originated several theories that would become part of both academic and popular consciousness around the nature of stones throughout the classical, medieval, and early modern periods. Following Theophrastus, the next important work in the development of Western lapidary theory appears around 64 C.E. by the Greek physician Pedanius Dioscorides (40–90 C.E.), imperial surgeon to Nero and the legions of the Roman army. *De Materia Medica* consists of a list of more than one thousand medicinal substances, including a number of metals and minerals, along with information for their preparation and use.[27]

Dioscorides provides a detailed account of the medicinal properties and practical applications of a wide range of crystals that later became integrated into medieval pharmacological knowledge. He recommends the use of *aëtites*, hollow geodes that were tied to a woman's arm or thigh in order to aid in childbirth. He also asserts that this stone could be used as an anti-epilepsy agent and that it would "betray a thief" when mixed with meat; however, only the gynecological cures achieved great popularity.

As one of the most popular medical texts for 16 centuries after its compilation, the work of Dioscorides firmly established stones as natural substances with medicinal properties. The text set the standard for early modern apothecaries, who integrated lapidary materials into pharmacology.[28]

The writings of Pliny the Elder, a Roman, are the most influential classical texts in the development and production of medieval and early modern lapidaries.[29] Pliny the Elder (23–79 C.E.), in his 37-volume *Naturalis Historia* ("Natural History"), gathered all the information of his predecessors together with Roman wisdom and folkloric belief; however, only the final volume contains information on precious stones. Pliny describes the healing effects of rock crystal over the emperor Nero, whose love of gems was well known.

Pliny is credited with early attempts to classify gems according to color and observable external characteristics. This led to the practice of assigning the attributes of one stone to all stones of similar color or appearance. Pliny's *Naturalis Historia* is the first text to address the classification of therapeutic uses of gemstones as "medicinal" or "magical," providing insight into how classical culture perceived practices of crystal healing.

The later text of Damigeron, entitled *De Virtutibus Lapidum* ("The Virtue of Stones"), was written in the second century B.C.E. and is the first lapidary that examines the medicinal properties of stones in a Christian context. It combines both Christian and pagan values— appealing to the saints and the Virgin Mary in one passage and referring to the symbols of Hellenistic mystery cults in the next.[30]

Damigeron also offers advice to his readers on how to use gems to manipulate the spiritual and physical world to their advantage. Unlike previous authors, Damigeron provides information about which stones can be used to gain great wealth, resist the threats of kings and rulers, and ensure favorable outcomes in lawsuits.

Below is a table of stones and their corresponding curative properties. Even though the corresponding meanings of the stones may seem magical or arbitrary, in truth, they were based on observation or experience rather than theory or pure logic. The table is a clear example of the different meanings that stones assume when seen through the veil of the beliefs and mind-sets of the time.

The Ancients' Magical/Curative Properties of Stones	
Stone	**Magical or Curative Property**
Agate	The wearer of an agate was believed to be made "agreeable and persuasive to man, and have the favour of God"[31]; agate was also believed to avert storms if burned[32] and to bring victory[33]
Amethyst	Neutralizes the effects of alcohol and prevents inebriation; represses evil thoughts; grants good understanding; makes a barren wife fruitful[34]; grants riches and makes one humble, courteous, gracious, and wise[35]; protects from lightning and hailstorms[36]; offers the ability to control virtue by way of dreams or visions
Carnelian	A charm for actors and other public speakers[37]; expels fear and cultivates courage[38]; protects from the evil eye[39]
Cat's Eye	Draws wealth and prevents its loss[40]
Chalcedony	Protects against bad weapons and deceptions and gives victory in argument and in battle; helps with merchandise and other needs; works against illusions and frivolity stemming from melancholy; gives good eloquence in speaking; protects from fire and water and should be mounted in gold[41]
Chrysoprase	Overcomes enemies; protects from betrayal; increases wealth[42]
Citrine	A talisman against alcoholism, evil thoughts, overindulgence, scandal, libel, and treachery[43]; protects from dangers in traveling[44]

Clear Quartz	Repels bad dreams; strengthens meditation; develops the higher mind and soul[45]
Heliotrope	Could make a person invisible if combined with the plant of the same name
Jasper	An amulet against evil spells and illness[46]
Onyx	Cools desire and passion[47]
Peridot	Dispels darkness when worn around the neck or left arm; dispels night terrors; cures cowardice; calms anger and madness[48]
Sardonyx	Restrains lascivious emotions; makes men merry and agreeable[49]; ensures happy marriage and attracts friends[50]
Smoky Quartz	Dissolves problems; shifts consciousness to higher levels[51]

Other ancient cultures around the world also incorporated minerals and rocks in their remedies. The *Rasaratna Samuccaya* is a 13th-century Tantric alchemical treatise, named after the Hindu and Buddhist scriptures produced at the time. Written by Vāgbhaṭa, this work explains the preparation and properties of mineral drugs. For example, ashes of aquamarine were believed to cure fever, lung diseases, and anemia.[52]

The Chinese, who called quartz *shi ying* (or "outstanding stone"), believed that it was a great harmonizer and excellent conductor of energy that could intensify the effects of other stones. Quartz had the power to conduct *qi* (energy) and strengthen the lung-kidney relationship. Rolling quartz on the bottom of the feet could improve kidney-and-lung dynamics.[53]

Overall, we have ample evidence that the belief in the curative properties of precious stones was at one time universal among all those to whom gems were known.

The Symbolic Meaning of Color for Our Ancestors

Color is an intimate part of our being. Every visual stimulus processed by human perception contains color information. Color influences you psychologically and physically, consciously and subconsciously. Colors carry nonverbal communication that can symbolize and trigger aspects of us that we are not even aware of. Consciously or not, we are constantly resonating with colors. We are attracted to certain colors and reject others. Some colors make certain emotions arise, and others connect us with inner peace.

Naturally, the meaning of colors corresponding to gems and crystals has changed throughout the centuries. The lapidaries of the medieval and early modern periods offer a significant amount of information about these symbolic meanings, which were passed down from antiquity.

In ancient and medieval times, remedies for illness and disease were prized because of their rarity, and also because it was believed that certain spiritual or planetary influences had aided in their production and were latent in them. Besides this, the symbolism of color played a very important part in the recommendation of the use of particular stones for special diseases, particularly red or reddish stones, such as carnelian, bloodstone, etc. These were thought to be remedies for any blood-related imbalance, from hemorrhages of all kinds to bleeding gums, hemorrhoids, and menstruation.

De Laet wrote in 1647 that carnelian has the power to stop bleeding from the nose. He states that rings were cut from carnelian and worn for this purpose.[54]

The medicinal use of bloodstone was reinforced when early Spanish explorers found Native Americans using it for the same purpose—to restrain the flow of blood and to heal wounds: "And as concerning the Indians they have it for certain that touching the same Stone in some part where the blood runneth, that it doth restrain; and in this they have great trust; for that the effect hath been seen."[55]

Stone used to stop nose bleeding, from *Hortus Sanitatis,* the first natural history encyclopedia, 1491. Reproduced with the permission of the Wellcome Library, London.

Use of stones to cure blindness from the *Hortus Sanitatis,* the first natural history encyclopedia, 1491. Reproduced with the permission of the Wellcome Library, London.

The red hue of these stones was believed to indicate their fitness for such use, upon the principle *similia similibus curantur*[56] (or "like cures like," which is a predecessor of what we know today as resonance).

In the same way, yellow stones were prescribed for the cure of bilious disorders, for jaundice in all its forms, and for other diseases of the liver. The second-century B.C.E. writer Damigeron states, "The Agate has great powers, and if it has a color like that of a lion's skin it is powerful against scorpion bites, for if it's tided on, or rubbed on with water it immediately takes away all the pain and it cures the bite of a viper." He adds: "Ground and sprinkled on the wound and taken in drink, it cures."[57]

The use of green stones to relieve diseases of the eye was evidently suggested by the beneficial influence exerted by this color upon the sight. One of the earliest references in Greek writing regarding the therapeutic value of gems appears in the works of Theophrastus, who wrote in the third century B.C.E. Here, we are told of the beneficial effect exercised by green stones upon the eyes. In the 14th century, chevalier Jean de Mandeville mentions: "Chrysoprase comes from

India, it has a green color, mixed like leek juice, and sometimes with golden drops. It is hard to find and gives graces to he who wears it, and it's good for the eyes."[58]

According to Marbod, Bishop of Rennes, there are 17 different kinds of jasper (a number that varies in the literature of the time about these stones), but the best is shining green. When carried, it cured the stomach and was used by early physicians as an astringent.[59]

Claudius Galen (130–216 A.D.), a physician to the school of gladiators, states that the green jasper benefits the chest if tied upon it.[60] Roman athletes also used the stone as a talisman to protect them from injury.

Blue stones resembling the blue of the heavens were believed to exert a tonic influence and were supposed to counteract the wiles of the spirits of darkness and procure the aid and favor of the spirits of light and wisdom. These gems were associated with chastity.

Among purple stones, the amethyst is noteworthy. The well-known belief that this gem counteracted the effects of undue indulgence in intoxicating beverages is indicated by its name, derived from an ancient Greek term meaning "to be intoxicated." It is not unlikely that a resemblance between the hue of these stones and that of certain kinds of wine first gave rise to the name and to the idea of the peculiar virtues of the amethyst.

Amethyst was also believed to make women fertile and expel poison. It also banished headaches, prevented nightmares, and granted memory.[61]

Clear and milky quartz stones were associated with the color white. As we have seen, at one time, it was the universal conviction that rock crystal or transparent quartz was a form of ice, hardened or petrified so that it never melted. Romans used quartz crystals to reduce glandular swelling, fevers, and to relieve pain. In the first century A.D., the medical men of Rome used rock crystal balls to heal wounds. They prescribed allowing the sun's rays to pass through the ball and onto the wound as the best method of cauterizing and promoting healing.[62] The belief that quartz is made of congealed water may have also led to its use as a remedy for dehydration.[63]

Colors were also accorded a symbolic significance according to the Christianity of medieval and early modern Europe. The Christian symbolism of colors has in many cases determined the use of certain colored gems for religious ornaments, as follows:

- White: purity, innocence, virginity, faith, life, light
- Red: suffering, martyrdom, Christ's sacrifice, divine love
- Blue: celestial virtue
- Yellow: God's goodness, faith (bright yellow); treachery, envy (dull yellow)
- Green: hope, joy, youth
- Violet: chastening, purification, Lent, Advent Sunday
- Black: death, mourning, sorrow, Good Friday[64]

These many interpretations of colors, unfortunately, are part of our unconscious false information. They are symbols linked to our upbringing, society, culture, history, and biased learned experiences and knowledge. It is important to be aware when we choose stones in a prescriptive way, as they may encode learned meanings that do not coincide with our authentic ones. Being completely conscious and discerning is the key, as crystals can also help us decipher and disable our unwanted contents.

Stones and Religion

According to anthropologist and scholar Mircea Eliade, "For religious man, nature is never only 'natural'; it is always fraught with a religious value. This is easy to understand, for the cosmos is a divine creation; coming from the hands of the gods, the world is impregnated with sacredness. It is not simply a sacrality *communicated* by the gods, as is the case, for example, with a place or an object consecrated by the divine presence. The gods did more; *they manifested the different modalities of the sacred in the very structure of the world and of cosmic phenomena* . . . . Above all the world exists, it is there, and it has structure; it is not a chaos but a cosmos, hence it presents itself as a creation, as work of the gods."[65]

Over time, the wisdom of crystals spread throughout the world and was mixed with other practices, such as religious worship. Just as they were used by different cultures, crystals were part of the celestial language of some religions. Throughout the Middle and Near East, kings, priests, and other dignitaries adorned themselves with breastplates inlaid with precious gems, as numerous burial finds from the Pharaonic Period reveal. In the Bible, the Book of Exodus, within Chapter 28, Verses 15 to 21, also refers to the 12 stones on the breastplate of the high priest Aaron, the brother of Moses. Sardonyx or carnelian, aquamarine, and emerald were part of the first row; ruby or garnet, sapphire, and jasper were part of the second; jacinth, agate, and amethyst were in the third one; and chrysolithus, onyx, and aquamarine made up the fourth row.[66]

High priest showing the stone breastplate. Photo: akg-images | Heritage-images | The Print Collector.

During that time, people would come to the great priest to ask questions of the stones. Each question would activate light in a specific stone or group of stones, indicating God's answer. According to the Talmud, a collection of writings compiled between the third and sixth centuries C.E. that cover Jewish law, these crystals allowed people to become aware of what they needed to do in order to address their afflictions and restore their peace.

According to the Torah, or Old Testament, crystals are related to creation. One section in the Old Testament contains the description of "the Son of Man," who, on the day of his creation, was decorated with precious gems: "In Eden, the garden of God you were; every precious stone was [set in] your covering; ruby, topaz, diamond, chrysolite, onyx, and jasper, sapphire, carbuncle, and crystal and gold; the work of your drums and your orifices is in you; on the day of your creation they were established."[67]

The Old Testament also gives us many other instances of the use and meaning of precious gems in ancient Israel. The prophet Ezekiel had a vision in which he saw, behind the "foundations of the heavens" above the earth, "seven mountains made of precious stones." Similarly, the prophet Enoch spied a heaven made of crystal.

Although the Christian Church has always maintained a rather ambivalent stance toward crystals and the superstitions surrounding them, stones are mentioned within Christianity and its sacred writings.

Saint Epiphanius (315–403 c.e.), Bishop of Constantia in Cyprus, wrote the first treatise about the gemstones in Biblical writings, thus serving as a model for how Biblical gems were considered in future lapidaries. His writings included one of the first explicit references to the significance of the 12 stones in the breastplate of the high priest Aaron.[68] Lynn Thorndike writes that these early opinions concerning the stones of Aaron's breastplate "perhaps [give] an excuse and [set] the fashion for the Christian medieval lapidaries."[69]

Between 443 and 452 c.e., the Council of Arles condemned anybody who worshiped stones; later, in 506, the Council of Agde forbade anyone from swearing oaths to stones. The condemnation continued in tenth-century England, when the Law of the Northumbrian Priests condemned all those who gathered around stones.[70]

Dorothy Wyckoff writes in her studies of lapidaries that although the Church had banned the practice of heathen worship and superstitious practices, "even devout Christians could not entirely shake off the old beliefs that precious stones possess some sort of supernatural powers or significance."[71]

Other early Christian writers included the bishop Isidore of Seville (560–636 c.e.). One book in his encyclopedia, the *Etymologiarum Sive Originum Libri XX* ("Etymologies"), is devoted to stones and metals, and worked powerfully to spread lapidary medicine throughout medieval Europe.

After Isidore of Seville, a break in the tradition of Western lapidaries occurred. There are no existing new lapidaries from the period between the seventh and eleventh centuries, and medieval authors reference none. The first independent composition after this period, written by Marbod (1035–1123 c.e.), Bishop of Rennes, would become the single most important text in the development and circulation of lapidary medicine during the later Middle Ages. His *De lapidibus* addressed the physical appearance and healing properties of 60 stones and was one of the most popular lapidaries of its time. Marbod expressed two beliefs closely integrated into the idea and practice of lapidary medicine in the Middle Ages: first, that the therapeutic use of gems is an orthodox practice of healing and "scientific" in the sense that it combines human wisdom with healing agents found in nature; second, that the medicinal virtues of stones are "hidden" yet effective.

In Islamic practices, Muslims still worship the black stone of *al-Ka'bah*, the House of Allah on Earth, in Mecca. The Prophet Muhammad embraced this 50-foot stone, and Muslims salute it whenever they do pilgrimage. It is believed that all those who touch the stone are forgiven for their sins.

Islam strongly recommends that its followers wear rings made from different stones to increase faith, piety, and endurance. Muhammad used *aqiq* (carnelian) in his ring. It was believed that praying two *rakats* (daily prayers) while wearing a carnelian ring was better than praying a thousand *rakats* without it.

In Tibet, clear quartz is also used among the Tibetan Buddhists to sink into deep meditation and to find the path to enlightenment, and this crystal placed over the head is used in conscious dying practices to guide the soul out of the body.[72]

In the Vedic period of Indian history (1500–500 B.C.E.), the early sacred Hindu texts known as the Vedas were written as hymns and prayers. This mythology was further developed in a series of lengthy versified medieval texts called the Puranas. The Puranas, especially the Garuda Purana, contain numerous references to geological materials, sometimes used medicinally.[73] The Puranas describe the *spatikam* as a divine gemstone that is conducive to meditation, mantra recitation, and worship of the goddess of knowledge, Saraswati. People in India make their *japa malas*, or prayer beads, from rock crystal, and they call them *spatik malas*. These are used to enhance the efficacy of their prayers and for meditation, healing, and purification. It is very important to wear a *spatik mala* when attending or performing *puja* (religious ceremonies), as the beads help retain the sacred energy from any spiritual practice.[74]

The Sacred Geometry of Stones

For the Greeks, and the Egyptians and Phoenicians before them, mathematics was the language of the divine, and geometry brought order and balance to the world. Concepts of sacred geometry continued to influence philosophers, mathematicians, and scientists in the medieval and Renaissance periods. The five so-called "Platonic solids" were made famous by the ancient Greek philosopher Plato. They are the tetrahedron, the cube or hexahedron, the octahedron, the dodecahedron, and the icosahedron.

To the Greeks, spheres represented the divine because they had no end or beginning. And because the Platonic solids were the only figures that could be nested within a sphere, they too carried the attributes of the Creator. The Greeks were fascinated by these figures and considered them "perfect."[75]

Plato saw all five forms as sources of great wisdom. To him—as well as Aristotle, Pythagoras, and, later, Euclid—the geometric figures were the secret to understanding the mysteries of the universe and the celestial realm.

The Greeks knew that the geometric patterns and codes were symbolic of our own inner realm and what we call the authentic self. These ancients believed that the experience of sacred geometry was essential to the education of the soul, a bridge between God and man.

Plato believed that God continually geometrizes. He had such a reverence for geometry (the word itself comes from *geo*, meaning Earth, and *metron*, meaning measurement) that he engraved above the door of his Academy the phrase: "Let no one who is ignorant of geometry enter here."

This image illustrates what Plato meant by "God geometrizing." *The Ancient Days*, by William Blake, 1793. Photo: akg-images | Fitzwilliam Museum, Cambridge, UK.

For ancients, geometry was a sacred language to understand and communicate with the cosmos. Contemplating geometric patterns, we can compare them to codes that allow us to gaze into the deep wisdom and inner working of the universe itself, the intrinsic design that created and unifies all things.

What does sacred geometry have to do with healing? How can sacred geometry help to alleviate suffering? We know that suffering begins in the mind. We also know that the mind works with repetitive patterns. In the same way that sacred geometry brought a sense of order to the chaotic world of our ancestors, today these geometric patterns continue to resonate with us and bring order and healing. Ancient structures used divine proportions and geometric patterns specifically intended to create balance and harmony and to bring God closer to human beings.

Egypt's pyramids were built on the basis of sacred geometry. Photo: 15505768©Dan Breckwoldt | Dreamstime.

Professor Robert Moon, at the University of Chicago, demonstrated that the entire periodic table of elements, literally everything in the physical world, is based on the same Platonic geometric forms. Every natural pattern of growth or movement conforms inevitably to one or more geometric shapes. Even water has a perfect geometric configuration when it originates from a natural source.[76]

From the spiral configuration of massive galaxies, to the intricate patterns of plants and leaves, to the molecules of DNA responsible for all living things, the blueprint of the universe could be found in the graceful lines and curves of geometry. Beehives, some bonds of the DNA structure, and crystals have the same hexagonal pattern:

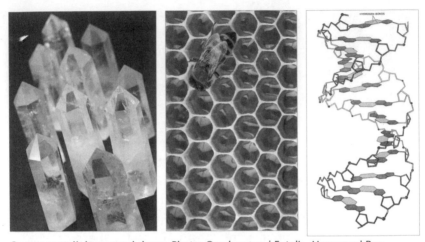

Quartz crystal's hexagonal shape. Photo: ©mykeyruna | Fotolia. Hexagonal Bee Honeycombs. Photo: 3240914©Alexandr Anastasin | Dreamstime. Illustration: [NYPL] | Science Source.

The shapes and proportions observed in nature bear the universal signature of what came to be known as the "golden ratio," or "golden mean." This number, approximately 1.61803399, often represented by the Greek letter Phi, dates back to Euclid, who wrote about it in his mathematical treatise, *Elements*, around 300 B.C.E. Both the Greeks and Egyptians believed the golden ratio was a sacred, spiritual code embedded in all forms of creation. The golden ratio is another way of talking about the repeating patterns that make up the universal. These are the same universal codes that enable the resonance to our deep cosmic origins through crystals.

The ancient axiom, "as above, so below," can be extended to "as in the atoms, so in their properties." Quartz crystals form stable structures that reflect the arrangement of their atoms. Tetrahedrons are the natural repeating patterns of quartz crystals' inner structure. They grow out at predictable intervals and form perfect geometric structures.

Simply put, a tetrahedron is a triangular pyramid with a triangular base. To Euclid, who is considered the father of geometry, the tetrahedron was the most special of all the Platonic solids. How so? If you look at the *other* four Platonic solids, each of them can also fit inside one another and be perfectly nested. The tetrahedron is different. It is the only solid that *cannot* nest other solids. Rather, the tetrahedron has the ability to "give birth to itself" endlessly, through a process of regeneration (or as healers would put it, "transformation"). Although for Pythagoreans, triangles were the most stable of geometric figures, modern science has shown that the tetrahedron alone produces not equilibrium but instability. No wonder Plato associated it with fire. Fire is the *only* element that possesses the power to change all that it touches. That is why tetrahedrons are associated with transformation.

To create balance, tetrahedrons must be in pairs or sets of pairs. A 64-tetrahedron cluster creates equilibrium in the vacuum of space. When tetrahedrons work in pairs, they also create the star tetrahedron, which is associated with balance. The star tetrahedron consists of two inverted tetrahedrons contained within each other.[77]

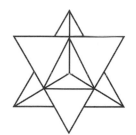

The Star Tetrahedron represents complete equilibrium, whether it is in inanimate matter or a living creature.

This represents our polar world and the inseparable relationship between the two complementary halves: the positive and negative, the manifest and unmanifest, the masculine and feminine, spirit and matter, heaven and earth, which form a perfect equilibrium. According to the ancients, when we are able to integrate the polarities within us, we can achieve "oneness" of our unlimited selves: in other words, the authenticity that is inside each one of us.

In our modern world, a star tetrahedron is the geometric shape of silicon computer chips, which demonstrates how data is stored so efficiently within a computer.

Quartz, found deep within the earth's crust, is not only a manifestation of sacred geometry but, in its very constitution, also a classic example of the golden mean in nature. Although the ancients might not have talked about it in these exact terms, they used quartz crystals in the same way that today's healers do—as a means of connecting with the authentic self.

Recognizing that there is an invisible order in the universe that ranges from the smallest known particle to the formation of the cosmos, and that everything is in constant vibration, we can deduce that numbers also transmit and transform energy. The earliest known systematic cult based on the rule of numbers was that of the Pythagoreans, created by the mathematician Pythagoras. For him, numbers symbolized unity and the origin of all things.

Although most of us associate numerology with names and birthdates, its symbolic meaning can also be applied to healing. Using the energy of numbers and crystals according to their specific meanings, certain energy fields can be created for the purpose of healing. This is done with crystal grids, which are crystals arranged in specific geometric forms and using specific numbers. We see such patterns in ancient megalithic configurations (large collections of stones) around the world, and also in the configuration of ancient temples. Stones were placed by taking into consideration the symbolic meaning of numbers.

Below is a table of the different meanings of numbers, all of which originated in antiquity and were considered in geometric crystal grids and mandala configurations:

Numbers and Meanings	
Number	Meaning
1	Unity and indivisibility; also relates to the ego
2	Division, polarity, duality, opposition; the feminine and masculine; inside and outside; up and down; Earth and heaven; conscious and unconscious; can integrate and complement, reflects but also can create conflict due to immobility when forces are equal; the initial movement that spurs the evolution of any process
3	The presence of the Trinity; creation and evolution from the beginning; the center and end of all things; generative processes; happiness and joy

4	Structure; matter; the earth; cardinal directions (east, west, north, south); the elements (air, water, earth, and fire); the energy bodies (physical, emotional, mental, and spiritual); the ages of humans (infancy, childhood, adulthood, old age); manifestation
5	Human life (one head, two arms, two legs); imbalance; change
6	Balance; co-creation; the relationship of the divine and the human; harmony and balance; unconditional love; integration of feminine and masculine
7	Authentic self; intuition; illuminated intellect; the truth of reality; the void; higher vibrations; universal cycles; days of the week; musical notes
8	Infinity; surrender to higher consciousness; cause and effect; purity; responsibility
9	Completion; realization; fulfillment; wisdom; new beginnings; gestation and formation of a human
10	Perfection and completion; God energy and eternity
11	Mastery; integration of learning; transcending the limits of the mind and achieving mastery
12	The universe and universal truths

Astrology and Crystals

For ancients, one's disposition was predetermined according to the configuration of planets and constellations in the sky when one was born. Astrology can be defined as the study of the movements of the solar system, its various positions in the zodiacal circle, and the possible influence of the cosmos on terrestrial events and humanity.

The Babylonians have the greatest reputation of any ancient peoples for their astronomical study, and the contemporary zodiac system had its origin in their observations. The zodiac itself originated as a time-measuring device. It was much more useful to early civilizations as a calendar, as the study of the stars and planets provided important data. The zodiac was also a predictive instrument, not only for external situations but also for the unconscious.

Patterns of thinking, or archetypes, as Jung called them, could be related to planets. Each planet had its own personality and corresponding abilities, events, occupations, and unconscious patterns. For example, the sun was connected to God and father; Mars was connected to such characteristics as vitality and aggression; and Venus was connected to femininity, love, and fertility. The moon was the "planet" that represented the archetype of the mother. In a person's individual birth chart, the placement of the moon will speak about his or her relationship with his or her mother—and if the individual is a mother, the relationship she has with her own children. Many astrologers feel that the relationship between the sun and the moon in the natal chart reveals the types of messages we received from our parents or parental figures.

The talismanic influence of the stones associated with the planets and also with the signs of the zodiac is closely connected with ancient ideas regarding the formation of precious stones. In an anonymous ancient work on the occult properties of gems, we read: "The nature of the magnet is in the iron, and the nature of the iron is in the magnet, and the nature of both polar stars is in both iron and magnet, and hence the nature of the iron and the magnet is also in both polar stars, and since they are Martian, that is to say, their region belongs to Mars, so do both iron and magnet belong to Mars."[78]

The author then proceeds to describe an analogous relationship between a human and any natural object or product to which his imagination draws him, and shows that, if this object stands in a sympathetic connection with the star beneath which the man was born, the man, the star, and the object will constitute a helpful "triplicity."

The wearing of the appropriate zodiacal gem was always believed to strengthen the influence of the zodiacal sign upon those born under it and to afford a sympathetic medium for the transmission of stellar influences. The gem was thus more than a mere symbol of the sign. When Christianity gained ascendancy throughout Europe, the same was true of the stone of the saint who ruled the month and that of the holy guardian angel set over those born in that particular month. In each and every case, the material form and color of the stone was believed to resonate and attract the favor and grace of the saint or angel.

Ancient authors insisted that while the image graven upon a stone was in itself dead and inactive, the influence of the stars and stones amplified material talismanic qualities and virtues. Even in the case of the amethyst, a generally recognized antidote for all sorts of poisons, it was held that the scorpion's bite could be most effectively healed by a crystal upon which this creature's figure had been cut during the time when the constellation Scorpio was in its ascendancy.[79]

Reichelt, who wrote *De Amuletis* in 1676, finds in the hardness of precious stones a reason for their retaining the celestial virtues they receive. After they have been extracted, these virtues persist in the stones, and they keep "the traces and gifts of mundane life which they possessed while clinging to the earth."[80] These "gifts of mundane life" signify the stored-up energy derived from the stars and planets, which penetrates the stone.

The stones associated with the signs of the zodiac have varied throughout the centuries. On the next page, you will find a list of zodiacal stones from various ancient sources and some from the first half of the 20th century and thus unknown to the ancients:

Stones and Astrological Correspondences		
Quartz	**Zodiac Sign**	**Planet**
Amethyst[81], Sardonyx[82], Bloodstone[83]	Aries	Mars
Heliotrope[84], Carnelian	Taurus	Venus
Chrysoprase, Keraunos (Reddish Onyx), Heliotrope[85], Agate	Gemini	Mercury
Green Jasper, Chalcedony	Cancer	Moon
Agate, Jasper, Onyx, Cat's Eye[86]	Leo	Sun
Chrysolite, Carnelian, Peridot	Virgo	Mercury
Sard, Chrysolite	Libra	Venus
Sardonyx, Jasper, Amethyst	Scorpio	Pluto
Rock Crystal, Amethyst,	Sagittarius	Jupiter
Chalcedony, Chrysoprase	Capricorn	Saturn
Rock Crystal	Aquarius	Uranus
Jasper, Amethyst	Pisces	Neptune

Because the sages of ancient times believed that stones were highly sensitive to the vibrations or emanations of planets and constellations, they were thought to exert an influence on the different parts of the body by the respective zodiacal signs. This belief often determined the administration of precious stone remedies by physicians of the 17th and earlier centuries.[87]

The following table corresponds to quartz equivalents used by the ancients to heal different parts of the body:

Zodiac Signs, Body Parts, and Quartz		
Zodiac Sign	**Part of the Body**	**Quartz**
Aries	Head, Brain, Face, Eyes	Bloodstone
Taurus	Neck, Throat, Thyroid, Vocal Tract	Blue Quartz
Gemini	Arms, Lungs, Shoulders, Elbow, Hands, Fingers, Nervous System	Agate
Cancer	Breast, Stomach, Alimentary Canal	Chrysoprase
Leo	Heart, Chest, Upper Back	Onyx
Virgo	Digestive System, Intestines, Spleen	Carnelian
Libra	Kidneys, Lumbar Region, Buttocks	Chrysolite
Scorpio	Reproductive System, Sexual Organs, Excretory System	Chalcedony
Sagittarius	Hips, Thighs	Citrine
Capricorn	Knee, Joints, Skin, Skeletal System	Red Jasper
Aquarius	Circulatory System	Red Quartz
Pisces	Feet, Toes, Lymphatic System	Amethyst

The Age of Reason

So what happened to all this ancient wisdom, rich in the symbolism of crystals? Classical works sought to reveal the properties of gems as one of many marvelous products of nature; medieval writers built upon these ideas, integrating them with a Christian cosmology that saw them as gifts from God provided for the use and benefit of humanity. For several thousand years, the art of crystal healing was seen as a natural part of medicine, a tradition that continued through the Renaissance. In the Enlightenment period of the 17th and 18th centuries (also known as the Age of Reason), the knowledge of stones was expanded upon, and minerals became the subject of scientific observation.

One of the early predecessors of the Enlightenment period was the physician and philosopher Paracelsus (1493–1541 c.e.), considered the father of holistic medicine. He influenced a deep interest in the healing power of precious stones during the 16th century. He perceived human beings and minerals as part of a world seen as a whole and as a work ordered by God.

During the early modern age, stone texts continued to be produced; these included Georgius Agricola's *De Natura Fossilium*, published in 1546, a text that historians of science often name the first modern mineralogical work of all time. Agricola provided comments of considerable accuracy on the nature, properties, and treatment of gemstones.

His work was followed by *Gemmarum et Lapidum Historia* (1609), by Anselmus Boëtius de Boodt, a physician to the royal court of Rudolf II of Prague. This lapidary includes gems of the New World and compares them to those in Europe and Asia. It differentiates stones according to five degrees of hardness and speculates the existence of a distinct atomic structure in minerals. His information includes the best scientific knowledge of the time and is considered the most important lapidary of the 17th century.[88]

In later centuries, medieval mineralogy began to be viewed not as a true science but as something mired in myth. Scientists and citizens influenced by the new "Age of Reason" rejected anything linked to superstition, religion, or the inexplicable, crystals and stones included. Although it was known that, in practice, ancient methods of working with crystals generated results, the problem for this new era of thinkers was their inability to scientifically rationalize the healing process with crystals.

Robert Boyle (1627–1691), English philosopher, chemist, and physicist, wrote *An Essay About the Origine and Virtues of Gems* in 1672. It was considered the most scientific work of its time. It covers the formation of minerals and their crystals. Important new work was included on crystal formation and crystallization from solutions as reported by direct observation. Boyle doubted the remedial ability of gems but admitted that some soluble materials might be of benefit.[89] In his 1703 book *The Craft and Frauds of Physick Expos'd*, English physician Robert Pitt reiterated the insolubility of gems and the fact that this would make it impossible for them to affect the body.[90]

Danish anatomist and naturalist Nicolas Steno (1638–1686) was the first to note in 1669 that the faces of a crystal are always arranged in specific angles, displaying a characteristic symmetry. Many scientists began to study these properties under the microscope and devise new theories. For example, René-Just Haüy (1743–1822), a French mineralogist and Catholic priest considered the father of modern crystallography, discovered the geometric law of crystallization. He found that crystals are made up of smaller, basic chemical units that have the same shape, but when they are joined, they produce different structures. In 1784 he published his observations in the book *Essai d'une Théorie sur la Structure des Cristaux*.[91]

During this period, the tradition of using precious stones in healing was still accepted, but scientists were bringing the efficacy of such treatment into question. The "Age of Skepticism" then pervaded the late 19th and 20th centuries.

As time passed, much of the symbolism of stones was lost and forgotten. People still used signets of crystals, but only for decorative affect. The legends and metaphysical properties of gems were perceived merely as good practice in the business of selling stones. A comprehensive study of lapidary medicine was notably absent. The ability of science to explain many things previously accepted as miracles brought a sense of doubt to the so-called attributes of gems—which remained difficult to prove.

It would not be until the discovery of electromagnetism by James Clerk Maxwell in 1865 that humanity would be able to explore the scientific applications of crystals and finally prove the healing process through energy frequencies imperceptible to the human eye.

Today, as science has revolutionized our understanding of stones, quartz crystal itself can be considered an amulet that balances the vibration of mind and body; it works as an energy shield, as it automatically creates resonance—sending our balanced vibrations to our surroundings and, in this way, bringing balance to any unstable or negative thoughts or energy.

Although, as we have seen throughout this chapter, many of the uses of crystals in antiquity are linked to the ancients' beliefs, their applications have many similarities with those of our times. Just like the healers of old, we use crystals today to protect against negative energies, thoughts, and emotions, as well as modern diseases and misfortunes of all varieties.

Today crystal healers are continuing to gain ground as they join scientific awareness to the knowledge that our ancestors cultivated so painstakingly over the course of human history. As we dive into Chapter 4, you'll make the connection between the stone wisdom of our ancestors, native and aboriginal peoples, and modern crystal healers. You will also see how crystal healers are receptacles of ancestral wisdom and tribal practices. You will recognize the influence of this ancient wisdom in their different techniques, such as crystal resonance, mandalas, grids, essences, jewelry, and art, and how they help us reconnect with our authentic crystal blueprint.

CHAPTER 4

Modern Tribes

---

*"In the body of the Earth Mother, crystals are akin to brain cells,
gemstones are the organs, rocks the muscles . . ."*

— CHEROKEE SAYING[1]

IT IS ALSO THROUGH CRYSTALS that Earth communicates with
its brothers and sisters—the other planets, and perhaps celestial
phenomena beyond the solar system. Each crystal taken from the
earth maintains its contact with the heart of the earth. In many
ways, crystals are the proverbial "eye of God," communicating to the
heavens and the earth the thoughts and actions of humanity.

Contemporary approaches to quartz crystals are associated
with the diverse approaches of Western civilization, from ancient
Mesopotamia to the "Age of Reason." Indigenous and aboriginal
peoples are believed to be the original people of the world who
retained in their oral traditions the ancient use of crystals. Their
shamanic practices must be examined, as they continue to impact
our understanding and awareness of crystals and their power today.

Quartz crystals and their use in contemporary crystal healing are
integrally associated with shamanism. From ceremonial rattles and
costume artifacts to initiatory rites and healing tools, crystals pervade
shamanism throughout Australia, East Asia, North America, South
America, and Africa. As shamanic practices become more common
among contemporary healers, we cannot underestimate crystals'

survival in ritual use and healing today. On all continents of the earth, indigenous wisdom keepers have been stepping forward and presenting oral histories about crystals that have long been kept in small, tight circles of initiates. Much of the work of today's crystal healers is derived from these ancient secrets.

Indigenous shamans relied on the power of their ancestors, their intuition, and their ingenuity to discover the properties of crystals, and what they learned was transmitted down through the centuries from generation to generation, offering an ever-expanding base of knowledge. This wealth of knowledge and experience is the main source of modern tribal wisdom, which persists today in a variety of crystal healing protocols and practices.

Crystals and Indigenous Knowledge

The archetypal cosmology of shamanism portrays crystals as solidified light originating in the supernal realms. Although fallen or brought down to Earth, crystals offer the shaman both a bridge to the heavens and a key to supernormal powers associated with celestial beings. Shamans generally ascribe a singular importance to quartz above all other power objects, perceiving it to be the bones of the earth, a "live rock," a living being. As such, crystals are regarded as among the most powerful of the shaman's "spirit helpers."

Among Native Americans, clear quartz is placed in the cradles of newborn babies as a symbol of the connection of their souls to the physical body and the energy of the Earth. In medicine bags, crystals are used as a tool for self-empowerment, as they emanate their light- and life-giving properties through a diverse medley of power objects, and act to energizing them and maintain their full potency. In ecstatic trance states, crystals are used as a catalyst and a rainbow bridge to project the soul to the otherworlds beyond this human realm. This is true for the Sea Dayaks in Borneo; their shamans use crystals to reach a patient's soul.[2]

While many Native American tribes have produced and used fetishes made of stone through the ages, the most renowned animal fetish carvers are the Zuni. The Zuni believe that the world was once covered with floodwaters. The Sun Father, revered by the Zuni as the giver of life and light, created twin sons, who recognized that the world was too wet for humankind to survive. The Sun Father gave his sons a magic shield, a bow (the rainbow), and arrows (lightning). The twins placed their shield on the earth, crossed the rainbow and lightning arrows on top of it, and shot an arrow into the place where they crossed. Lightning flew out in every direction, creating a tremendous fire. Although this dried the earth, it made it too easy for predators to catch and eat people. To save humanity, the twins struck these predatory animals with their lightning, burning and shriveling them into stone. But deep within the stone, the animals' hearts remained alive, with instructions to help humankind with the magic in their hearts. So when a Zuni finds a stone that naturally resembles an animal, he or she correlates it with one of the ancient stone beasts. Here are some Zuni animal fetishes:

Quartz Bear carved by Dee Edaakie. Photo: Grey Dog Trading, Old Town Albuquerque, New Mexico.
Montana Quartz Buffalo carved by Gibbs Othole. Photo: Grey Dog Trading, Old Town Albuquerque, New Mexico.
Quartz Eagle carved by Dee Edaakie. Photo: Grey Dog Trading, Old Town Albuquerque, New Mexico.

The Cherokee legends speak specifically to the transformative power of crystals. Early in creation, each mineral agreed to help humankind by offering its powers in service to healing. The ruby, worn as an amulet, would heal the heart, while the emerald would heal the eyes. The chief of the mineral tribe, quartz crystal, was clear, like the light of creation itself. Quartz declared, "I will be the sacred mineral. I will heal the mind. I will help human beings see the origin of disease. I will help to bring wisdom and clarity in dreams. And I will record their spiritual history . . . so that in the future, if humans gaze into me, they may see their origin and the way of harmony."[3]

This Cherokee legend has been retold in almost every tribe in the Americas. It tells of an ancient time of peace, a mythical homeland known to every culture on Earth.

No one medicine person and no one tribe should or can say that their structure is the exclusive Native American method of working with crystals, but what all these peoples have in common is that they see crystals as a holder and determiner of energy. In the tradition of the medicine wheel (the great cosmic compass that relates the cycles of all that exists—of matter and thought, space and time—with the aim of achieving cosmic harmony), crystals played a significant role.

Medicine wheels themselves acted as the ceremonial focal points of many cultures. They were also astronomical laboratories and places where indigenous peoples would come to mark cycles in their own lives, as well as that of the Earth. Here, they could pray, contemplate, and amplify their connection to nature and creation. Usually, medicine wheels were positioned over areas with geomagnetic activity; using these in ceremony made the energy and aftereffects stronger.

Each stone placed in the medicine wheel can offer clues about our ties with the ancient past and with the earth. In one example of a medicine wheel, the center of the wheel holds the creator stone symbol. From this center radiates the energy that creates the rest of the wheel. The stones that surround the creator form the foundation of all life. In the southeast is the stone that represents Earth Mother; clockwise is the stone honoring Father Sun; next comes Grandmother Moon; and she is followed by different stones that represent the elements of earth, water, fire, and air. The outer circle is made of four stones honoring the spirit keepers of the four cardinal directions. These spirit keeper stones divide the circle into the quadrants that set the boundaries for the 12 moon stones in the outer circle, which represent the cycle of moons of the year. Complementing the medicine wheel are four spirit paths, each consisting of three stones. These paths go from the spirit keeper stones toward the center circle. They represent qualities that take us from daily life into the sacred space of the creator.[4]

That simple physical description of the wheel helps us understand that everything is interconnected, and that the sacred is within *all* of us.

Forms of the medicine wheel exist all around the globe, from ancient archaeological rock-cairn circles like Stonehenge and Medicine Bend to stone calendars and zodiacal systems.

A Lakota Sioux medicine woman relates the use of white crystal medicine in creating her own wheel and administering healing practices: "First, I will counsel with a prospective patient to determine what they think is wrong with them, although often the problem lies elsewhere. I then ask Spirit which instruments (crystals, feathers, etc.) to use, and then I ask the whole Sioux Nation (which includes those in Spirit form) to help me energize them through the Will of my hands and heart. The choice of crystals and/or feathers is often a function of the patient's consciousness (whichever instrument they have the most faith in accepting). I generally use either interchangeably, although I personally find crystals to be slightly more solid retainers of energy than feathers."[5]

According to ancient wisdom, crystals and stones are ancient living beings. That is why some Native American tribes today refer to them as elders. They say that within the memories of the stones are ancient stories, crystallized from the origin of our planet, here to cure all discomforts. They can take you on a sacred journey to retrieve all the pieces of your soul that have been lost through your identification with civilization. According to the Cherokees and Apaches, meditation, prayer, and physical exercises are all appropriate ways to work on ourselves while working with crystals.

The Paipai Indians of Northern Baja California refer to rock crystal as *wii'ipay*, which means "living rock" or "live rock." For them, the *wii'ipay* is one of the most potent objects used by the *hechicero* (shaman). They believe that the power of the *wii'ipay* is neutral and that it is the responsibility of the shaman to channel this power.[6]

The Huichol Indians, who live in the Sierra Madre Mountains of West Central Mexico, believe that five years after death, the souls of humans turn into a rock crystal. Others believe that the *urukáme*, or crystals, actually form while the person is alive and that they can become crystallized through the intercession of a shaman. The Papago in the north of Arizona believe that crystals grow inside the heart of the shaman.[7]

As we travel across the continents, we see that shamans of other tribes view crystals as holders of sacred qualities. The Warao shamans of the south of Venezuela place quartz crystals in their big medicine rattle, or *hebu-mataro*, because they believe that they are "spirit helpers" that assist in extracting harmful intrusions from the bodies of their patients.[8]

The Kogi people of Colombia understand the earth to be a living being. Through meditation, they communicate with all living things, including stones. They live in their authentic selves, or *aluna*, an inner world of thought and potential. Kogi also have sacred stones that they refer to as their fathers. The place where the sacred stone resides is called *Duanama*. The daily work of the *mamos*, or Kogi priests, is to offer their *pagamentos*, or tribute with prayers and intentions, at sacred sites to assist the earth's energetic balance.[9]

Africa's Dagara tribespeople are also well known for their spiritual healing practices, which include quartz crystal. According to the Dagara, minerals evoke the life purpose that is linked to each human being. Overall, indigenous peoples across the world know that there is collective memory and individual memory. According to Dagara healer Malidoma Somé, "Collective memory is not a vast well that exists separate from individual people. It is the sum total of the personal memories of each person. In other words, for a village, a tribe, and a culture to remember, each individual must master the ability to remember the knowledge that lives in his or her bones."[10]

For the Dagara, stones stimulate individual and collective memory, as well as a deep sense of authentic connection. One of the ways that the Dagara work with stones is by placing them on an individual altar and praying to be shown one's life purpose. After three days of placing the stone on the shrine, the practitioner then brings food and water, adding a request of nourishment for both the stone and the practitioner. Then the person waits and listens to what the stone wishes to share with him or her.

Rock crystals also play an essential role in the magic and religion of the Australian Aborigines. They believe that quartz crystals connect all people with their highest level of personal power. The Aborigines connect their powers with the presence of rock crystals in their own bodies.[11]

The Aborigines sought quartz crystals with internal fractures that produce vivid rainbow light refractions. These fractures signal that the stone resonates powerfully with the primordial energies of the Rainbow Serpent, a symbol of the creative forces of the Great Spirit. Quartz crystals were a very important part of the Aboriginal initiation process, which connected initiates to the power of the Rainbow Serpent. After young Aboriginal men were initiated into manhood, some of them would undergo a voluntary journey toward becoming medicine men, or they would be elected to go on this journey by divine beings. The initiate would go with a medicine man to an area where he could connect with the essence of the Rainbow Serpent. The initiate would see the Rainbow Serpent rise out of the ground or the water, and then he would faint. He'd then be led by the Rainbow Serpent to a cool and dry area of a subterranean cave, where a sort of "psychic surgery" would then be done on him.

The Rainbow Serpent would give the initiate a new brain and also place white quartz crystals in his body. This powerful symbolic descent and rebirth, and the presence of these rock crystals in the medicine men's own bodies, differentiated them from ordinary humans and provided them with supernatural powers. The young medicine man would be able to see before his inner eye past and future events and "happenings in other worlds." He would also learn to read other people's thoughts and recognize their secret worries, to cure illnesses with the "medicine" stones, to put himself in a trance, and to send his *ya-yari* (his dream) from his body to gather information.[12]

Quartz crystals could also be used by anyone who wished to be cleansed by smudging themselves with quartz, a special chant, and the smoke of fragrant herbs and woods like pituri (native tobacco) and bush cherry bark.

Geomancy: The Ancient Way of Healing the Earth

In the past, we had a deep connection to the earth. In a way, this connection was linked to our consciousness, which resonated with the divine (the whole of the universe) and nature (its parts). Aboriginals and indigenous peoples around the world were the Earthkeepers.

According to author and scholar Drunvalo Melchizedek, Mongolian shamans, Native American Hopis, the Kogi people of Colombia, and the Arawak and other tribes of the Caribbean speak of an ancient story that has been passed through generations since the times of Atlantis.[13] They say that during those times everyone had a very high consciousness. But because of something that happened, consciousness fell. Through their desire to control the world, a small group of people created low-frequency electromagnetic fields that went out of control and led to the eruption of disease and illness. According to indigenous peoples, this imbalanced field is the cause of much of the chaos of the world. At this time, there were ascended masters on Earth who did all they could to heal the conditions of the planet. According to these higher beings, who were in charge of restoring Earth frequencies, the only way to recover our higher consciousness was to work in partnership with the earth.

That is why they decided to create a planetary grid, which is an etheric crystalline structure that envelops the planet and holds consciousness. The grid has an electromagnetic field that can work in both lower and higher dimensions. The grid started in Egypt near the Great Pyramid. From Machu Picchu to Stonehenge, the locations of the sacred places are no accident. Edfu Building Texts explain how groups of sages and creator gods after a global flood began to build temples throughout the world at carefully chosen locations.

The ascended masters decided to create a grid of pyramids, temples, stone circles, and sacred sites along mountains and lakes, all with large contents of quartz over certain electromagnetic alignments built into the earth. The entire globe is wrapped in a series of what is known as ley line grids, which is a macrocosmic equivalent to the acupuncture meridian system in our human body that can be tapped into to produce balance. "Spot of the fawn" was the name given by the Hopis to these places with a higher concentration of power. All these sacred sites were meant to act as mirrors of the heavens so that ordinary men and women might be transformed into gods, or the best version of themselves. Texts have even been found that mention how leading away from these sites may lead to people not knowing their truth.

The combination of quartz and geomagnetic energy together with the sun's rays is what allows concentrating and amplifying electromagnetic energy in this grid around the planet. Through oral traditions, we know that this energy web has been around for 13,000 years and that we can tap into this energy through the power of crystals. Also, by leaving crystals in these sacred sites, we can connect to these places and increase our frequency and awareness.

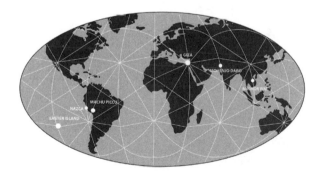

The planetary energetic grid operates through sacred geometric patterns. Grids meet at various intersecting points and are alleged alignments of ancient sites and megaliths. Some of the strongest power spots on the planet, where you can tap into your own process of transformation, have quartz within their structures.

Believe it or not, there is a scientific explanation for this.

Today we know that Earth's electromagnetic fields are produced by the planet's quartz core. (We'll explore this in more detail in Chapter 7.)

According to Joe Kirschvink, a geophysicist at the California Institute of Technology, human beings are magnetoreceptors, meaning that we are susceptible to electromagnetic fields. In fact, magnetic fields can induce electric currents in the brain that mimic an electroencephalogram (EEG) signal.[14]

Dr. Rick Strassman, researcher and psychiatrist, conducted U.S. government–approved clinical research in the 1990s that found that certain electromagnetic fields could release N,N-Dimethyltryptamine (DMT). A small amount of these molecules can produce altered states of consciousness that some know as shamanic or psychic states. In 1972, Nobel Prize–winning scientist Julius Axelrod found that DMT is also produced by the human pineal gland. According to Strassman, DMT exists in our brains as a spirit molecule, allowing us to gain access to nonmaterial realms.[15]

In many experiments, it has been evidenced that exposure to certain magnetic fields and frequencies can stimulate the brain to release DMT.[16] It is possible that the electromagnetic fields amplified by quartz have this power, and their geometric configurations in grids around the earth have the ability to reconnect us to our original higher frequency.

Crystals used in grids around the earth can create energy alternatives and harness a perpetual pulse to restore our original frequencies. Within the periphery of most Kogi settlements, for example, we can see scattered stones and boulders of different sizes, apparently forming part of the natural landscape, placed there to restore the original flow of energy.

Indigenous peoples around the world are still making use of the original grid by placing crystals and stones on the earth, just as crystal healers today place crystals to restore the balance of our minds and bodies.

Crystal Healers Today

The symbolic meanings accorded to stones by our forebears are valuable in considering the evolution of crystal knowledge and the history of how they worked with stones. However, as the universe is made up of energy that is in constant motion, it's inaccurate to say that we all resonate with the same frequency or information—or that the meanings of certain stones should remain static and unquestioned. And if we add to this that our individual life stories and experiences are not the same, we will end up understanding why crystals that work for us may not work for others and vice versa.

But according to many contemporary crystal healers who draw their practices from indigenous peoples around the world, as well as contemporary scientific knowledge, protocols of crystal healing are as diverse as the planet we live on. Each healer has his or her own way of healing because each resonates with something different and develops his or her own technique.

You might see one healer specializing in essences and crystal grids, another in prescriptive crystal work, and yet other in resonance and intuitive crystal work. I myself work with crystals through resonance by recognizing unconscious patterns in a client and guiding that person to reconnect with the authentic self. For me, crystals are symbols or mirrors that bridge our outer world with our inner world.

The stone that a client chooses specifically shows me what that person is resonating with. The stone is pointing to a pattern in the client's unconscious that is preventing the client from living the full expression of who he or she really is beyond his or her learned beliefs. Crystals will direct their energy toward this place where the client needs to work on him- or herself for transformation to occur.

In the following pages, you will find some information I have collected through the years in my crystal practice, as well as my personal understanding of the connection between crystals and the authentic self. For me, the journey from opaque to transparent forms of quartz is the symbolic path of transcendence from false learned information to the discovery of who we really are.

Just as vaccines are made from antigens that produce antibodies, the same crystal may contain the conflict (false information pattern) that we may need to work with but also the solution (authentic pattern) to help us resonate with the best choices that will help us dissolve the conflict. Once again, these are suggested meanings from my own experience, and I encourage you to explore your own personal symbolic resonance with stones via observation and exploration.

Quartz and the Path of Reconnection to the Authentic Self		
Type of Quartz Crystal	False Pattern	Authentic Pattern
Smoky Quartz	Collective paradigm wounds (family, society, and culture)	Filters information and establishes boundaries
Tangerine Quartz	Mother wounds since the moment of conception; gender and separation wounds	Reconnects with our authentic mother (the authentic model we create of our mother within ourselves after we release the original wound and expand our limited learned perspective that comes from our mother, female ancestors, and patriarchal society) and sexuality
Citrine	Father wounds	Reconnects with our authentic father (the healthy image of the father we create within beyond the learned father wounds, masculine ancestors, and patriarchal society)
Pink Quartz	Relationship wounds	Reconnects us with authentic love

Blue Quartz	Media wounds (the wounds unconsciously learned from biased information outlets, including television and social media, which become templates that resonate and create our reality and wounds)	Reconnects us with our authentic voice
Amethyst	Learned mental rigidity and negative bias wounds	Reconnects us with our true intuition and inner wisdom
Clear Quartz	Attachment to false reality	Reconnects us with our authentic reality

Modern Crystal Symbols

Symbols and patterns are the language of the unconscious mind. Crystal patterns can resonate and communicate with the unconscious and be translated as a client's relationship to their mothers or fathers, or even as a physical illness. For example, smoky quartz and amethyst might point to a learned negative pattern from my mother that I need to transform, or an addiction that needs to be worked through by instituting proper boundaries. I once had a client who had cancer in the stomach and kept choosing citrine and smoky quartz. Citrine resonates with the stomach and smoky quartz with lower frequencies, indicating the possibility of illness in this organ.

Another client, Susan, had infertility problems and kept choosing carnelian and amethyst. She had mentioned that she had done everything to get pregnant without results. The shape and color of carnelian resonate with the womb. The presence of amethyst was telling me that the problem wasn't originating in Susan's physical body but in her mind. Both of the stones together indicated that her mind was affecting her womb. After persistent inner work, Susan became pregnant.

The following is a table that generalizes the most common contemporary meanings of colors and their association with stones, which I have also discovered through years of offering crystal readings:

The Meanings behind Stones and Their Colors		
Color	Associated Stone	Meaning
Black	Tibetan Black Quartz	The darkness or absence of light; mourning; the end; secrets; magic; force; violence; evil; elegance; sophistication; power control; the unknown; the unconscious; depression; pessimism; self-denial and negativity; insecurity If you have an excess of black, you are overly negative, unconsciously dissatisfied with your life and inviting change, sad and don't want to admit it, and/or tend to play a victim role. A lack of black signifies a denial of one's shadow side.
Brown	Smoky Quartz	Stability; structure; practicality and support; common sense; protection and support of family; security and belonging; hard work; attachment to the material; order; strength and maturity If you have an excess of brown, you have self-imposed limits and are overly inflexible and dogmatic. You might tend to favor others' learned beliefs and paradigms and remain in your comfort zone. A lack of brown signifies a lack of clarity, discernment, structure, and practicality. You may not be discerning of your boundaries and could be drawn toward addictive and abusive behavior.
Red	Red Quartz	Blood; vitality; basic survival; warning and danger; demanding attention; hyperactivity; aggression; impulsiveness; domination; love; sexuality; passion If you have an excess of red, you may be hyperactive or overly attention-seeking. You might also be overly focused on the physical aspects of life—the body, sexuality, conventional success, and money—and neglect inner development and reconnection to your authenticity. A lack of red signifies health issues or a block to your vitality and life energy.

Orange	Carnelian	Joy; spontaneity; creativity; enthusiasm; fascination; happiness; lack of inhibition; group bonding; inspiration; new ideas; transcending life's setbacks; deep fear (and overcoming it) If you have an excess of orange, you might tend toward rudeness or unkindness. You might be harboring unconscious fears that require release. You might also be inconsistent, superficial, and insincere. A lack of orange signifies a closed mind, a lack of creativity, and a tendency to withdraw from social situations.
Yellow	Citrine	Acquired knowledge; left side of the brain; academic and intellectual pursuits; pragmatism; the ego; self-worth; material wealth; a quick temper If you have an excess of yellow, you might have a superiority complex or a bad temper. You might also tend toward being tyrannical, judgmental, or deceitful. A lack of yellow signifies low self-esteem, as well as a tendency toward irrational behavior and emotional fragility.
Green	Green Aventurine	Balancing of love and will; equality; self-confidence; optimism; harmony; growth; taking responsibility; good health; balance If you have an excess of green, you might tend toward workaholism. You might also be unbalanced or disconnected from reality. A lack of green signifies stagnation, indifference, poor health, and a disturbed sense of inner tranquility.
Pink	Rose Quartz	Intimacy; caring; gentleness; unconditional love; compassion; gratitude; sharing; nurturing of self and others; appreciation; intuition; hope; safety; the healing of wounds If you have an excess of pink, this can indicate oversensitivity and immaturity, as well as emotional volatility. A lack of pink can signify emotional neediness, unrealistic expectations, a lack of willpower and self-worth, codependency, and a fear of commitment.

Blue	Blue Lace Agate	Clarity; meditation and contemplation; clear communication; authentic voice; enhanced learning; higher ideals If you have an excess of blue, this can indicate the tendency to talk excessively and be imprudent or destructive with one's words. It can also point to coldness, a lack of emotion, and a tendency toward solitude. A lack of blue signifies excessive thinking, difficulty with self-expression, and gullibility.
Violet	Amethyst	High vibration; intuition; co-creation; wisdom; transformation; clarity of mind If you have an excess of violet, you might be suffering from addiction or unhealthy boundaries, a limited or fixed mind-set. You might tend to see life as you imagine it rather than how it is. A lack of violet signifies doubting in the existence of one's authentic self and true gifts.
White	Clear Quartz	Completion; wholeness; the authentic self; the culminating stage of evolution; independence; neutrality; clarity; amplification; expansion; openness; opening to a new cycle If you have an excess of white, this could indicate feelings of loneliness and frustration, as well as a lack of vitality. A lack of white signifies lack of transparency, a belief in absolute truths and a tendency to identify with the world of the five senses and false unconscious programming.

One can also work by choosing the stone according to the attributes of the planet with which the stone is related, which was a practice favored by the ancients. In my crystal healing sessions, I complement the reading of stones with astrology. I use the client's chart to map his or her internal work and gifts and as a starting point to develop strategies to help the client reconnect with the authentic self. Generally, I look for the sun and the moon in the astrological chart, and all the aspects with other planets. The sun is the archetype of the conscious mind, while the moon represents the unconscious and hidden part of us. I also look for Saturn and Pluto, which are "difficult" planets offering insight about the client's challenges, and Venus and Jupiter, which are more positive planets and can point to areas where the client can expand. (Interestingly, difficult planets such as Saturn can also show us where our mastery lies.)

Once you become aware that you have a bias to see things in a certain context, or that you have certain assumptions or beliefs, then you can start working within the framework of your chosen crystals to gradually expand the borders of an unbalanced pattern or limiting belief that is confining and preventing you from living your full self.

As you can see, much of crystal healing is about decoding symbols, an art in which an experienced crystal healer is well trained. By working internally and observing myself and clients for so many years, I developed the ability to recognize different patterns (thoughts, emotions, and illness) and to relate them to stones. But I have found that the same combination of stones can have different meanings according to what is resonating or being experienced internally by the client at that time. That is the main reason I support the selection of stones by resonance instead of prescription. Ancients also used to select stones in this way.

Leo McFee, crystal healer and founder of the Crystal Sun Academy, works in multiple ways with crystals. "I might create a grid that is just literally on a tabletop that would be up for a number of days. It's almost a focalizing way to intentionally send healing energy to someone. I can also make the room itself a grid by placing crystals around the perimeter."[17]

McFee refers to the work he does as "neo-indigenous." He says, "I feel like the purest relationship that I have any sense of, physically and emotionally, is with the various indigenous peoples of the world . . . that type of perspective which is not so available, especially to the Western mind. But on a heart level and a soul level, I feel a connection with that more on-the-ground relationship to the healing powers and the consciousness of stones and crystals. I'm always looking for connective points where the human scientific and geologic side meets with the metaphysical and spiritual side of the whole crystal journey."

McFee also notes that there is no clear or linear history of crystal healing, particularly in the shamanic traditions of indigenous cultures. "The history emerges from a more oral tradition and a non-Western or even nonhierarchical point of view; in this way, it doesn't lend itself to easily tracking or connecting to."

In his own work, Egyptologist Stephen Mehler, co-author of *The Crystal Skulls: Astonishing Portals to Man's Past*, considers the living intelligence of crystals, which is an integral aspect of many indigenous cultures: "When I got involved working with crystal skulls with Mayan elders, I discovered that they considered crystals to be alive. They considered a crystal to be the same as anything else with an essence or personality . . . a functioning being. In the modern day, we break down things according to whether they are inorganic or organic; we separate the so-called living and non-living, which is nonsense."[18]

Mehler notes that ancients who worked with crystals acknowledged that everything on Earth had consciousness and was alive. He says, "All the crystal skulls I've worked with, we have names for. When I worked with Native American elders, they referred to quartz crystal as the bones of their ancestors."

And crystal resonance therapist Naisha Ahsian notes that her practice has much in common with indigenous healing in that she is in service to the spirit, to its allies, and to their higher powers. She acts as a facilitator who helps her clients to reconnect with those powers.

Ahsian says, "I think that the power in crystal healing is that crystal healing allows us to reconnect with the greater consciousness of the geo-organism in which we are living. Indigenous cultures understand that connection—that they are conscious cells living inside of a greater organism, and communication within that entire organism is necessary for healing and balance. If we can use crystals and stones as a medium for reconnection with the geo-organism by empowering the client to reconnect to their spiritual connection, their energetic connection with that organism . . . then they will heal themselves."

Ahsian notes that, while indigenous peoples were steeped in the practices that were necessary for them to be connected to their authentic selves, the internal training required to be a crystal healer is what makes rigorous study so challenging for many people today: "People want simple, formulaic ways to understand crystals and stones, but as the ancients knew, this is not how spiritual growth is done. Spiritual growth is done through cultivating your ability to perceive, be present with, and understand whatever arises from consciousness—whether that comes through the physical or emotional body, through vibrations, or through physical objects. Meditating with them singularly and repeatedly, so that you revisit that stone's energy many different times in order to understand the consistencies of what it brings up, is a process. The way that true healing works is that we must identify where we are out of balance within ourselves and reconnect to our higher spiritual power through the medium of an ally. In this case, a crystal acts as a source of energy but also as a teacher, a mentor, a support that can give us guidance or assistance."

Ahsian works intuitively—first, by engaging with crystals personally in order to feel and understand their energy, and then by receiving a specific "mandate" or "direction" in which to work. "It was definitely an organic process of training with the crystals," she explains. "When I'm working with students, one of the things that they expect to receive when they are sitting with crystals or meditating with crystals is some sort of direct voice that says, 'Hi, I'm Amethyst. You put me on your third eye, and I heal addictions.' That is not the way crystals communicate. Crystals communicate vibrationally, and the primary way in which they communicate is by helping us to touch, feel, and perceive what needs to be healed. Crystals vibrate in resonance with some energy pattern within you, and that's going to be unique to you. It's not the same for everyone. The way the crystals communicate is through vibrations. Not through words. Not through stories in your head. As long as you are attentive to yourself and are able to own what comes up for you, then you can hear what they are telling you."

Ahsian has noticed that when people begin awakening to the idea of working with stones and start feeling drawn to crystals and stones, most of them will be specifically attracted to quartz first "because it's so present within the Earth's energy field but also because it's so present within our own bodies. Quartz is such an incredibly important material for connecting with the body of the earth and our own physical bodies, as well as finding commonality and communication there."

Like Ahsian, renowned crystal healer and author Judy Hall has made a lifelong study of crystals, ever since she was intuitively drawn to them as a child. "The stones always spoke to me and told me where they wanted to go. I've continued with them ever since," she says.

Although she was not formally trained, she practices by communicating with the "crystal oversouls," which she uses to assist her in her work with clients and in other situations, particularly with respect to resolving karmic, ancestral, personal, and environmental unrest.

Hall believes that crystals call to those whom they know they can assist: "It's a noninvasive, gentle form of healing that combines so well with other forms. It never competes. I use crystals all the time and am in awe of how they continue to evolve their consciousness. Each time a new form [of crystal] is discovered, it takes me further in my soul expansion and healing work."

Hall's workshops engage with a variety of forms of crystal healing and soul expansion, all of which incorporate ancient traditions, ranging from shamanic journeying to the laying out of stone grids in the environment.

She believes that crystals have continued to exert their influence on human consciousness, even if their presence might seem less obvious today. "Our modern world runs on silicon chips—in other words, crystals!" she says. "Planes would fall out of the sky without them. Cars would stall. Communications wouldn't work. Many of the drugs used every day are based on the minerals contained within crystals. So many people are becoming disenchanted with the side effects and resistance that is developing to conventional drugs that they are turning once again to Mother Nature's medicine chest. Our world still runs on crystals."

For artist Lawrence Stoller, crystals are more than tools for amplifying, condensing, and focusing electromagnetic energy; they also function as companions, forming an inter-kingdom friendship between us and them, between the mineral and human worlds. "In essence, my art strives to initiate a standing wave of resonance, as a sculpted artifact of beauty and a tool of light. Crystals are beautiful and beauty is a powerful force."

Stoller says that one of the aspects that links his work to that of the ancients is the notion of crystal conservancy, an ideal that acknowledges crystals as treasures of the earth. Conservation was often practiced among indigenous tribes, and many contemporary healers, likewise, revere crystals and are sensitive to unethical mining and extraction methods. Stoller adds, "Like a grove of majestic redwood trees, they need to be preserved, revered, and passed on to generations to come. They pass through our hands as they live on eternally into the future. We are infants in our relationship with these majestic ancient ones."

My former teacher JaneAnn Dow wrote, "When someone comes to you for healing, you are being invited into a sacred space. You will be opening up a corridor of light which extends from the physical consciousness to the spiritual body or soul of your client."[19]

Crystal healers seek in some way to incorporate shamanic ways into our modern world through the symbolic language of crystals and the influence they exert over our unconscious. Real healing, as shamanism proposes, doesn't come from our limited perspective or treating in isolation the physical part—it comes from connecting with our invisible true essence and expanding our vision of reality and the whole.

As the Earthkeepers of the world know, there is a spiritual responsibility that comes from working with crystals—a responsibility to the stones that come to us as gifts from the earth, to the energy they hold and the role they play in the healing process, and to the planet itself as the source of all life. Our ultimate responsibility is to *be* the quartz crystal. We need to be very clear and focused as we interact with the subtle energies of the mineral kingdom. We need to be aware that in healing ourselves and raising our frequency, we contribute in a small way to healing planetary consciousness.

As we have explored in this chapter, there is a clear bridge between indigenous crystal healing practices and the work of contemporary crystal healers who recognize the power of reconnecting with the earth through rituals and geomancy—particularly as we consider the power of responding to environmental devastation by recognizing our planet as one cohesive organism rather than a series of separate ones.

And now we move into Part 3, which reveals that the concept of interconnectedness that was embraced by indigenous peoples across the world is *supported* by modern science and technology. Together, we will explore the crystal blueprint on a quantum, sub-particle level. In Chapter 5, you will learn all about how quantum theory offers a thorough explanation of crystals' unique properties—and you will see how the language of energy is the perfect expression of crystals' healing power.

PART III

THE SCIENCE BEHIND CRYSTAL HEALING

.

CHAPTER 5

Crystal Healing and Quantum Theory:

Understanding Energy in the Sub-particle World

"For most of the twentieth century, science and religion have dwelt in separate houses, suspiciously peeking through the curtains at one another. But the mystical side of man cannot be long locked away, and many mystical hearts beat in the bodies of pure scientists."

— RA BONEWITZ[1]

TO TRULY UNDERSTAND CRYSTAL ENERGY HEALING, you must recognize that it works at an invisible, subatomic level. If your chosen paradigms rely on the see-to-believe paradigm, your mind can offer much resistance in believing in the benefits of crystal energy.

This part of the book seeks to clarify the way crystal healing works by offering a thorough overview of the nature and behavior of energy on the subatomic level studied in quantum theory. You will find evidence of energy manipulation in the constant application of quartz in today's technology—and in healing techniques. In this chapter, you will learn the basic language of energy, as well as its properties and how they act on the body and mind in such a way that allows crystal healing to restore wellness and connection to the authentic self.

In today's world, you will find two different paradigms for looking at reality. One of them is based on the physical reality that everything in the universe is made out of matter, and this is the point of view that some scientists still follow to this day—a cosmos of linear and finite systems with highly defined boundaries. The other model is based on the energetic foundation of all phenomena; this is the model that many metaphysical and spiritual people follow and that we are rediscovering through a new science, which tends to view the world in an infinite way.

Although there can sometimes seem to be a conflict between science and mysticism, both scientists and mystics are essentially in search of the same thing: the truth. It is only today, particularly as recent advances in science have offered us an opportunity to discover that matter is just a specialized arrangement of energy (which is what the mystics have been saying for thousands of years), that we can discover common ground between these seemingly different disciplines. However, with the discoveries made since Einstein and the advent of quantum physics, we can see that the world is very different from what we have been told and that it is much closer to what the ancients described.

As physicist Max Planck once said, "Science cannot solve the ultimate mystery of nature. And that is because, in the last analysis, we ourselves are . . . part of the mystery that we are trying to solve."[2] In fact, during the quantum revolution of the early 20th century, advances in science revealed a mysterious, invisible world to our eyes, as we discovered that the world of seemingly solid matter around us is 99.999 percent space.[3] Niels Bohr, who received the Nobel Prize for physics in 1922 for his contributions to our understanding of atomic structure, revealed that the atom, the basic unit of matter, is mostly empty space filled with energy. So what many of us define as our material world is only 0.0000001 percent of the known universe, yet we spend most of our lives only paying attention to that aspect. In fact, if we were to compare the nucleus of an average atom to a tennis ball, the atom's electrons would be smaller than a grain of sand—and the outmost layer of electrons would be circling the tennis ball at a distance of four miles. If you were to squeeze out all the empty space from your body, what would remain of you would be microscopic in size.

Although we are not always aware of it, we live immersed within an ocean of energy.

This means that the truth is not necessarily written in stone. We see this in the history of humanity. How many battles were fought for rigid beliefs? Beliefs change. Earth, once believed to be the center of the universe, eventually ceded its place to the sun and, after being considered flat for centuries, was eventually recognized as round and then as an oblate spheroid. The same thing is happening today with matter. The solid and tangible realm of matter is giving way to the transparent realm of energy.

We now have a convincing scientific model that gives us an explanation of the nature of matter and energy on atomic and subatomic levels. This "quantum field" offers a framework for what the mystics knew of as the blueprint for everything in creation. The very foundation of quantum physics—that the universe is made up mostly of energy, which pervades all space—applies to everything from galaxies, stars, and planets to the body, thoughts, and emotions. This energy moves in space in the form of waves and frequencies, and clusters in a number of different energy fields, each one conveying specific information. This also means that the body—each organ, each thought, each crystalline structure—also clusters in a specific energy field that gives it unique and specific properties.

The energetic fields—which are made up of infinite, boundary-less waves—constantly intermingle with and affect one another in an invisible, pulsating dance. This means that thoughts can affect our emotions, our emotions can affect our bodies, our bodies can affect our environments, and vice versa. Quite literally, we are all connected by virtue of energy.

Like everything in the quantum universe, humans are made of energy. We can think of ourselves as a group of cells made up of trillions of atoms per cell. Likewise, crystals are also formed by trillions of subatomic particles. Physicist Nassim Haramein, who has been questioned by mainstream physicists for challenging existing quantum mechanics paradigms, demonstrated that the tetrahedron is involved in the geometric structure of the vacuum of space since it's a very stable structure. According to Haramein, the 64-tetrahedron grid is the seed geometry of what eventually becomes "the infinite holofractographic vacuum structure of the entire universe."[4] Crystals' unique molecular structure also consists of a tetrahedron grid that has the ability to resonate with space and to balance, transform, and amplify energy that it interacts with. Using crystals as tools, you can literally change your reality.

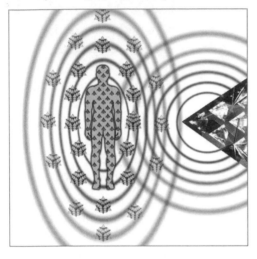

Quartz geometry resonates with the geometry of the body's energy field.

Quantum Theory and Consciousness

In 1931, Max Planck, the father of quantum theory, said, "I regard consciousness as fundamental."[5] Due to the existence of the quantum field, he suggested that our physical world was sustained by a greater intelligence. "We must assume behind this force [that we see as matter] is the existence of a conscious and intelligent mind." And then he concluded, "This Mind is the matrix of all matter."[6]

Consciousness is important in the study of crystal healing, as the energy of our focused, conscious mind is amplified through crystalline properties. Within the unlimited margins of quantum theory, this is possible because no phenomena are ever truly separate. At the sub-particle level, crystals and humans are immersed and interacting in an invisible, continuous ocean of energy. From this perspective, our consciousness can be useful, as we can direct it to transform energy within and around us and eventually make it perceptible to our eyes. Consciousness enables the energy of the crystals to interact with the energy of the body at a level imperceptible to the human eye;

this later materializes in our physical world through healing and the sudden changes we experience in our lives.

Physicist David Joseph Bohm developed the concept of the *holomovement* in the 1970s. In one of his books, *Wholeness and the Implicate Order,* he describes the universe as a single unified system of "undivided wholeness" where the "implicate" and "explicate" orders are interconnected as a flowing stream. He defines the "explicate" as phenomena we can perceive with our five senses and that appear separate—such as crystals and people—and "implicate" as a deeper and more fundamental order of reality from which everything originates: a greater wholeness in which everything is interconnected through energy.

The implicate and explicate orders are connected. Bohm compared this connection with a flowing stream that includes ripples, splashes, and waves; although the water disturbances may look separate to us, they are connected and part of the same body of water. In the same way, although crystals and the body may seem separated, they are connected through energy fields and waves. For Bohm, wholeness wasn't static but was part of a dynamic state of becoming that he called the "universal flux," which allowed everything to move together in a connected evolutionary process.[7] This process, which connects our energy to the energy of crystals, is what allows the healing process to occur.

The universe is constantly changing or flowing from the implicate to the explicate, from the unseen to the seen. Although many of us define ourselves on the basis of our physical bodies, the truth is so much bigger. Animate and inanimate matter are inseparably interwoven, and life, too, is enfolded throughout the totality of the universe. As author Michael Talbot put it: "Even a rock is in some way alive, said Bohm, for life and intelligence are present not only in all of matter, but in 'energy.'"[8]

This undivided wholeness has been described in the Hindu scriptures known as the Vedas, which many scholars believe date back to 5000 B.C.E. The Vedas speak of a unified field of "pure consciousness" embedded in all creation. According to this ancient tradition, any thought is seen as a perturbation within this field: a ripple in the water of consciousness.[9]

If our natural state is to be in constant motion, or transformation, our fixed mind-set—created by false information—creates resistance to the natural flow of energy within us. The tension that can result in this perturbation in the field can be expressed in many ways, including suffering.

From this point of view, our reality can be seen as a never-ending cycle of our inner creations unconsciously learned from others. Our actions (explicate) originate first in the realm of our thoughts (implicate) on the energetic level. Our ability to use the energy field consciously empowers us to transform and heal our inner reality to co-create a better world for ourselves.

Bohm's description of holographic information is especially pertinent when we look at crystal healing. Bohm was convinced that the universe works as a hologram, wherein patterns are contained within patterns and any individual element could reveal information about every other element in the universe.

Crystal energy healing is also holographic in that healing one part benefits all parts. Choosing quartz crystals can reveal information about the mind and body, and healing ourselves can result in healing those around us.

While not claiming knowledge of the mystical implications of his holomovement theory, Bohm says, "The implicate order has many levels of subtlety. If our attention can go to those levels of subtlety, then we should be able to see more than we ordinarily see."[10] In other words, energy (the implicate order) does not have the boundaries present in matter (the explicate order). This allows us to interact and exchange energy with crystals on a subatomic level during crystal healing. The implicate order also explains the concept of our authentic selves, on a quantum level, as our untouched and pristine nature.

Bohm's idea that every part contains the information of the whole, and vice versa, points to another important concept in quantum theory: nonlocality.

Dean Radin, chief scientist for the Institute of Noetic Sciences, explains that nonlocality means that "there are ways in which things that appear to be separate are, in fact, not separate."[11] This supports Bohm's model of universal flux, which enables us to see that seemingly disparate events are, in fact, connected.

For example, a quantum particle can be in one place only, two places at once, or even many places simultaneously. No matter how far apart these locations are, the particle can be connected to *all* of them!

Nonlocality explains how all parts within the whole are connected. And although the fixed mind-set might view life as disconnected, this is not so on the level of energy. Through the perspective of nonlocality, everything leaves a mark on our lives, and we leave a mark on everything else. We are constantly affecting each other even if we are not aware of it. The information we receive from our parents and our environment affects us in unthinkable ways. Nonlocality also explains how can we reconnect with our authentic selves, as we remain connected to our true origin beyond learned false information. Within us, the authentic self is an underlying, omnipresent force.

This can also be explained through entanglement, another important principle of quantum theory. Entanglement posits that particles that interact with each other become permanently connected, or dependent on each other's states and properties, to the extent that they lose their individuality and in many ways behave as a single entity. For example, one particle that is seemingly at an immeasurable distance from another particle can still influence the actions and behaviors of that distant, faraway particle with no time delay. When two particles are entangled, they stay that way, and no matter how far apart those two particles become, information passes between them instantaneously.

Quantum particles can also communicate with themselves at different points in time. They are not limited by concepts of the past, present, and future. This is why, during a crystal healing in the present, we have the power to heal the past and create the future—through the principle of entanglement.

Entanglement explains how our thoughts affect our bodies and our reality, but also how crystals can heal the body and mind. This might also explain the power and efficacy of distant crystal healing.

Entanglement is also the quantum property that will help you to understand your connection to the universe, but also your disconnection, which is caused by the influence of your learned beliefs. The purpose of crystal healing is to reestablish your connection.

Energy Language

One of the great revelations of 20th-century science is that all existence can be broken down into simple wave functions—from photons to elementary particles to color.

Energy communicates, and crystals interact, through waves. Waves are part of the electromagnetic spectrum known as light, a collective range of frequencies of electromagnetic radiation and their associated wavelengths, which travel at the speed of light ($3.0 * 10^8$ meters per second) through a vacuum. This includes the invisible electromagnetic waves of the spectrum: radio waves, infrared, ultraviolet, X-rays, and gamma rays.

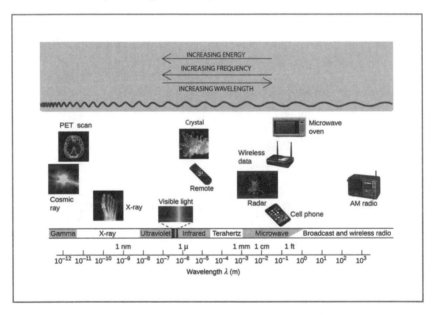

All forms of light are energy, and the term scientists use to describe this energy is "electromagnetic radiation." This illustration shows some everyday examples of various types of light, from cosmic rays to cell phones. From radio waves to gamma rays, the human eye is only capable of seeing the visible light in this spectrum.
The frequency we see is a tiny fraction of the available light in the universe. Radio, microwave, wireless data, radar, cell phones, remote controls, and infrared waves have longer wavelengths and lower frequencies; ultraviolet, X-rays, PET scans, and cosmic rays have shorter wavelengths and higher frequencies. The energy of quartz crystals is in the infrared part of the spectrum, which is why we cannot see their energy but can feel it. Sunlight is also electromagnetic and covers the ultraviolet, visible and infrared region of the electromagnetic spectrum. Crystals, as well as our bodies, resonate within the infrared region.

"Most of the radiation emitted by [the] human body [and, likewise, by crystals] is in the infrared region, mainly at the wavelength of 12 micron[s]. The wavelength of infrared radiation is between 0.75 to 1,000 micron[s] (1 micron = 10^{-6} meters). This wavelength is longer than that of red visible light."[12]

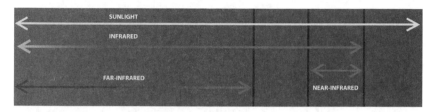

Infrared light lies beyond the color red in the visible spectrum; it's wider than the range that makes up visible light. Scientists often use "far" infrared and "near" infrared to differentiate between the two ends of the range, with near infrared just below the kind of light we can see and far infrared closer to the microwaves in the electromagnetic spectrum. Quartz crystals work within this frequency range.

In the scientific world, crystals are mostly known for their properties to transform mechanical and electrical energy, but crystals also emit energy. At a sub-particle level, crystalline structures are also energy and respond in unique ways to a variety of energies, including heat, light, pressure, sound, electricity, gamma rays, microwaves, bioelectricity, and consciousness. With these different inputs of energy, the atomic structure of crystals can oscillate and lead to the emission of radiation.[13]

In order for quartz crystal to emit energy, it must be exposed to an external source of energy, such as the human body. As mentioned, the body and quartz crystals both emit infrared energy at about 12 microns. Because of this similarity between the human body and quartz crystal, the body gains the capacity to easily assimilate the crystal's infrared energy during a healing. The kinship between quartz and our bodies is what allows energy exchange and healing to occur.

The body's infrared energy has the capacity to affect the crystal's inner electrical environment, and vice versa. External energy makes the quartz lose its inner electrical balance, which produces vibration and waves. The atoms in all our cells are continuously in motion, also sending waves. The warmth and tingling sensations we feel while experiencing crystal healing is the exchange of infrared energy between crystals and our bodies.

In this way, crystal healing can be explained by looking at exchanges of wavelengths on a subatomic level.

Light itself is a wave of alternating electric and magnetic fields. The propagation of light isn't that different from waves crossing an ocean. Every element has a certain amount of light that gets released when an electron falls from one orbit to another. The energy released is called a photon. Photons move at the speed of light (186,000 miles per second) and carry no mass or electrical charge.[14] Indeed, the human body emits biophotons invisible to us but detectable via sophisticated modern instrumentation. In effect, we are literally beings of light.

The limitations of our senses prevent us from perceiving the electromagnetic spectrum at a variety of frequencies and wavelengths. If our eyes were to see the whole range of visible light at once, they would read it as "white." In fact, the human eye is sensitive to a narrow band of frequency of the overall electromagnetic spectrum: we can detect light at wavelengths between 400 to 900 nanometers. The only part of the spectrum that we can see is from violet and red through the rainbow color bands of indigo, blue, green, yellow, and orange. This is what we see in the visible light segment of the electromagnetic spectrum.

According to science, color doesn't really exist. Color is a function of the human visual system rather than an intrinsic property of light. Technically speaking, colors are the way our brains, by virtue of our eyes, interpret the electromagnetic radiation of a wavelength within the visible spectrum.

When you choose a crystal, what you are really choosing is the wavelength and frequency that resonates with your own wavelength and frequency. It's important to understand what waves and frequencies are to understand the energy language of crystal healing.

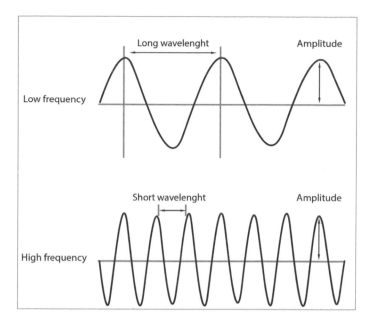

Scientists use frequency and wavelength to determine how much energy a certain type of light has. Light with shorter wavelengths (or higher frequencies) carries more energy than light with longer wavelengths (or lower frequencies).

Energy moves in a wave pattern. Frequency measures how many wave peaks pass by over a certain period of time—for example, one second. We usually measure this as the number of wavelength cycles that pass per second. Hertz (hz) are the units for this measurement. Wavelength is the distance from the peak of one wave to the peak of the next. Longer wavelength means a lower frequency and shorter wavelength a higher frequency. For you to understand it better: if the wavelength of a light wave is shorter, the frequency will be higher. More cycles can pass by the set point in one second. But if the light wave has a longer wavelength, it will have a lower frequency because each cycle takes longer time to complete.

Another key characteristic of an energy wave is the measurement along its other axis, from top to bottom of a wave. This is called the amplitude. While the wavelength will tell us what type of radiation we are looking at, the amplitude will tell us about its intensity, or brightness. The higher the amplitude, the farther the wave will propagate and the more energy it carries. In most cases, higher amplitude is associated with high-energy waves and lower amplitude with low-energy waves. The amount of energy is usually proportional to its frequency, but this isn't always the case. Loud sounds (like those made by ocean waves crashing against the cliffs on the shore) are made by high-amplitude waves.

The brain interprets various wavelengths of light as different colors. Colors originate in light and work through various wavelengths and frequencies. In fact, frequency and wavelength determine the color of visible light. We know, for example, that red has the lowest frequency and longest wavelength of visible light; violet has the highest frequency and shortest wavelength. The HeartMath Institute talks about how negative and positive emotions can have a corresponding vibratory frequency. Lower-level vibrations can occur in connection with frustration, anger, disappointment, sadness, judgment, comparison, and much more (correlated with low-frequency colors such as red, orange, and yellow). They have a very long wavelength and slow vibration, while love, care, compassion, kindness, appreciation, forgiveness, and more (correlated with high-frequency colors such as violet, blue, and green) have a very rapid and high frequency.[15]

Through the language of frequency, we can relate colors with emotions and feelings and translate what our unconscious is trying to communicate to us on a deeper level. Colors usually exert their influence automatically. When we choose quartz crystals by resonance, color plays a fundamental role by helping us to decipher what is inside our unconscious mind that needs to be transformed.

When some of the wavelengths are missing, we see an object as "colored." So if an object absorbs all of the frequencies of visible light except for the frequency associated with green light, then the object will appear green. When you see a green crystal, the color is the result of the crystal having absorbed the red and orange wavelengths from the white light around it while rejecting the green; the green frequency of light is what bounces off the object, allowing us to "see" it.

Color is not a property of electromagnetic radiation but a feature of visual perception by an observer. In other words, color exists only in the mind of the beholder. A person's perception of colors is a subjective process; different people see the same illuminated object or light source in different ways and have their own unique ways of perceiving the world.

The process through which the brain encodes white light into color and the association with already-existing information within our minds offers us an important pattern that decodes information in our unconscious that can lead toward our healing.

In the same way that the brain decodes light into color, it decodes the waves of our daily experiences based on resonance with waves of previous experiences. These pulses are then decoded by the brain to transform frequencies and waves into a literal hologram of our reality.

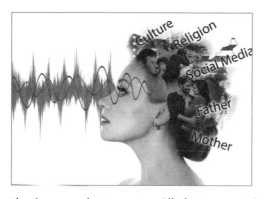

The brain and learned beliefs converting the frequency and waves into our familiar reality.

To better under-stand this, think of how television cameras collect light and convert it into electronic pulses decoded by television sets to produce the images that we see. All that we see is merely a wave interpretation of electromagnetic energy. As scientist Nikola Tesla is reported to have said, "If you want to find the secrets of the universe, think in terms of energy, frequency, and vibration."

Everything in the universe exists in a state of vibration, and every electromagnetic field is characterized by measurable rates of vibration, or frequencies. Humans, crystals, and anything else you can think of exists at a particular vibrational frequency, and this may change at any moment, in accordance with mental and emotional state, internal or external stressors, and other factors.

The electric and magnetic fields of the human body are complex and dynamic and are associated with processes such as heart and brain function, blood and lymph flow, and a variety of other biological processes on many scales. These phenomena all contribute various components to the biofield, or the human energy field.

The Human Energy Field

From the time of Hippocrates, conventional medicine has tried to convince us that symptoms are physiological consequences of malfunction in our bodies and that we must carefully investigate them, avoiding any subjective interpretation, thus leaving no room for inconsistency in the prognosis.

In truth, the body is never ill or healthy in and of itself; it simply expresses messages that our authentic selves are attempting to transmit to us.

According to Thorwald Dethlefsen and Ruediger Dahlke, in their book *The Healing Power of Illness: The Meaning of Symptoms and How to Interpret Them*, the body does not do anything by itself. The body of a living person owes its performance to the *biofield*. The biofield is a term coined by scientists from the National Institute of Health in 1994, describing the energetic "field" of information that surrounds and penetrates the body. It consists of a number of fields, including electromagnetic fields, biophotons or very low-level particles of light, infrared emissions, brain waves, and heart waves.

Living cells are made up of a large number of interacting molecules. The health and vitality of a person are reflected within the flow of energy in their cells and their various organs. The flow of energy in the body results in a comprehensive electromagnetic field around it, with many smaller fields in which energy patterns and electron pathways flow to the entire body. This network of energy is the biofield. Ancients knew that the biofield carries information in the form of patterns.

Disease can be seen as a pattern in the biofield that produces imbalance in the body. Illness becomes the twinkling lights of our dashboard, warning us that something within us is not resonating with our true essence. Interestingly, all the chemical reactions of matter studied by current medicine are reduced to energy exchanges at the subatomic level. Unfortunately, conventional or allopathic medicine focuses only on matter and its chemical reactions. Crystal healing attunes us directly to the energy of the subatomic particles that make up matter.

Contrary to the knowledge offered to us by conventional medicine, there is not a diversity of incurable illnesses. Rather, there is a single illness that arises from a disconnection with the authentic self. This disconnection is manifested through symptoms whose sole purpose is to show us that we are out of sync with our authentic nature. In other words, symptoms are messages of the implicate order (the authentic self) that are expressed in the explicate order (our bodies).

Thus, to eradicate any symptom, we must address it from the energy perspective.

A wonderful opportunity arises when we experience illness. Illness interrupts our normal flow of life. It brings our awareness inward and begins a self-questioning process that could lead to reconnecting with the true self.

When we shift our attitude from fighting disease to accepting it as a teacher, we see that it is not an obstacle but rather the path toward healing and transformation.

In our healthcare system, we have two vastly different models of human biology. One of them is based on the Newtonian view, which posits the physical reality that everything in the universe is made of matter. According to this view, the body is a machine full of chemicals and genes; if there is anything wrong with the machine, you adjust the chemicals and genes, which are the primary source of the problem.

The view that is most aligned with alternative forms of medicine is based on quantum physics; it shows us that the universe is actually made up of energy, and everything we see as matter is actually energy . . . including ourselves.

According to Lynne McTaggart, an award-winning journalist and the author of many books, including the bestsellers *The Field* and *The Intention Experiment*, this is the new medicine. "The new medicine is all about looking at the body as a dynamic system and understanding that if you affect one part of the body, you affect the rest of it. You put medicine on your arm and you create changes in your leg, in your liver, everywhere. So the new approach is to approach the body as a holistic system and also an energy system. So, we don't have to do things grossly to our physicality. We can treat ourselves through energy, and treat ourselves through things that we cannot really see."[16]

Crystals are part of this new medicine modality, as they work vibrationally through crystalline energy.

Although this concept of the new medicine is gaining ground, in truth, it has been around for thousands of years. The Chinese began to document it approximately 5,000 years ago. Today, it is becoming a more common paradigm for various reasons: efficacy, non-invasive methods that render fewer side effects, and alignment with both science and spiritual methodologies. About 55 percent of the population are using alternative and integrative medicine because they are getting results.[17]

According to Dr. Bruce Lipton, "The fates of our cells are controlled by the chemistry of our blood, and the chemistry of our blood is adjusted by the way we perceive life." He says, "If we open up our eyes and see love in our presence, we release chemistry in the blood such as oxytocin, dopamine, serotonin. These chemicals promote health and vitality of the system. In contrast, however, if I open my eyes and I see something that threatens me or scares me, I release a completely different set of chemicals into the blood, such as stress hormones and histamine. The difference is these chemicals actually shut down my growth and prepare me for protection. So it becomes very critical on how we see the world because our perceptions are converted into chemistry, and the chemistry directly controls not just our behavior but our genetic expression as well."[18]

When we shift the biofield, we shift the body's dynamic toward wellness. In fact, we realize that our atoms themselves are vibrational fields that offer us "energy profiles" of our bodies. According to Dr. Lipton, adjusting our energy is "hundreds of times more efficient in controlling biology than our chemical signals." The result is that we move from a pharmaceutical paradigm for healing and into a more effective way of introducing long-lasting health. If our bodies are made up of energy particles, the solution to our diseases and imbalances should be in treatments based on energy.

In fact, biochemical processes are energy exchanges at a sub-particle level. The emerging field of energy medicine proposes that these processes are regulated by changes in the human biofield. Early diagnosis and treatment of disease can be achieved by balancing a disturbed biofield.[19]

According to biophysicist Beverly Rubik, "I like to think of the biofield as an orchestra of different energies, different frequencies. Just like you hear, literally, a symphony. Complex fields of infrared magnetic energy, visible light, bioelectricity, and probably more. And then you may ask: 'Well, who is the conductor?' The mind is. Where mind goes, energy flows, and blood and flesh follow. So the mind is the supreme conductor of the symphony of the biofield, and the biofield literally moves at the speed of light, because fields do this. And makes the body a coherent whole in response to thoughts. . . . So if we can work at that level with our medicine, then we can shift ourselves, and self-healing will happen."[20]

The human biofield possesses qualities unlike the kinds of energy with which we are normally familiar. One of these is the ability to manifest as an amorphous blur of energy around our bodies. Talented psychics often report seeing a "hologram" around people. These images are usually of objects and ideas that hold a prominent position in the thoughts of the person around whom they are seen.

In 1911, Dr. Walter Kilner looked at the etheric body by using colored filters and coal tar. He noted that there appeared to be three regions: next to the skin, a dark layer; a wispier layer at a 90-degree angle to the body; and another ethereal layer contouring the body about six inches out. He noted that the etheric body, which he called the "aura," changed depending on a person's thoughts and physical and emotional health.[21]

In the early 1900s, Dr. Wilhelm Reich also studied this mysterious aura, which he named "orgone" and referred to as a universal energy that surrounds everyone and everything, from humans to inanimate objects. His later work revealed that where there were areas of blockage in the orgone, our mental and emotional patterns could work to clear and release them. Reich's body of research was invested in the subtle connections between physical, emotional, mental, and etheric energies, which are constantly interacting.[22]

Dr. Zheng Rongliang of Lanzhou University in China similarly studied subtle energy in the human energy field by measuring it with a detector that revealed that the aura of the human body has a pulse. However, the rate and intensity of this pulse varies for everyone's field. The study was repeated and validated by researchers at the Shanghai Atomic Nuclear Institute of Academia Sinica.[23]

In the 1930s, Russian scientist Semyon Kirlian and his wife, Valentina, invented Kirlian photography. This photographic process captures the human energy field on film by projecting a high-frequency electrical field at an object. Today, people still use Kirlian photography to demonstrate how the aura can shift depending on specific emotional and mental states. Practitioners even use it to diagnose specific illnesses and disorders. Interestingly, while not the same as Kirlian photography, medical science looks at "heat auras" and other ways of imaging and mapping the body's processes to study its electromagnetic and biochemical functions and map any corresponding irregularities.[24]

The physical body can be viewed as a complex pattern of energetic interference that is penetrated by the organizing biofield of a person's etheric, or energetic, body. Physician Richard Gerber speculated that "the 'etheric body' is a holographic energy template [a.k.a. morphic field] that guides the growth and development of the physical body."[25]

Crystal healing is based on the recognition that matter is energy; therefore, we can heal the body through the manipulation of different energetic vibrations and patterns through the network of interwoven energy fields. We have already learned of the importance of working with the patterns encoded within our energy fields on a symbolic level, but we must also act with them on an energetic level.

As we have seen, all beliefs and experiences are imprinted in the biofield—an energy bubble surrounding our physical bodies that is connected to the cellular expression of the physical body and, as such, the continuous creation of either health or illness.

Crystal energy healing attempts to heal illness and transform human beliefs and experiences recorded in the biofield by manipulating symbols and energy patterns. As Bohm's concept of holography revealed, within each pattern, every piece contains the whole. In this way, crystal energy healing seeks to restore the flow of universal energies within us.

What does it mean for flow to be restored? It simply means that our energetic systems are distributed throughout our bodies and their energy fields. According to Dr. Valerie Hunt, the hologram itself is part of a dynamic system, not a static one.[26] In order for the system to be in balance, a constant flow of energy is necessary. This means that everything has to flow, including our thoughts. Any fixed thought could bring instability, and ultimately disease, to the biofield. As Bohm pointed out, universal flux is a universal property and our natural state of being.

Our Holography

Any wavelike phenomenon, including the energy fields of our body and mind, can create an interference pattern. Destructive interference in our body might be linked to the fixed learned beliefs in our minds, which can impact the flux of energy and our health.

According to scientist Jon Whale: "On the physical plane the human body is a formation of billions of constantly vibrating atoms. All the vibrating quantum particles entering humans and living systems create quantum energy waves." One can view the (healthy) human energy field as the result of the interference of the energies of *all* oscillating wave particles, atoms, and cells that make up the human body.[27]

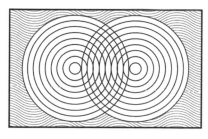

INTERFERENCE PATTERN
Created by dropping two stones into water

When we throw a stone into a pond, the expansive waves it produces illustrate how the energetic vibrations propagate through space. When we throw another stone, the waves that both objects produce intersect. This occurs in a similar way when our vibrations and the vibrations of crystals intersect; however, unlike the stones in water, we do not perceive these intersections because energy is imperceptible to the human eye. This is what is known as an interference pattern.

Interference can be explained by an image of two pebbles thrown into a pond. Both will radiate ripples or waves in the water. When waves expand and pass through one another, interference occurs. When two waves meet in such a way that their crests (tops of the waves) line up together, this is constructive interference. For two waves of equal amplitude interfering constructively, the resulting amplitude is twice as large as the amplitude of an individual wave. The resulting wave has higher amplitude and frequency.

Scientists recently discovered that calcite and zinc oxide crystals contain rhythmic fluctuations; when the crystals dissolve, the fluctuations spread out, similar to ripples that spread out from the center when you drop a pebble into a body of water. It is believed that such activity, which is a prime example of constructive interference, can help researchers in a number of fields, from pharmaceutical manufacturing to corrosive prevention.[28]

In destructive interference, the crest of one wave meets the trough (bottom) of another, thus canceling it out. When two waves interfere destructively, the result is lower total amplitude. A high-amplitude wave is a high-energy wave, and a low-amplitude wave is a low-energy wave.

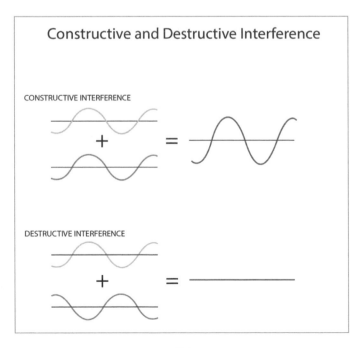

Constructive and Destructive Interference

CONSTRUCTIVE INTERFERENCE

DESTRUCTIVE INTERFERENCE

Destructive interference produced by our learned false beliefs may stagnate energy, producing energy blockages in the long run that might translate as different imbalances in our bodies and lives.

The double-slit experiment is a famous experiment that shows how a hologram is produced. We know that light travels in waves. When those waves pass in the form of a laser light through two parallel slits, a single wave gets separated into two waves that run into each other, forming interference patterns that are recorded on a piece of film.

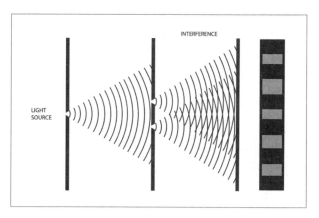

The resulting image on the film doesn't actually resemble the object that was just photographed but rather looks like a series of radiating concentric rings. But when one shines an additional light source onto the film, a three-dimensional image of the object will magically appear. However, it is impossible to touch or grab it, as it is mere light rather than a solid form.[29]

The hologram is an energy interference pattern. Within this pattern, *every* piece contains the whole. Consequently the body also operates: as an interference pattern where each part contains the information of the entire system.

The late neuroscientist and researcher Karl Pribram believed that the brain itself was like a hologram. That is, any part of a hologram contains the whole of the stored information. This also points back to the nonlocality of human consciousness, which cannot be found in any one specific location, such as a part of the brain, but rather in its energy field.

Pribram was originally struck by the similarity of his ideas and Bohms's concept of the implicate order, and contacted him with the desire to collaborate. In 1991 Pribram worked with Bohm to develop the holonomic brain theory, a model that describes the brain as a holographic storage network.

If we are unable to perceive the macrocosm of reality—with its vast ocean of waves and frequencies—that is only because our brains take that "holographic blur" and convert it into familiar objects and ideas that make up our world. For example, if you were to take a common object such as a teacup and filter it through the lens of the brain, it would manifest as what we know of as a cup. However, if we removed that lens, we'd experience the cup in an entirely different way: as an interference pattern caused by the interaction of different waves of energy.

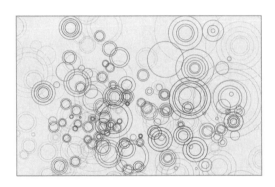

This is a representation of how the world would look without the brain's filters.

In this way, objective reality does not exist in the way that we think it does. Pribram himself suspected that perhaps the beliefs of the sages of ancient times were based in truth, and that the entire world was *maya*, or a grand illusion. In fact, Pribram believed that the limitless realm of waves and frequencies was filtered through our senses, thus offering us an image of our "reality" that is, by definition, limited.[30]

Pribram showed that energy fields are decoded by our brains into a 3D picture to give us the illusion of a physical world of discrete objects. Additionally, the brain interprets the world according to our learned information. From this perspective, it seems obvious why we all seem to view the world so differently from one another—literally!

Something known as the "observer effect" can also dictate our perception of reality. In science, the observer effect relates to the fact that simply observing any particular phenomenon will influence that phenomenon.

Dr. Joe Dispenza has noted, "Quantum experiments demonstrated that electrons exist simultaneously in an infinite array of possibilities or probabilities in an invisible field of energy. But only when an observer focuses attention on any location of any one electron does that electron appear. In other words, a particle cannot manifest in reality—that is, ordinary space-time as we know it—until we observe it."[31]

The observer literally transforms waves into particles and our reality. Physicist Nick Herbert, a supporter of this interpretation, says that this has sometimes caused him to imagine that behind his back, the world is always "a radically ambiguous and ceaselessly flowing quantum soup."[32] He adds, "Likewise, humans can never experience the true texture of quantum reality because everything we touch turns to matter."[33]

We are literally creating our own reality!

Strange as it may sound, constructive interference or energy waves can only occur when no one is watching. In the moment we observe them, destructive interference occurs; thus, so does our experience of matter.

We don't perceive our holographic universe transparently; we perceive it through the filters of our minds' learned information. Through observation, our minds' contents rearrange atoms in the energy fields to create what we know as our reality.

The unconscious mind can't distinguish between an imagined event and a real one. In our brains' energy fields—in which all experiences, real or imagined, are reduced to organized waveforms—our memories and imagination can play just as big a role as an actual event.

The observer effect points to the interconnectedness and entanglement of all things. Our capacity to observe beyond the limits of our mental filters impacts what we are able to see—as well as the wholeness we are able to experience.

We can achieve healing by linking the implicate ("enfolded," invisible, or deeper and more fundamental) order and the explicate ("unfolded" and including the phenomena that most humans perceive) order. Crystals can be the perfect links between these orders, guiding us to transform our awareness of reality.

In a brain that operates holographically, symbolic meaning plays an important part, as there are no divisions between mind and matter. That is why crystals as symbols can move and transform energy. According to Bohm, consciousness isn't the only thing that responds to meaning. The body also responds, so meaning is simultaneously physical and mental and can serve as a bridge between these two experiences of reality.[34]

A color, a shape, and the sensation of holding a crystal may link the explicate and implicate orders and guide us to transform our reality.

In quantum theory, all boundaries are illusory. Additionally, as we explored with the concept of entanglement, a healing experience is not bound by spatial or temporal limitations. The client is able to experience other places and other timelines. The symbolism of crystals connects us with different experiences in time and space. During a crystal session, the time and space gap disappears. We might experience something that happened in our early childhood as a real-time occurrence. The difference is that, this time, we can choose a different approach, one that generates a constructive response—or interference that will transform and improve our lives.

Bohm has said, "Every action starts from an intention in the implicate order. The imagination is already the creation of the form; it already has the intention and the germs of all the movements needed to carry it out. And it affects the body and so on, so that as creation takes place in that way from the subtler levels of the implicate order, it goes through them until it manifests in the explicate."[35]

In other words, in the implicate order, as in the brain itself, imagination is just as real as what we deem "reality," and it should therefore come as no surprise to us that images in the mind can ultimately manifest as symptoms in the physical body and healing during a crystal energy session.

The electromagnetic field of an atom can change with any of our thoughts. This affects other atoms—and our world. Atoms are in constant motion when they are exposed to the electromagnetic fields of our minds—continuously creating our reality. Using crystals as tools for healing gives us the opportunity to amplify and transform our minds' contents to create the best version of reality.

If our mind has the capacity to influence the appearance of an electron, in theory, its conscious intervention can increase the range of possibilities in our lives. This could mean that the quantum field potentially contains the option that we are healthy rather than sick, that we have an abundant life rather than one deprived of well-being, and that we enjoy happiness instead of living in sorrow.

Crystals connect us to the quantum universe, which is just waiting for a conscious observer to influence it and bring it into reality!

If thoughts equal energy and energy equals matter, then thoughts *become* matter. By consciously reviewing a memory during a crystal energy session, we can transmute energy—and this new energy can materialize in our reality.

Physicist William Tiller concurs and has said that we create patterns in our minds. Illness manifests as the result of patterns in the mind and recurs because treatment occurs only on a physical rather than a mental level. Tiller has suggested that treating the human energy field would be more efficacious because this would modify our holographic reality on an energetic level.[36]

To understand what produces imbalances in the human mind and body, we have to look once again at patterns of electromagnetism, which are disturbed in the body due to lack of energy flow. In the language of frequency, our bodies and all the organs within them each have an optimal frequency corresponding to health. The frequencies related to illness tend to be on the lower side. This can also be applied to emotions, as our emotions are energy with a distinct vibratory frequency. Fear has been shown to have a very long and slow vibration, while love has a very rapid and high frequency.[37]

Our bodies have a certain frequency when healthy (typically, 62 to 78 MHz) and a different frequency when sick (58 MHz and lower). At this lower level, minor illnesses such as the flu can show up. At even lower levels, terminal illnesses can appear.[38]

Researchers who have studied the effect of various frequencies on human cells have revealed that the body can be impacted by frequencies on a subatomic level. This is because cells respond directly to changes in light and sound. Some of the remarkable discoveries they made include the fact that specific frequencies had the power to eradicate illness within cells and to preserve the health of nearby cells.[39]

In order to support our health, we must remain within the range of healthy frequency or near to it.

According to the HeartMath Institute, in our literal higher vibration, we can experience easy decision-making, a flow of solutions, intuitive wisdom, better discernment, and clearer and more effective choices—all qualities of the authentic self.[40]

Crystals are wonderful tools for helping us to work with our frequencies, as their internal structures have the ability to balance our energy and help us support and recover our healthy frequencies.

The Waves of the Body

Since we are speaking about energy, waves, and health, it's important to include the waves of our hearts and brains—the two largest electromagnetic fields of the body—and how crystals interact with them.

According to HeartMath Institute director of research Rollin McCraty, in his paper *The Energetic Heart*: "The heart generates the largest electromagnetic field in the body. The electrical field as measured in an electrocardiogram (ECG) is about 60 times greater in amplitude than the brain waves recorded in an encephalogram (EEG)."[41]

The HeartMath Institute has demonstrated that 0.1 Hz is the frequency of the human heart. Heart rate variability gives us an enormous amount of information about health. It indicates psychological resiliency, behavioral flexibility, and our ability to adapt to the changing demands of our environment. It also helps us to see health not simply as the absence of illness but as a process through which we maintain a sense of meaning and coherence, and through which we function in the face of change and other challenges.[42]

Researchers at the HeartMath Institute have noted that when we are focused on inner love and peace, the heart sends coherent energy patterns to the rest of the body, including the brain. Crystals can aid in this activity, as they resonate with the heart's crystalline structures and can help balance and create a coherent state and invite well-being into our lives.

And then there are the waves of the brain, which are similarly connected to our health in that they reveal information about our relationships to fear, anxiety, depression, and suffering, but also about our wellness. Brain waves are electrical impulses produced by our neurons, which also communicate with each other by means of electrical impulses. These brain waves can be observed with an electroencephalogram (EEG). The lower the brain wave frequency, the slower the brain activity.

There are four brain wave states, ranging from deep, dreamless sleep to high arousal. The same four states are common to the human species.

The beta wave state (13 to 30 Hz) is associated with active engagement in mental activities. However, it's also related to overthinking and fear, stress, paranoia, and addiction.

The alpha wave state (7 to 13 Hz) represents a state of relaxation or concentration. It relates to self-observation, eliminating physical and psychic tensions, rapid learning, and a positive, reflective attitude. Your stresses and worries drift away when you enter the alpha state. Tension and nervousness also disappear as your brain's thought process is calmed down and the mind becomes clearer. The "feel good" effect of alpha waves leads to the production of happy and well-functioning cells in your body, as well as the release of serotonin.

The theta wave state (4 to 7 Hz) is connected with mental trances, dreaming, imagination, visualization, and creativity. This type of brain activity has been suggested to improve inner awareness and insight.

The delta wave state (1.5 to 4 Hz) is most common in deep sleep, as well as among infants and young children, who are involved in unconscious learning. This wave state is also associated with deep levels of consciousness, relaxation, empathy, intuition and extreme bliss.

Finally, the gamma wave state (31 to 200 Hz) is associated with the brain's optimal frequency of functioning. Gamma brain waves are commonly associated with increased levels of compassion and feelings of happiness. Gamma brain waves are also associated with a conscious awareness of reality. They have a tiny (virtually unnoticeable) amplitude and can be found in every part of the brain while in minimum electrical voltage (if we consider that the average neuron's resting voltage is 0.07 volts).[43] Gamma waves are also associated with holographic thinking and the unification of all the different information we receive.[44]

Crystal healing can help us connect with different waves, from alpha and theta to delta and gamma; it all depends on our level of commitment to our inner work. Slow brain frequencies help the production of endorphins and aid in the reduction of suffering. Moreover, the same structures that can be found in crystals can also be found in various areas of the brain, providing the kind of resonance that can aid in our healing.

Vibratory Resonance and Crystal Healing

We are made of nothing but patterns of resonant energy! All matter is simply energy modified by electromagnetic wave forms. These encompass the limiting thoughts that originate in our minds.

Ancients believed that emotions and diseases were mirrors that reflected something deeper within, and that all diseases could be prevented and healed from within by removing the original wound.

In Plato's *Timaeus and Critias*, we find: "When the mind is too big for the body its energy shakes [vibrates] the whole frame and fills it with inner disorders." [45]

Emotions are energy patterns generated by our minds that imprint energy patterns in our biofield. When these patterns are negative and not managed in time, they create disease. When we are ill, our bodies are communicating something we need to address. Something is off balance within us and requires our immediate attention to work it out and heal it. When the false information in the energetic field of our minds comes into contact with the the biofield, this produces destructive interference—negating the natural flow of waves in the energy of our bodies and producing what healers know as blocks in the flow of universal energies. This is what creates disease and all sorts of abnormalities.

According to Samuel Hahnemann, the founder of homeopathy, this is how disease is viewed from an electromagnetic point of view. He believed that "if the person's constitutional state is quite strong and the harmful stimulus weak, the electromagnetic field changes vibration rate only slightly and only for a short time. The individual is not aware that anything has happened at all.

"But if the stimulus is powerful enough to overwhelm the vital force, the electromagnetic field undergoes a greater change in vibration rate, and effects are eventually felt by the individual. . . . The symptoms of a disease are nothing but reactions trying to rid the organism of harmful influences which are merely the material manifestations of earlier disturbances on a dynamic electromagnetic level."[46]

As far as promoting healing is concerned, sluggish cells, organs, and glands that are vibrating too slowly will benefit from any method that increases and unifies their rhythms—while those cells, organs, and glands that are overexcited will benefit from any method that helps to reduce and unify their rhythms.[47]

The task, of course, is to find that substance whose vibration rate most closely matches the imbalance of the person to be healed.

This is what crystals can do.

In crystal healing, it is not necessary to use electronic devices. While our rational minds cannot discern the exact frequency of a given crystal, we are naturally drawn to the crystal with the particular frequency, color, thickness, and shape needed to balance our own frequency and bring us back into energetic balance.

Crystals resonate with the body and operate on the principle of wave interaction; that is, researchers have discovered that even low-powered oscillations can have an enormous impact on standing waves, physical structures, and the human body. A constant resonant frequency, when applied to a standing wave, can intensify, reinforce, and prolong the frequency of that wave. This has the power to induce altered brain states.[48]

Resonance occurs when an object vibrating at the same natural frequency of a second object forces that second object into vibrational motion. In this way, the second object (in this case, the body and mind) can vibrate and tune in to a healthy frequency—and in some cases, our original frequency: the authentic self.

The remarkable thing about crystal energy healing is that every stone has the power to balance an unbalanced frequency. When crystals are placed over the body, the body's energy interacts with the crystals, producing constructive interference patterns, which then recalibrate the biofield.

Crystals can help you recognize and resonate with your unbroken wholeness and produce changes in your body. When your focus is on your natural state of oneness and interconnection, and moves away from fragmentation and isolation, health naturally occurs.

If you compare your body to a musical instrument, crystal healing is a tool that enables you to play that instrument. As you master the notes, your life and mind-set expand—and so does your understanding of the holographic universe. You will even come to learn new octaves, as well as notes in those octaves. The more access you have to infinite universal flow, the greater your potential to discover your own crystal blueprint and to create and live from your authentic self.

Just as you have discovered in this chapter, the crystal blueprint is the electromagnetic field that permeates everything. You also learned that crystals' electromagnetic properties offer a holographic understanding of energy and consciousness—one that quantum physicists have explored in great depth over the last century. You will discover in Chapter 6 the manner in which crystals power both our electronic devices and our bodily processes. You will also learn that many of the facets of modern technology that make everything from healing the body to communicating across great distances possible are the same facets that have made crystals desirable to healers for millennia.

CHAPTER 6

The Properties of Quartz: From Electronic Devices to Our Bodies

---

"The crystal is a neutral object whose inner structure exhibits a state of perfection and balance."

— MARCEL VOGEL[1]

ARCHAEOLOGICAL EXCAVATIONS around the world have revealed that quartz knowledge was known to many civilizations around the world, as we discovered in Chapter 3. Progress and technology have given us the opportunity to incorporate quartz crystals' power into our daily lives in the form of electronic devices.

Interestingly, the very same qualities that make crystals so desirable in modern technology are what have drawn different cultures and philosophies around the world, as well as energy healers, to quartz for millennia. A deeper understanding of these qualities is precisely what will allow *us* to use crystals to reconnect with the authentic self.

What Is Quartz?

Quartz is a crystal. According to scientist and inventor Harry Oldfield, "In modern understanding a crystal is a solid material in which the atoms are arranged in a regular pattern."[2]

Quartz is also a mineral, which is an inorganic substance that naturally occurs deep in the earth's crust and is assembled of one element or a combination of many elements. The hardness of a mineral is graded on the Mohs' scale from 1 to 10; quartz is at a 7, making it relatively hard and solid.[3]

Quartz crystal, also known as silica, is naturally abundant on our planet. Quartz can be found in virtually every geological environment known to us, and its appearance can give us clues as to how it was formed. Enormous swaths of the earth's surface and other layers are abundant with quartz, which is especially profuse in granite and similar rocks.

Overall, the crust of the earth harbors 12 percent quartz, most of it in the planet's continental crust. Although the quartz tends to be hard and solid at the surface, it softens and enters a more fluid form as it moves into layers of the Earth that contain higher temperatures and pressures.[4] (We'll discuss the geological formation of quartz further in Part IV).

Quartz consists of tetrahedral molecules of four oxygen atoms and one silicon atom. According to Dr. Richard Gerber, author of *Vibrational Medicine*, "Crystals represent the lowest state of entropy possible because they have the most orderly structure in nature."[5]

Although the atoms that make up a substance are separated by microscopic distances (and the atoms themselves would look like cloudy spheres of quickly moving electrons), scientists have still been able to study the geometric structure of quartz on a microscopic and macroscopic level. If we were to look at the geometry of quartz, we'd see four different axes, which we could designate as a1, a2, a3, and c. The a-axes are all in the same plane and of equal length, with 120° angles between them. The c-axis is perpendicular to the a-axes and is roughly 1.1 times the length of the a-axes.[6]

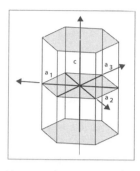

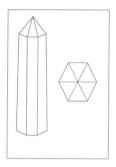

Hexagonal quartz crystal structure with axes

Quartz crystals commonly grow into the form of a six-sided prism that terminates in a point or apex.

Quartz occurs in a number of varieties that differ in form and color. Quartz crystals can also be found in different formations that reflect the environment and conditions in which the crystallization process occurred. Below, you can see a selection of crystal formations:

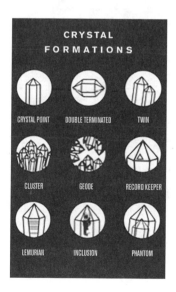

When it is pure, quartz is colorless. As you might recall from Chapter 5, visible light occurs at a specific range of frequencies in the electromagnetic spectrum; the color of light is determined by these different wavelengths. All electromagnetic waves, including light, travel in straight lines until they hit matter. If the crystal is opaque, that wave-length that hits it is reflected back or absorbed; if the crystal is translucent, light is diffused in many directions. But if the crystal is completely transparent, the wavelengths of light are all transmitted.

Pure light is an electromagnetic wave cause by high-energy electrons. The light wave will travel through the entire crystal and beyond it in the same straight line in which entered. The clearness of quartz is what makes it a unique and effective healing instrument and transmitter of energy. When we see a piece of crystal that has color, we know that the color we see is a product of the differences between transmission, reflection, and absorption.[7]

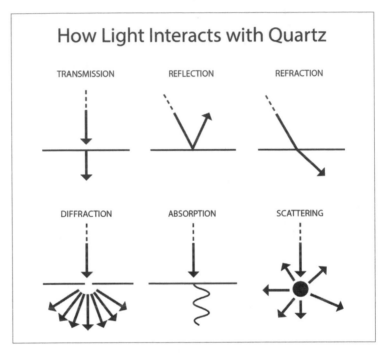

What determines the color of a crystal? In most instances, color arises from the absorption of certain wavelengths of light energy by the atoms making up the crystal. The wavelengths of white light that are not absorbed are what give us the experience of color. When we see a black crystal, such as Tibetan black quartz or dark smoky quartz, we know that it has absorbed all the light traveling toward it, while a white crystal, such as milky quartz, reflects this light. The electrons that are affected in an object absorbing light are the ones in the outer shell, as well as electrons associated with defects (also known as color centers) in the lattice. These defects in the lattice occur because of the inclusion of other minerals, as well as built-in trace elements and natural radiation.[8] The defects are the reason that quartz can appear in a number of colored varieties, like amethyst (violet), citrine (yellow), or smoky quartz (gray, brown to black).

Just a few atoms per million can change the perfect internal structure of a crystal enough to color it. Imagine a cube of quartz crystal (composed of silicon and oxygen atoms) that is one square foot. By introducing a pinch of iron to the lattice, atoms can turn normally clear quartz violet; thus, amethyst is formed. Quartz also occurs in dense rocks with no visible crystals, like agate and flint.[9]

When most people think of quartz, they are usually thinking about macrocrystalline quartz varieties, which have an obvious crystalline structure; these include clear quartz, smoky quartz, amethyst, ametrine, aventurine, citrine, pink quartz, prase, chrysoprase, red quartz, prasiolite, milky quartz, black quartz, blue quartz, rose quartz, tiger's eye, hawk's eye, and cat's eye. In contrast, microcrystalline varieties of quartz don't show any visible structures, as they are made of microcrystals ingrained in a much denser structure. They include flint, jasper, agate, chalcedony, plasma, sard, carnelian, chrysoprase, onyx, and heliotrope. True granite has over 45 percent quartz, and metamorphic rocks such as gneiss, schist, slate, and quartzite may also contain quartz.

Quartz on a Subatomic Level

Most of the effects observed in the use of quartz crystals in our technology and healing are related to their unique arrangement of atoms. The description given here of the mechanics of the atom covers the essentials necessary for a general understanding of crystal energies.

The atom consists of three primary building blocks: protons, neutrons, and electrons. Protons and neutrons are approximately the same size and weight, and they form the central part of the atom, the nucleus. While the proton has a positive electrical charge, the neutron is neutral. Electrons, which circle the nucleus at a relatively far distance, are much smaller in mass than protons or neutrons and have a negative charge.

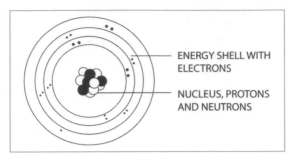

ENERGY SHELL WITH
ELECTRONS

NUCLEUS, PROTONS
AND NEUTRONS

To understand the properties of crystals, it is important to know the modern understanding of the structure of the atom. The atomic structure consists of the atomic cloud, formed by orbits with pairs of electrons, and the nucleus, a small, dense region at the center made up of protons and neutrons.

Electrons travel in pairs and arrange themselves in layers, or shells, around the nucleus. Each progressive layer corresponds to a different energy level. These layers of electrons fill from the center outward. The electrons in the outermost orbitals are known as valence electrons and are in charge of forming bonds with other chemical elements. In quartz, silicon has four valence electrons and oxygen has six.[10]

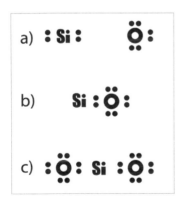

The formation of a
quartz molecule

The chemical equation for a single quartz molecule is SiO_4, although in a group of tetrahedrons, each oxygen atom is actually shared between two different tetrahedrons, making the underlying chemical composition SiO_2. The chemical bonds in quartz are also covalent, meaning that electrons are shared between the outer shells of the atoms, making the molecule a balanced, powerful, continuous network of covalently bonded atoms that extend throughout the entire structure.

Since the atom tries to always maintain electrical balance, the positive charges of the nucleus are generally balanced by the negative charges of the electrons. In the mineral kingdom, the outer layers of the atom are important, as they are responsible for many of the properties and energetic effects we find in crystals. Also, it is here that bonding between different atoms takes place and forms a unit cell, which is the building block of crystalline matter.

It is important to recognize that electrons don't simply move from layer to layer; they do so only when their energy has been increased or decreased by a specific amount of energy, known as a quantum. A quantum is a multiple of the energy produced by a photon of light. To picture this, think of each of the electron layers, and the quantum leap from one layer to another, as rungs on a ladder.

We know that protons, neutrons, and electrons are the basic building blocks of the atom, but recently, scientists have discovered even smaller particles, including quarks, neutrinos, and mesons—all of which are infinitesimal and can move easily through solid matter.

Matter takes on three forms: solid, liquid, and gas. In a solid, the atoms tend to be attracted to each other and cohere tightly to one another, forming distinct patterns. Crystalline matter is solid matter. To understand crystal energy, we have to understand the forces that attach atoms to one another in the crystal; disturbances in these attaching energies are responsible for so many of the properties we see in quartz.

The Geometric Inner Structure of Quartz

In *Timaeus,* Plato suggested that the pyramid is one of the four building blocks of creation. He ascribed the pyramid to fire, writing: "Logic and likelihood thus both require us to regard the pyramid as the solid figure that is the basic unit or seed of fire . . . . We must . . . think of the individual units . . . as being far too small to be visible, and only becoming visible when massed together in large numbers."[11]

It seems as if Plato, more than 2,000 years ago, was referring to the internal crystalline geometric structure and its electric properties.

Quartz's geometric inner structure can help us understand the mysterious connection between technology and crystal healing, as it's one of the most valued qualities when it comes to creating high-precision devices. It's also one of the reasons materials such as quartz are considered to be powerful holders of energy—something that the ancients demonstrated in their remarkable architecture and rock formations.

The structure of quartz was discovered by Bragg and Gibbs in 1925. Quartz crystals are the ones that bear the most potential in manipulating subtle energies. As we mentioned earlier, quartz crystal is made up of a precise and orderly giant lattice arrangement of atoms; this arrangement repeats regularly in all three dimensions up to the outermost physical boundaries of a crystal.

The internal tetrahedral grid structure of quartz

The shape of the crystal itself also reflects its internal structure; that is, the macrocosm reflects the microcosm and vice versa.

In many ways, when we look at a giant crystal lattice arrangement, we are seeing matter in one of its most stable and balanced states. Quartz is one of the most stable energies on Earth and has the ability to balance everything that it touches. At an atomic level, the crystal lattice of quartz is made up of one silicon atom surrounded by four oxygen atoms. This creates the shape known as the tetrahedron. Basically, silicon is in the center of a microscopic pyramid, and the four oxygen atoms are located in the corners of the pyramid. [12] So quartz can be described as a regular, three-dimensional lattice of networked SiO_4 tetrahedrons.

SiO_4 tetrahedron—the building block of quartz

The patterns of vibration of the molecule affect the atoms within it, and since the electrons are electrically charged, the atoms are in a pulsating electromagnetic field. The crystal lattice of molecules also vibrates in harmonic patterns, creating electromagnetic fields within the nested hierarchy of vibrating fields.

Quartz also contains several threefold and sixfold helical chains of SiO_4 tetrahedrons running parallel to the c-axis. These helices spiral both clockwise and counterclockwise.

Each group of SiO_4 is connected to two neighboring groups above and below it. This pattern is repeated vertically, forming spiral columns parallel to the c-axis that resemble the structure of DNA.

As author Stephen Skinner has written, "What all spirals have in common is expansion and growth."[13] The helices within quartz even resemble DNA. In fact, after 1953, when Watson and Crick discovered the structure of DNA, Maurice Wilkins used X-ray diffraction to demonstrate that some biological molecules, such as DNA, can form crystals if treated in certain ways, revealing the same regularity one would find in a quartz crystal.

Just as DNA transfers genetic information, is it possible that the tetrahedral helices within quartz crystals serve a similar purpose of transferring information? What we do know is that the spiral structures can generate a great deal of energy. The spiral form that causes each atom of the crystal to line up in a structure is similar to a serial battery. While each single crystal atom has the smallest ability to generate energy, millions of atoms working together can create a power equal to the sum of their parts.[14]

In our quantum world, energy frequencies move in geometric patterns. When the geometric patterns are altered, so is the way they manifest in the world. Crystals, due to their inner structure and resonance with geometric patterns—including the basic tetrahedral geometry of space itself—can completely repattern the geometry of any unbalanced energy.

We already understand that suffering begins in the mind. We also know that the mind works with repetitive patterns that stop the normal flow of energy within us and produce imbalances. Through resonance, the geometry of crystals can help us restore and balance the geometry in our biofield and reconnect us with our original frequency: that of our authentic selves.

From psychology to healing, the influence of sacred geometry cannot be overstated. Research has shown that when people view geometric patterns, the cells in their opiate-rich neural pathways become active. According to scientists at Japan's Kyoto University, geometry can create measurable effects in our brains and bring us feelings of peace, connection, and well-being.[15]

A crystal itself, due to its internal sacred geometry, is in a state of perfect equilibrium in which it seems not to be giving off energy or taking it in. In truth, crystals are constantly releasing and absorbing energy—but they always do so in perfect balance, with vibratory oscillations that are regular and precise, so that the crystal remains unchanged.[16]

The regularity of quartz's internal structure is one of the main reasons it is so desirable in the high-tech world. For example, this regularity is what enables it to maintain a high degree of precision, which aids in the accuracy of timepieces that utilize quartz.[17] On an energetic level, quartz crystals have the ability to organize discordant vibrations and to bring into balance different kinds of information (including learned data and the inauthentic information from the outside world that we discussed earlier).

This is why holding or being in the presence of a quartz crystal is the easiest and fastest way to rebalance chaotic energies.

The Electromagnetic Properties of Quartz

Ancients believed that quartz had a mysterious force with alchemical properties capable of transforming the nature of things. Today, science has the ability to explain this mysterious force through something known as the piezoelectric effect.

Piezoelectricity is the ability of certain materials, most notably quartz, to generate an alternating current (AC) voltage when they are exposed to an external vibration or mechanical stressor. Quartz is the most common piezoelectric substance. When we place quartz in contact with the body, this creates a mechanical force that awakens quartz's piezoelectric properties. The resulting friction between the skin and the crystal is what enables the geometry of quartz's crystal lattice to alter and give rise to an electrical current. This contact literally generates charges and vibrations in the sub-particle world within both the quartz and our bodies.

At a subatomic level, electrical charges are produced as some of the atoms making up the inner structure of the quartz's tetrahedral grid are pushed together when they come in contact with the skin. This upsets the inner balance of quartz, causing electrical charges to appear. When electrons are freed from the outermost layer of the crystal, moving to the surface, this transfer releases energy. This in turn creates a flow of new energy that unblocks stagnant energy within our bodies. Afterward, the crystal springs back to its original dimensions, replacing the lost electrons that created an electrical imbalance in quartz by bringing them back from the surface of the crystal or from the air.[18] This is demonstrated in the illustration below:

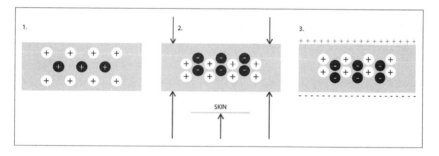

How quartz generates and transforms energy at a subatomic level

This conversion from mechanical to electrical energy, and vice versa, is what enables our transformation. This transmission of energy is precisely what healers refer to as "crystal energy."

Quartz crystal's piezoelectric properties became the foundation of 20th-century digital technologies. Piezoelectricity is the property that is responsible for keeping regular time in a quartz watch. Additionally, the microphone in your computer most likely uses piezoelectricity to turn the sound or vibrations of your voice into electrical signals that your computer can then interpret and transmit.[19]

The reverse piezoelectric effect happens when an electric current (that is, a flow of electrons into the crystal) causes the crystal's inner structure to expand. The influx of electrons briefly overloads the outer layer of the atoms, causing the atoms to drift apart somewhat. The overall movement of the electrons as they pass through the layers of the atom to achieve stability creates an oscillatory effect. This alternating expansion and contraction of the crystal structure via the flow of electrons is what we know of as vibration.[20]

As we discussed in the previous chapter, neuroscientist Karl Pribram, in collaboration with physicist David Bohm, described the brain as a holographic storage network that works through interference patterns from neurons. Neuroscientists still don't know exactly how the brain generates thoughts, but today we know that electrical signals and electromagnetic energy are involved in our thoughts as brain waves that oscillate at specific frequencies. Thanks to recent discoveries in quantum physics, we also know that the mind has the power to influence the behavior of subatomic particles and physical matter through the observer effect.

Energetically, both thoughts and crystals can be mutually affected by each other. That is, crystals can be influenced by the energy of our thoughts, while our thoughts can be transformed by the energy of crystals.

Crystals that impact us by releasing energy are operating on the piezoelectric effect. By subjecting the atoms inside the crystals to the electrical flow of our thoughts, we are creating a reverse piezoelectric effect. The latter is the same effect we see in quartz watches and ultrasound equipment, where a transducer (that is, a device that can convert energy from one form into another) made of crystals uses the reverse piezoelectric effect to convert electrical energy into rapid mechanical vibration.

Through either the piezoelectric or reverse piezoelectric effect, electrons return to their initial positions to reestablish their stability, and it is this very process by which the quartz works to restore equilibrium.

When applied to healing, this is what produces the effect of balancing our biofield. Crystals have the capacity to vibrate to and with even the subtlest energies; in this way, they can transform us when we are exposed to their energies.

The laws of physics suggest that the larger the crystal, the greater its potential for moving electromagnetic energy. In general, larger stones have a greater effect than smaller ones, as the power of their energy increases in proportion to mass. Larger stones also increase in efficacy across distance. While a small amethyst might be effective at a radius of a few inches, a large crystal cluster can "irradiate" an entire room.[21] Whenever large crystals are excited by electromagnetism, they emit more energy than a smaller crystal. Healing can still occur by using a smaller crystal. According to Harry Oldfield and Roger Coghill, in their book *The Dark Side of the Brain,* "The rule seems to be that the larger the crystal, the lower the frequency and the smaller the crystal, the higher the frequency."[22] So it's better to use large crystals because they emit more energy when stimulated, but it is the smaller crystals that have higher frequencies. High-frequency stones are recommended for working the internal patterns of the mind, as well as treating ill organs or anything that requires balance due to lack or shortage of energy. In quartz oscillators within electronic devices, thin slices of quartz will resonate at millions of cycles per second.[23]

The naturally amplifying properties of quartz crystals have deep ramifications for our healing. The light waves are slowed down and bent in a different direction when they pass from the air (a gas) to the crystal (a solid). When light strikes the surface of quartz, the beam is split into two and refracted at different angles that are emitted parallel to each other. Refraction is always accompanied by a wavelength and speed change, as in the image below.

Refraction of light by a quartz crystal

WHITE LIGHT

Diffraction is also a constructive interference pattern. One beam of light is transformed into two, thus amplifying the effect of light. In this way, crystals have the power to magnify frequencies and rebroadcast a healthy wavelength that retunes our energies. As an amplifying channel, quartz crystal can turn the weak energy signals of our thoughts into a strong signal so that we become aware of them.[24]

When we work with quartz crystals, it's as if we are reviewing our lives through a magnifying glass. We have access to information far from our present time and beyond our conscious minds; we also gain the possibility of amplifying energy. We can access all our seeds of suffering to uproot them and sow new seeds that reconnect us with our authentic path. As Randall and Vicki Baer tell us in their book *Windows of Light: Quartz Crystals and Self-Transformation*: "The ways in which energy can be processed through the crystals are numerous and include the function of reception, reflection, refraction, magnification, transduction, amplification, focusing, transmutation, transference, transformation, storage, capacitance, stabilization, modulation, balancing, and transmittance."[25]

Crystals are quantum convertors. It is little wonder that both tribal shamans and the modern high-tech industry include quartz crystals among their collection of "power" objects.

The Morphic Resonance of Quartz

In 1981 Rupert Sheldrake, a Cambridge University biologist, published a book called *A New Science of Life*, where he proposed his hypothesis that organisms were able to pick up patterns of learning that could progress their behavior, even if they did so from a far distance and with no direct contact with this knowledge. According to Sheldrake's theory of morphic resonance, similar forms (which he referred to as "morphs," or fields of information) can resonate with each other and exchange information within a universal energy field. (This also takes us back to the quantum principle of entanglement from Chapter 5, which posits that we can be influenced via resonance through space and time.)[26]

According to developmental biology, a morphogenetic field is simply a group of cells that can respond together to biochemical signals that lead to the development of coherent structures and organs. Sheldrake believed that morphogenetic fields are actually connected across time and space, and this is what contributes to the evolution of an organism. That is, we are impacted by the behavior of past organisms of the same species, regardless of whether or not we've had direct physical contact. The information of the past is intimately connected to that of the present and future. Sheldrake cited such evidence as the fact that rats of a particular species are able to perform better on a test in England after rats of the same species (but different genetic lines) have learned to perform the same test in the United States. Thus, the learning processes of a species are interconnected because of morphic resonance.

Morphic resonance is analogous to energetic resonance in that it takes place between vibrating systems. Atoms, molecules, crystals, organelles, cells, tissues, organs, and organisms are all made up of parts that are in a state of vibration. So all morphic units, including crystals and groups of cells, are constantly vibrating. Quartz also has the power, through its own morphogenetic field, to acquire and retain large quantities of information, as well as transmit it. Because of this, biochemist Alexander Graham Cairns-Smith believed that quartz crystals are very likely the most ancient progenitors of life (which we will discuss further in Chapter 7).[27]

Through morphic resonance, the presence of a healer who has healed her own stories can assist a client in attuning to his or her own healing of similar issues. Crystals can aid by sorting out nearby human signals and amplifying them for the benefit of the client.

Proof of Crystal Energy

The method of photography developed by the Kirlians originated when Semyon Kirlian, an electronics engineer living at Krasnodar in southern Russia, was asked to collect an instrument for repair from a research institute. Kirlian noticed that a small flash of light persistently jumped between the electrodes and the patient's skin. He wondered if he could document the sparks he saw by placing a photographic plate between the patient and the electrode.[28] The resulting Kirlian device is a high-frequency spark generator, vibrating at between 75,000 and 200,000 electrical oscillations per second. This generator enables the object to radiate a bioluminescent "aura" onto the emulsion of the photographic paper. For Kirlian, a camera wasn't even necessary.[29]

The most famous Kirlian photograph details the phantom leaf effect, which reveals a living leaf with a large part removed from it. However, the removed part can still be seen in its energetic form. This suggests the existence of a morphogenetic field that continues to hold the plant's cellular tissue in a coherent form.[30]

In Kirlian photography, quartz requires longer exposure times: that is, 60 seconds for a two- to three-inch quartz crystal. Many experiments have been conducted by photographing specific objects alongside quartz crystals. What these experiments revealed was that, as several photos were taken, the energy field around the crystal and the object alongside it increased. This did not happen when control photos of the object and crystal were taken separately.[31]

Scientist Harry Oldfield, who used Kirlian photography, firmly believed that crystals had the power to heal: "I knew that most scientists would be skeptical of any suggestions that crystals can be used for healing purposes, especially in the absence of any attempt at an explanation within the parameters of conventional science.

So I set about experimenting with crystals in order to see what they could do therapeutically and, at least as importantly, to find an acceptable explanation in order to satisfy any criticisms from scientific colleagues."[32]

Oldfield noted that crystals gave off enormous amounts of energy when stimulated and measured with Kirlian photography. "I then used the Kirlian apparatus to see the effects of the energized crystals on the human body. I studied these effects for years, comparing the effects with those of natural crystals. The energized crystals had very different effects from the natural crystals.

Then I found that by stimulating different crystals with certain compatible frequencies you could amplify each crystal's effects. In other words, each crystal harmonically resonated with particular frequencies."[33]

After many years of research, Oldfield also realized that changes could be produced in brain wave patterns, which can be measured by EEG monitors. When holding a crystal in your hand, your macromolecules (large molecules, composed of many atoms, that include proteins and nucleic acids), which have their own frequency and wave form, imprint on a crystal lattice and influence the oscillation of its micromolecules (molecules with a low molecular weight that include inorganic compounds). The crystal then copies your specific waveform through resonance and alters your frequency by means of its internal structure. [34]

In this way, crystals have the power to balance frequencies.

Electrocrystal Therapy

Harry Oldfield, who was a leading researcher on electrocrystal therapy, reasoned that if energy was symptomatic of disease, it could also be used to correct it. He found that applying an electrical field to amplify the effect of naturally occurring crystals had a therapeutic effect on his subjects. Thus, he treated disorders, ranging from migraines to multiple sclerosis, with a high success rate.[35]

He believed that when an electrical field passed through the various stones he chose, it picked up the healing vibration of the stone and carried it to the patient. After electrocrystal therapy, people reported being either tired or overly relaxed; others, after several sessions, noticed an increase in their vitality and a decrease in their illness. Another effect was that people who came in with a particular disorder reported afterwards that other conditions unrelated to that disorder had also been alleviated.

This kind of result convinces us of not only the value of the electrocrystal therapy but also its holistic results. In the early days when Oldfield only treated patients symptomatically, he discovered that not only did their physical well-being improve, but so did their mental and psychic stability.

Sound Generated by Crystals

Crystals can also be activated through sound, as their piezoelectric properties are triggered via sound.

As sound is vibration, it has the power to move the atoms inside the crystal. When atoms bounce into each other, they emit electrical energy. The curious thing is that these bouncing atoms can also produce sound—the sound of crystal. Highly tuned electromagnetic waves such as sunlight can excite the individual crystals to such an extent that they start to emit audible sound waves with long individual notes.[36]

This occurs at their resonant frequency, which refers to the natural frequency at which it is easiest for the crystal to vibrate. And even if we don't hear it (which occurs when the pitch is below the audible level and the amplitude of the wave form is high), we will still feel it. In fact, this is usually what occurs with crystals, in that we can feel them even when we cannot hear them.

The sound of crystals themselves appears to have a therapeutic effect on people who hear it. Even deaf people, or those with hearing difficulties, have received benefits, proving that the harmonic vibrations of crystals can create beneficial results in the body.

Sound has been overlooked in the study of crystals, but sonics have played an important role in crystal healing since ancient times. In healing temples, trained priests or healers sang into crystals; it is believed that in the lost civilization of Atlantis, simply doing so had the power to restore organs and limbs to health. Nowadays, sound and quartz crystals are used in medical ultrasounds for diagnostic purposes and to remove tumors. High-frequency sound pulses or ultrasonic waves are transmitted into our bodies to obtain images of our inner anatomy and break apart malignancies by using transducer probes that work through the piezoelectricity of crystals.[37]

How Quartz Works in Electronic Devices

It is estimated that 200 metric tons of cultured quartz is produced each year in our electronics.[38] It is not an exaggeration to say that the Digital Revolution created a true global mass market for quartz.

Certainly, there had been demand for quartz earlier in our history, too, as in the period when the U.S. needed large quantities for radio communication technology during World War II. Today, however, it is impossible to imagine modern life without the many devices that now rely on quartz crystals—from smartphones to medical technology and much more (including time crystals used in computers, built on quantum-physics principles). Most quartz is used within crystal oscillators for consumer devices such as wristwatches, clocks, radios, computers, and cell phones. As an essential ingredient in all of these electronic items—and a major element in the overall technology boom—quartz is what made the Digital Age possible.

Walter Guyton Cady built the first quartz crystal oscillator in 1921. A crystal oscillator is an electronic circuit or device that periodically generates oscillating electrical signals. This converts direct current (DC) signals into alternating current (AC) signals, thereby creating an electrical signal with a precise frequency.[39] Prior to crystal oscillators, radio stations controlled their frequencies with tuned circuits, which could easily drift off frequency. But in 1920 crystal oscillators began to be used to control the frequencies of broadcasting stations.[40]

As we know, quartz oscillations are so regular and precise that they form a handy reference for keeping track of time, as in quartz wristwatches. This is what provides a stable clock signal, and also stabilizes frequencies for radio and television transmitters and receivers.

The quartz oscillator circuit can be represented as follows:

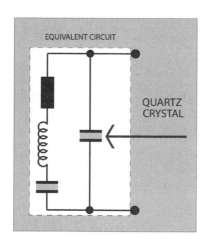

EQUIVALENT CIRCUIT

QUARTZ CRYSTAL

When electricity is applied to a crystal oscillator circuit through reverse piezoelectricity, the crystal vibrates in a precise frequency. This is the reason quartz crystals are so desirable in our modern technology.

Crystal oscillator circuits work on the principle of reverse piezoelectricity. An applied electric current causes the structure of the crystal lattice to deform and oscillate back and forth at a precise, resonant frequency. The crystal within the oscillator filters out the frequencies that come in while allowing only the resonant frequency to remain. The signals coming out of crystal are amplified by the oscillator, making them strong enough so that the resonance band of the oscillator can remove any unwanted frequencies.

The most common material for crystal oscillators is quartz. Although quartz crystals were originally used, today synthetically created crystalline quartz predominates due to the low cost and high convenience.

The frequency of a quartz crystal is important in its usage. Frequency is dependent on the thickness of the quartz: The thicker the crystal, the lower the frequency; the thinner the crystal, the higher the frequency. Crystals can be manufactured for oscillation over a wide range of frequencies, from a few kilohertz up to several hundred megahertz. Typically, 8-MHz crystal oscillators are used in microprocessors and microcontrollers, which provide clock signals and generate pulses that synchronize internal functions. Crystal oscillators have also been used for communication systems (in navigation and electronic warfare), research and management (in satellites, medical devices, and electronic measuring instruments), industrial applications (computers, digital systems, modems, sensors, and telecommunication), and consumer applications (cable television systems, video cameras, toys, video games, and cellular phones), among other things.[41]

The Body as a Crystal Oscillator of Electromagnetic Energy

When the body is at rest, the average human produces 100 watts of power.[42] Just as a crystal oscillator uses a vibrating crystal to create a signal with a precise frequency, our bodies' inner crystalline structures also aid in the transmission and reception of crystal's electromagnetic energy within and outside our bodies.[43]

Many of our bodies' physiological functions depend on electricity. Our cells are bathed in a crystalline, conductive saline solution, and measurable electricity flows between them.[44] Moreover, many of our biological macromolecules (including proteins, nucleic acids, and enzymes, to name a few) have piezeoelectric properties.[45] Piezoelectricity can also be found in the bones, tendons, skin, and nerve conduction, among many other biological systems. Scientists have reported that many of the problems we experience with bioelectricity, mechanical deformation, and physiological activity and wound healing can be managed by electric stimulation.[46]

The structural elements of the human body that contain piezoelectric substances can take mechanical energy and transduce it into an electric current. This current can then flow toward the internal organs. An electric current induced either by piezoelectricity or directly applied from an external source may in turn stimulate individual cells in the target organ and bring about healing.[47] In this way, the piezoelectric properties of quartz crystals resonate with our own bodyies' crystalline structures and bring transformation and balance to the body.

The main component of quartz is silicon dioxide (SiO_2). Sixty-five percent of the body is composed of oxygen, while silicon can be found in our bones, teeth, skin, muscles, and connective tissues. Although natural quartz is 99.7 percent pure SiO_2, its minor impurities can include magnesium, manganese, chromium, calcium, sodium, water, potassium, iron, and lithium, all of which resonate with our bodies.[48]

Additionally, the colors of crystals (which correspond to their frequencies) can also resonate with pigments or chemicals with a specific color. Most cells in our bodies are clear and colorless, much like clear quartz. This is because of the fact that proteins and DNA within the cells have wavelengths that are shorter than those of visible light.[49]

Pigments may play vital roles in the daily operations of the body. For example, hemoglobin is a red pigment that carries oxygen from our lungs to our cells and is connected with life force. Biliverdin is a green pigment related to the liver and spleen, while bilirubin is yellow and related to the liver. Stercobilin is a brown pigment associated with the large intestines. Urobilin is yellow and resonates with the kidneys.[50] Rhodopsin is a purple pigment in our eyes.[51] Melanopsin is another pigment that resonates with violet and blue short-wave frequencies in the eyes, pineal gland, and eighteen sites in the human brain, including the cerebral cortex, cerebellum, and neurons.[52] By using crystals of specific colors, one can heal corresponding ailments in the same-colored parts of one's body.

This natural resonance is compounded by the fact that there are several structures similar to quartz within our bodies. As we learned earlier in the book, the human body contains numerous crystalline structures that are fundamental to our proper functioning. The straightness of our posture is the result of the calcium phosphate crystals in the human skeleton. Our sense of balance and orientation to our gravitational field can be attributed to calcite crystals in the inner ear. Roughly 65 percent of an adult's bone mass is constituted of hydroxyapatite crystals. These crystals all contribute to our overall stability.[53] Moreover, we know that the human bone structure is a solid crystal structure with piezoelectric properties.[54]

The pineal gland of the human brain also consists of small crystals. These crystals contain calcium, carbon, and oxygen. The complex structure of these microcrystals may lead to piezoelectricity.[55] Within the pineal gland, the secretion of melatonin, a hormone that impacts our sleeping and waking cycles, is in fact impacted by exposure to electromagnetic fields. The presence of such a field can result in a buzzing or humming sound, which we hear when our pineal glands are activated. The sound waves are then transformed into electrical currents, and even light, which is then picked up as visual images by the pineal gland.[56]

It's also believed that crystal can pattern the water within our bodies, as quartz (SiO_2) and water (H_2O) have similar tetrahedral geometries. The late scientist Marcel Vogel, who worked as IBM's researcher in the application of quartz, discovered that he could structure water by spinning it around a tuned crystal, altering the characteristics of the water and converting it into an information system.[57] Remarkably, the brain and heart are made up of 73 percent water, and our lungs are 83 percent water. The skin has 64 percent water, while the muscles and kidneys are 79 percent. Even our bones comprise 31 percent water.[58] The average adult human body is 50–65 percent water. Given that our bodies are primarily made up of water, it is likely that crystals can repattern our interior processes and assist us in our transformation.

Within our living tissues (including bone, cartilage, tendons, ligaments, and skin), crystalline arrangements that lead to electric pulsations are commonplace.[59] In fact, the living cell includes properties that are both liquid and crystalline. Liquid crystals have both the mobility and flexibility of water and the structural order of quartz. Similar to quartz crystals, they can respond to many external stimuli, such as light, sound, mechanical pressure, temperature, and electric and magnetic fields.[60] Many proteins (essential for life), lipids (part of the molecules), polysaccharides (the source of energy for living organisms), hemes (a component of hemoglobin and other hemoproteins), and nucleic acids (main constituents of genes) in water exhibit liquid crystalline structures.[61]

According to an early paper on liquid crystals: "A liquid crystal in a cell, through its own structure, becomes a proto-organ for mechanical or electrical activity, and when associated in specialized cells (with others) in higher animals gives rise to true organs, such as muscle and nerve."[62] Liquid crystals can transmit light waves of different velocities in different directions and, in this way, transfer energy and information as it occurs in the cells and cellular membranes. One of the most important liquid crystals is myoglobin, a hemoprotein that is related to the electricity of the heart and allows the muscles of the myocardium to expand and contract and, in this way, pump blood throughout the entire body.[63]

Other liquid crystals that work in our heart are L-3-hydroxyacyl-CoA dehydrogenase, an enzyme that catalyzes the chemical reaction, important for the normal function of the heart, that converts fats to energy;[64] and 6-phosphofructo2-kinase/fructose-2,6-biphosphatase, an enzyme that controls the breakdown of fructose to release energy.[65] According to Gregg Braden, the heart's energy is powered by crystalline structures, so it is no surprise that it is the strongest bioelectrical and biomagnetic field generator in the human body.

Recent findings in biology have also revealed that many biomolecules exhibit nonlocal properties that appear consistent with the body's ability to function at the quantum, energetic level. However, the presence of endogenous (internal) quantum fields in biological systems has not been examined in great detail.[66] If scientists were to observe the quantum properties that make both the human body and quartz crystal such extraordinary transducers—that is, converters of energy from one form into another—it is likely that our understanding of energy healing would increase substantially.

Electricity is what allows the nervous system to send signals to your brain. It also allows for communication between neurons; controls the rhythm of your heartbeat and the movement of blood around your body; allows you to see, feel, hear, and use your muscles to move; and regulates homeostasis, the body's ability to maintain constant balance within its internal environment when dealing with external changes. These functions are similar in electronic applications, in which crystal's oscillations, attained through piezoelectricity, maintain the stability of frequency and work to synchronize all internal operations.

Overall, crystals resonate with the many inner crystalline structures of our bodies, chemical composition, pigments, and internal tetrahedral geometry. This geometry includes pyramidal neurons with pyramid-shaped bodies, pyramidal pathways that supply neurons with nerves, renal pyramids (the kidneys' cone-shaped tissues), and so on.

As you have discovered in this chapter, the body's crystalline structures are similar to the technology that utilizes crystals' remarkable properties in that they are continuously receiving, transforming, and emitting energy. When we are healthy, our crystal blueprint resonates in unity and harmony with the universe.

The next part of the book, which explores the processes of crystal healing in depth, reveals that crystals themselves are the bridge between our understanding of the deep earth and the mechanisms of the deep unconscious. As electromagnetic, energetic beings intrinsically connected to the earth, we can learn a great deal from crystals. Without them, the technology we use cannot function. Neither can we, and nor can our planet.

PART IV

ESTABLISHING A CRYSTALLINE BODY AND MIND

CHAPTER 7

From Deep Earth
to the Deep Self

"As is the human body, so is the cosmic body.
As is the human mind, so is the cosmic mind.
As is the microcosm, so is the macrocosm.
As is the atom, so is the universe."

— UPANISHADS[1]

WHAT IS THE CONNECTION BETWEEN deep Earth (crystals and all processes that are hidden and unconscious to us) and our deepest wounds? What does it mean that crystals connect us to the deepest parts of the self? We can connect the electromagnetic field of the earth with our bodies' own electromagnetic fields. We can see, through thorough inquiry, how the brain's energetic fields are linked to our consciousness, and thus to our wounds. In understanding this link, we can also examine the origin of our deepest wounds and how we can use our understanding to take the necessary responsibility to work on ourselves and reconnect with our authentic selves.

Crystal healing uses quartz crystals and other stones as conduits for healing energy. However, no studies have yet demonstrated the therapeutic value of crystal healing. At the same time, we know that we live amid a universe of atoms, positive and negative charges, and chemical components that generate multiple unseen frequencies, each of which operates at levels that constantly affect us, whether we are conscious of it or not.

We know that crystals respond to stimuli from mechanical pressure, from sound, and from electromagnetism. And just as we are starting to see a paradigm shift in physics and biology, our model and view of Earth and her processes require an upgrade. Most geologists and scientists still view the earth as a six-sextillion-ton ball of inert rock and water, which is antithetical to what the ancients believed and knew.

However, new paradigms of science are revealing the earth itself as a living organism—a view that is consonant with that of indigenous tribes. According to the Gaia theory (named after the Greek goddess of the land) proposed by scientist James Lovelock, the earth is in its totality one superorganism that is capable of self-regulation. Overall, the Gaia theory is a compelling way of understanding life on our planet. It claims that Earth is more than just the third rock from the sun. It also asserts that living organisms and their geological surroundings have co-evolved as a single interconnected living system.

We have evolved and flourished on this planet and perhaps take for granted that we are surrounded by life itself . . . including crystals.

Although we live on the earth, most of us are disconnected from or unaware of its processes. What's more, most of us don't touch the earth anymore. In the past, humans maintained a direct physical connection with the earth, often speaking to it, walking barefoot on it, and tending its cycles and seasons. We were naturally charged and balanced with the healing energy of the planet and intimately acquainted with every aspect of our home. Today, we barely know what it even means to connect.

But it's possible for us to become reacquainted in a deeper way with the living earth. Have you ever noticed a subtle tingling or sensation of warmth rising up from your feet during a barefoot stroll? Did you feel revitalized at the end of your walk? If you did, you experienced the earth energizing your body. Earth is a large electromagnet in which energy can be measured. The ground beneath your feet is the result of the interconnection of different energy fields from a variety of minerals—among them, quartz.

Only recently has the knowledge and significance of this connection, which was so extolled by the ancients, been explored and explained by scientific experts in geophysics, biophysics, electrical engineering, electrophysiology, and medicine. From them, we are learning that the earth's electromagnetic energy maintains the order of our own bodily frequencies.

From the Big Bang to Quartz

Let us go back in time 13.7 billion years, to the very origins of the universe. At this time, billions of atoms were gathered in a uniform mass that not only began to expand rapidly but exploded to create what we now know of as matter, including countless galaxies and star systems.

Today, NASA technology such as the Hubble Space Telescope and the Spitzer Space Telescope continue to measure the expansion of the universe. They have offered us a firsthand vision of how the Big Bang was the starting point of the universe's continuous expansion, or what scientists refer to as "inflation." The inflationary model includes an initial phase of ultra-rapid expansion followed by a slower expansion.[2] We know that, for inflation to have occurred, at the time of the Big Bang, the universe had to have been filled with an unstable form of energy. This pattern would have been transferred to the matter of the universe.

Chaos was the origin of the universe's expansion, and this expansion is what created both human beings and crystals. Chaos is a fundamental part of our essence; with it comes expansion and new beginnings, life, death, and rebirth. Stars go through the same birth-life-death cycle in their physical bodies that we and crystals do. And it is in the death of stars that new birth takes place in the universe.

The so-called butterfly effect has become one of the most popular descriptions of chaos. The idea is that the flapping of a butterfly's wings in another part of the world can cause a tornado where we are. In other words, small disturbances have an explosive effect. They can produce substantial effects on a physical system's behavior. They can bring about transformation and a new order.

But the universe is not only about expansion; contraction is another important pattern in our cosmos.

About five billion years ago, a cloud of hydrogen and fragments from dead stars began to contract. Through gravitational attraction, it accreted into several dense parcels of matter. This is how our solar system and the Milky Way were formed. In our solar system, clouds of gas that were the residue of innumerable stars were drawn to the sun, while the heaviest elements were arranged in orbits that gradually settled and became planets.

In those dense gas patches, atoms collided and began to heat up, and nuclear fusion (in which the nuclei of two atoms join together and release tremendous amounts of energy) occurred. This is how the earth was created. This process is also the origin of quartz crystals. The force of gravity began to draw the heavier elements—iron and nickel—toward the center of the planet. Eventually, the pressure became so great that the rock melted. This central portion is known as the core. Earth's inner core is an enormous ball that constitutes half a percent of our planet's entire volume. It is slightly smaller than the moon and about 2 percent of our planet's overall mass. It's also one of the most idiosyncratic aspects of the planet. In order to envision it, think of the volume of water in all the oceans of the earth; multiply this by five, and you'll have the volume of the inner core—a metallic, crystalline solid that rotates at a rate slightly offset from the rest of the earth.

Although we still know very little about the inner core, we know that it is composed of iron crystals that range in size. We also know that this part of the earth is relatively new, having appeared between 500 million and 1,000 million years ago; it appears that it grew gradually from one single crystal of iron. In fact, the inner core continues to grow by half a millimeter each year. In time (a billion years from now), the iron core could get so big that it will have the power to switch off the entire magnetic field of the earth.[3]

The overall core of the Earth extends from the base of the mantle to the center of the earth and makes up 16 percent of the volume and 32 percent of the mass of the earth. Because we know that the outer core is liquid and the inner core is solid and crystalline, this slippage between the inner core and mantle (the layer of the earth just outside the core) is believed to be what generates the magnetic field of the earth.[4]

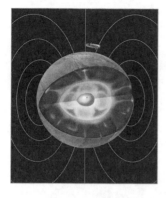

Earth's crystal core, which generates a magnetic field. Photo: Gary Hincks | Science Source.

Kei Hirose, director of the Earth-Life Science Institute (ELSI) at the Tokyo Institute of Technology, reported that the overall core of the earth—comprising mostly iron and nickel, but also light alloys like silicon, oxygen, and sulfur—most likely cooled by as much as 1,000 degrees Celsius since it formed 4.5 billion years ago.[5] When Hirose's team attempted to reproduce the earth's conditions during the initial formation of the planet, they were surprised to find that the tiny trace elements of silicon and oxygen that were present in the researchers' starting sample had merged to form silicon dioxide crystals—the same compound that we know of as mineral quartz, which we typically find at the earth's surface. In fact, the researchers believe that silicon dioxide crystals could very well be the powerhouse behind Earth's magnetic field.

Quartz itself is highly mutable; it can occur as a liquid (usually at an extremely high pressure and temperature) or even molten rock. Crystals often form in nature when liquids cool and begin to harden. One of the ways quartz is formed is when molten rock pours into natural cracks and fractures and flows through the open space of the earth's veins, depositing dissolved mineral matter. That is why some indigenous cultures refer to crystals as the bones or veins of Mother Earth.

Fire and transformation are part of crystal's nature. The extreme conditions that crystals endure are similar to those we experience in our own formation as human beings. When we are immersed in our suffering, pressures and high temperatures are akin to our life struggles. But if we take our cue from crystals, we can see that the heat, pressure, and "suffering" eventually result in the formation of a beautiful, transparent crystal that allows the light to shine through it, regardless of all the "information" to which it has been exposed: chaos, expansion, contraction, high temperatures, cooling. A new order is created that implies an advance, a step forward on an infinite path of evolution.

Whether or not a planet has a magnetic field goes a long way toward determining whether or not it is habitable. Quartz could be more important than we believe and closely related to life on this planet.

Earth's magnetic field shields our planet, protecting us against cosmic and solar radiation. Illustration: 57909103©Seveniwe | Dreamstime.]

Returning to Our Crystalline Origins

The story of crystals is related to the story of the universe and the stars; likewise, it is related to the story of Earth and humankind. In fact, there is a theory that life on this planet may have originated from these beautiful minerals.

The mantle is the thickest layer of the earth and represents 83 percent of the planet's volume and 67 percent of its mass. It is composed of many layers of fluids and dense, crystalline rocks—including silicates, iron, and magnesium. During the earliest period of the planet, the lighter mineral portions rose up from inside the earth to form what we know of as the crust, which is the hard outer layer of

Photo: Spencer Sutton | Science Source.

the earth. As this occurred, water was released from some of these recrystallized minerals to form the incipient oceans. (Recrystallization refers to the reorganization of a mineral's atoms due to temperature and pressure, although the chemical composition remains the same as before.) Also during this stage, large-scale currents carrying heat from the interior of Earth's surface aided in forming all the different continents.

The surface of the earth is our planet's thinnest layer, and it is the one upon which our continents formed. It is mostly composed of a granite-like rock known as granodiorite—a microcrystalline form of quartz. Although the crust is extremely thin beneath the ocean basins, beneath the continents it is particularly thick underneath our mountain ranges.[6]

The crust that we find beneath the oceans makes up 70 percent of the earth's surface. One major discovery by geologists was that the magnetic field found on the ocean bottom was arranged in a series of stripes running parallel to the tops of the ocean ridges and extending all the way to the continents. Some researchers believe that these stripes demonstrate that the ocean floor was actually recording fluctuations in Earth's magnetic field, which occurred as the continents moved farther apart from each other and liquid matter from the interior of the earth rose up to fill the spaces.

When Earth was still young and settling into the next stage of its journey—that is, the creation of organic, carbon-based life—the oceans consisted of a primordial soup of molecules. Ultraviolet light from the sun broke up the hydrogen-infused molecules that were in the atmosphere. The molecules then joined together to create more complex forms. As minerals broke down via chemical processes, they created even more rich material that became part of the foundations for organic life.[7]

It was the Scottish biochemist Alexander Cairns-Smith who suggested that the first living organisms originated due to crystals. This theory is known as the "crystals-as-genes hypothesis."[8] He said that the primordial soup of the early oceans was a harsh and reactive chemical bath, where any additional elements would have gone through rapid reactions and quickly transformed into something different. He did not believe that carbon-based life as we know it could have emerged from this kind of high-temperature, overly reactive environment. Thus, he suggested that life came not from biochemical processes in the primordial soup but from something else altogether.

He identified self-replication as one of the primary aspects of life. Self-replication is what allows for both the perpetuity of a species and that species' evolution. While many people see the DNA molecule as the primary building block of self-replication, Cairns-Smith disagreed. DNA on its own is actually quite fragile, he noted, as it breaks apart in the face of physical stressors—meaning it would have been destroyed by the early conditions of the earth.

Cairns-Smith examined some of the other qualities of primitive genes that developed during these early conditions. For starters, aside from self-replication, they needed to have the capacity to self-organize in the presence of simple rather than complex conditions. They had to obtain and store information and use that to develop a meaningful connection to the surrounding environment. They also had to be able to replicate themselves in such a way that this information would have continuity and be passed down to future forms.

Cairns-Smith realized that something even simpler than DNA meets all of the above criteria: crystals.

Crystals have the capacity to self-organize, to receive and transmit information through their geometric structure, and to self-replicate precise copies that have the same information. Their physical composition, due to their molecular structure, is also extremely stable—much more so than DNA. Thus, Cairns-Smith came to the conclusion that crystals are the originators of life as we know it. He thought that crystal mineral could be subject to a simple form of evolution by natural selection. In order to support his hypothesis, however, he recognized that he needed to demonstrate that crystals have the ability to use the information within them to interact meaningfully with the surrounding environment.

He found a link in clay minerals. Clay is made of tiny crystals. Clays can absorb and provide an incubating growth environment for a variety of other molecules—and they can also use this information to alter their own material. During the early periods of the earth, clay was abundant. For this reason, Cairns-Smith concluded that clay was the link between nonlife (crystals) and life (carbon-based organisms).[9] However, this theory was not approved by the larger scientific community because it lacked sufficient evidence, so it's seldom taught today.

Whatever the case, the patterns of creation that we know of include renewal, re-formation, movement, crystallization, and mergence. Earth as an organism is in a constant state of renewal and re-creation, so it makes perfect sense to draw parallels among our planet, crystals, and ourselves.

As Above, So Below: The Electromagnetic Field of the Earth and Its Connection to the Body

The electromagnetic field of the earth works similarly to the electromagnetic field of our bodies and brains. Both are emitted by crystalline structures and serve to sustain life. As described in Chapter 6, there are many crystalline structures within our bodies that may be serving a variety of purposes: supporting the body's electrical functions, transforming energy from one form to another, assisting in the formation of different energy fields within our bodies that feed the human biofield that surrounds us, and connecting with the many electromagnetic fields that are part of the earth and cosmos. In one way or another, the body's energetic anatomy resonates with that of the macrocosmos of cosmic phenomena and the microcosmos of unseen quantum processes—including those that occur in the human brain.

The scientific community has largely been content with assuming that consciousness is an emergent aspect of highly complex neural networks, specifically those comprising the neocortex of the human brain. But since the 1970s, it has been speculated that what we know of as consciousness may be the electromagnetic field itself. Biologist Rupert Sheldrake asserted that the nature of our minds is still mysterious to us. Whereas science has told us that the mind is equivalent to the brain, Sheldrake believed that the functions of the higher mind (including thoughts, dreams, and memories) transcended the physical body and existed in what he called "morphic fields." He compared our brains with our modern devices and said that the brain, just like our cell phones, can send out electromagnetic signals, acting as both a transmitter and a receiver in which the waves propagate beyond the constraints of the physical structure.[10]

Within these signals, consciousness exists. In other words, thoughts are not stored in the brain; rather, the brain tunes *in to* them. The brain doesn't "create" our thoughts; it's more like an antenna than a recording system. Likewise, according to Sheldrake, perception doesn't happen within our physical brains; rather, the process of perception comes from consciousness, which is facilitated by the brain but doesn't occur within it.[11]

Because we live in a holographic universe, the brain doesn't actually produce information; rather, with the help of biocrystalline microtubules, the brain gives meaning and shape to a universe of nonlocal information.[12]

A recent scientific study uncovered the presence of quantum vibrations (that is, tiny vibrations on a subatomic level) that arise from the harmonic oscillations of these biocrystalline microtubules in the brain, which are known to help with neurotransmission and the propagation of electrical signals.[13] These microtubules also resonate with oscillations in the quantum vacuum, which is present in everything. In other words, their vibration allows for communication with the cosmos, and our physical processes translate into the very language of the universe.

The piezoelectric effect that you learned about in Chapter 6 is occurring even at the level of the microtubules in our brains. Their vibratory pattern is the same one that can be found in the quantum vacuum, which is also a patterned sea of millions of vibrations. The resonance created within these crystalline structures allows our bodies to interact with the cosmos and for consciousness to take place.

Scientists believe that further study of these structures could help us to treat a number of neurological conditions, including Alzheimer's disease. We know that the healthy human brain has tens of billions of neurons that aid in transmitting information to the rest of the body; one neuron alone can have up to 7,000 connections with other neurons.[14] Neurological conditions like Alzheimer's arise, in part, when the biocrystalline microtubules of the brain begin to degenerate and stem the free flow of information and communication. But if we could reverse the loss of microtubules, this could potentially stave off neurological degeneration and improve cognitive health.[15] In other words, if we restored the crystal blueprint of the brain, we could help to restore the brain's ability to produce electrical vibrations and reinstate their resonance with memory and consciousness, which is nonlocal.

Depending on our experiences and patterns, which originate in either learned beliefs or authentic information, we will filter and resonate with specific information that comes through to us. Interestingly, new research corroborates this: scientists discovered that patients who'd previously harbored negative attitudes toward aging were more likely to develop degenerative neurological conditions associated with Alzheimer's disease. Dr. Becca Levy, an associate professor of public health and psychology at the Yale School of Public Health, says, "We believe it is the stress generated by the negative beliefs about aging that individuals sometimes internalize from society that can result in pathological brain changes . . . . It is encouraging to realize that these negative beliefs about aging can be mitigated and positive beliefs about aging can be reinforced, so that the adverse impact is not inevitable."[16]

Aside from resonating with experiences that conform to our preestablished ideas and learned information, our entire bio-organism resonates and harmonizes with the electromagnetic fields of the planet, serving to regulate the cycles of life and acting as engines for metabolic processes. It's also believed that the electromagnetic current in our bodies may activate inter- and intracellular communication. We also know that animals and humans innately and subconsciously use this field and its field lines for both navigation and spatial orientation.

Physicist W. O. Schumann discovered something known as the Schumann resonances, which are a series of peaks that can be found in the very low-frequency part of the earth's electromagnetic spectrum. The earth has a region that is referred to as its "cavity," which exists between the surface of the planet and the inner edge of the ionosphere. This is the area in which the Schumann resonances live; they aren't present all the time but rather must be "excited" in order for us to perceive them. They appear to be connected to electrical activity in the atmosphere and occur at a number of frequencies: 7.8, 14, 20, 26, 33, 39, and 45 Hz, with a variation of 0.5 Hz.[17]

Schumann's successor, Herbert König, noted that these resonances were correlated with observed rhythms in the brain. In fact, he found that the first five resonances (7.8 through 33 Hz) were actually in the same frequency range as the alpha and beta brain waves in a human electroencephalogram (EEG). The 7.8-Hz signal is more or less equivalent to the brain's alpha rhythm frequency. Further research also supports that the standing waves of the Schumann resonances are extremely important in terms of influencing various processes in our brains. In fact, we know that the brain can detect and respond to a Schumann resonance signal. Further, it is believed that external signals such as the Schumann resonances can help us to become synced up with the cycles and rhythms of the earth.

Research within the last decade reveals that the intensity and stability of a Schumann resonance signal can actually be altered by changes in solar and geomagnetic activity; in fact, by moving outside of its normal range, a Schumann resonance signal can generate significant alterations in the body. The negative effects might include cardiac and neurological issues, mental disorders, depression, tension, fear, and many other stress-related conditions.[18]

Thus, the activity of the body and biofield is mirrored by the activity of the earth and electromagnetic field.

At the same time, Schumann resonances, and variations within them, can trigger states of consciousness that are also linked to higher states of awareness. According to Dr. Robert C. Beck, "Oscillations of 7.8, 8.0, and 9.0 Hz produce anxiety-relieving and stress-reducing effects that mimic some meditative states." The cosmic waves colliding with the electromagnetic field of our planet effect many changes in our biological systems. Our DNA resonates with a 150-MHz frequency, which can also activate the pineal gland and the release of N,N-Dimethyltryptamine (DMT) in the brain. DMT has the capacity to change brain chemistry and open up consciousness to experience other levels of reality. In other words, it links the incorporeal to the material.[19]

Just as electromagnetic energy fields outside of us can affect our health and behavior, in the same way our learned mind programming—our inner electromagnetic fields—can affect us and generate suffering . . . or healing.

True Knowledge of the Self

Know thyself. This aphorism is an inscription that forms part of the ancient Greek Temple of Apollo in Delphi. It is an invitation to deepen into ourselves, to take an introspective look within, and to recognize who we are beyond who we superficially perceive ourselves to be. Only by knowing who we are can we recognize our learned patterns and consciously choose to change them.

But how can we discover who we *truly* are?

We come into the world without an instruction manual, but our bodies' biological functions still manage to operate in perfect synchrony. We breathe, our hearts beat, our trillions of cells metabolize energy and communicate, and the brain and its many parts take care that all is working properly within the body.

We know much about the body in terms of its physical structure: bones, tissues, flesh, cells. As we discussed in other chapters, this is the legacy left by Descartes—that is, the idea that our bodies are machines constituting measurable material mechanisms, governed by the laws of matter alone.

Descartes formulated the modern version of the mind–body problem that we experience so persistently in our world. We have a tendency to separate the mind and the body as different parts rather than recognizing the whole of who we are. In our modern context, however, this argument is clearly inconclusive. After all, we know that the atom, matter's fundamental pillar, is made purely out of energy.

The mind and the body create an interconnected whole. Mind and body cannot ultimately be separated, as energy is their true blueprint.

Although we know this information, unfortunately, Cartesian paradigms continue to rule our inner programming. They lead to greater disconnection, as well as a tendency to become addicted to material reality and identify only with all that is perceptible by the five senses—not at all taking into account the realms of the intangible and invisible.

This hinders us from the possibility of truly knowing ourselves. By recognizing ourselves only through the body, we are connecting to a part of our story, not our complete story.

According to some physicists, "When a quantum system interacts with the outside environment, the system loses its quantum coherence and everything that makes it quantum."[20] The infinite energy that we naturally possess and that is related to our well-being is bound by the limited nature of our thoughts.

Mind and body are entangled, which is why they are constantly affecting each other. If our thoughts flow with our authentic nature, they form constructive interference (which we learned about in Chapter 5) and we are healthy. Destructive interference is connected to false learned information. Additionally, our body–mind energy field is connected with surrounding energy fields, continuously shaping our reality.

Part of knowing ourselves better is recognizing all the learned information—from our families and peers, media, culture, and society—that has led us to become what we "think" we are today.

When we are in a state of suffering, we often feel disoriented, not centered, and not "ourselves." We are confused and cannot see clearly. We feel this as "chaos." But what exactly is chaos?

In order to understand chaos, first we must talk about its opposite: order. We know what it feels like to be in our comfort zone as a result of all our learned habits and beliefs. And we know that suffering is the tension or resistance that ensues when we diverge from this familiar sense of order. This tension is what cracks us out of our minds' false programming. It is the catalyst that lets us clear out all the accumulated data and make room for our authentic selves. If we compare the mind with a shell, suffering is what cracks us open so that we can realize what is inside.

If our familiar, comfortable world, our sense of order, is nothing but the projection of our minds, then what happens when our minds shut down? Our world falls into chaos because we don't recognize the new information. From this place, sadness can be seen as a mechanism to switch our attention from the outside to the inside and recognize that the information we have learned and with which we have identified so far doesn't fit what is actually true.

Chaos is the path by which we can liberate the contents of the holographic mind, which we explored in Chapter 5. Chaos brings to our awareness everything that needs to be let go of in order for us to become who we really are.

Suffering—or contraction, which is also connected with the processes of Earth's formation that generated life—takes us deep below the layers of learned false information to reconnect with our original being: that which existed prior to our imposed inner programming. Thus, suffering breaks the mind's old structures and brings in new information, which results in expansion and a new order.

The fear we experience during this process is the last attempt of the mind to cling to its known programming and reject whatever does not coincide with its inner data. In the world of energy—where our minds, thoughts, and reality are multiple interacting energy fields creating our reality—we can rely on the properties of crystals to facilitate the movement from false learned information to who we really are, from chaos to balance, from our wounds to our complete self-realization.

I know from firsthand experience that through crystal healing's inner work, you can transcend suffering and also raise your consciousness.

John's Story

Recently, I helped a client who was in deep emotional crisis. John had "woman problems." That is, his relationships were exciting and romantic at first but inevitably ended in pain and disappointment.

He looked back on all his relationships and noticed a common thread. One after another, he was dishonest with women. His lack of commitment to women had become a pattern. He knew the *what* but not the *why*. *Why* was this happening to him over and over again? *Why* did he keep finding himself in the same situation? John desperately wanted a life partner, but no matter how much he tried, he would fall back into dishonesty as if it were an addiction.

I bring up his story because what occurred in the days and weeks that followed was remarkable: using quartz crystals as a tool, he was able to gain a new kind of clarity.

John traced the roots of his problems back to his childhood and to his relationship with his father, who continually cheated on his mother with other women. This was the core wound that originated the repeating pattern. Sadly, the hypermasculine Latin American culture in which he had been raised didn't provide much help for my client in overcoming his own lack of commitment to women; on the contrary, it only helped to reinforce it.

He realized that the residue of his father issues and the friends and culture that also influenced him remained a heavy, unseen burden after so many years. He was 40, but the information recorded in his young mind had kept this wound fresh. In essence, he had been re-creating his father's dishonesty through all his subsequent relationships with women.

Although crystals helped John identify his core father wound, the process did not happen overnight. In the first crystal healing session, he resonated with citrine, smoky quartz, and amethyst—and during his visualization, he recalled different scenes where he was with different women in his life. In the last scene, he realized that instead of being himself, he was his father. At the beginning, he was still in denial. It was very difficult for him to understand what was wrong with this behavior so praised by the culture in which he was raised. Some time and crystal healing sessions passed, and his resonance had changed; now, amethyst and rose quartz were his chosen stones. His visualization was different this time. He felt the suffering of each woman he touched, as if the boundaries between him and the women had dissolved.

During this time of self-discovery, John also discovered that his grandfather had mistreated his grandmother—not with other women, but with his anger and bad attitude. He realized that he was part of the third generation of men in his family who mistreated women, and this is the piece of information that finally led to a breakthrough and permanent transformation. He didn't want his children or grandchildren to inherit this negative pattern.

After understanding both his own suffering and the suffering he had inflicted on others, John made the decision to be alone. During that time, he incorporated patterns—such as dancing and painting— that challenged the toxic masculinity of his culture; he also financially helped women in need. With crystals and inner work, he healed his patterns of masculinity and femininity, and this brought a feeling of general well-being into his life.

Decoding Our Chaos through Crystals

Where there is chaos, there is opportunity—and it's in times of chaos that crystals work best. This is because they help us to seize the opportunities that chaos brings. Crystals help us flow from contraction to expansion and resonate with our stellar crystalline nature so that we can shine again.

Crystals enable us to pervade the physical and energetic structures of our minds and our bodies, and to rewrite old patterns that we have inherited—and that take us further away from our authentic selves. Crystals also help us to comprehend the nature of the universe, the earth, and all the visible and invisible processes that shape our consciousness and life, as well as our own sense of connection.

The beloved astronomer Carl Sagan famously said, "The cosmos is within us. We are made of star-stuff. We are a way for the universe to know itself."[21] Crystals, with their unique properties and capacity to amplify energy and bring unconscious aspects of ourselves to light, provide a crucial key to knowing ourselves.

Crystals can guide us through our journey of inner self-exploration in a way that would otherwise be difficult. This is because they provide the ideal vibrational tool to tune the mind to specific channels, which then allow the necessary information to flow through. Crystals' abilities to balance, transform, and amplify frequencies make them excellent tools for supplementing a variety of spiritual practices: meditation, yoga, and any other healing modality.

According to crystal resonance therapist Naisha Ahsian, "The crystal is a spotlight and your mind is a dark room. You are able to use a crystal to spotlight areas of that dark room that you wouldn't normally look into because it allows your brain to process differently than it would normally process. We can hone in and focus on certain aspects of consciousness and awareness using crystals and stones that we can't do without them . . . because there is too much noise, too much chaos going on in the background of the mind. When we bring ourselves to resonance with the crystal and stones by engaging that physical law of resonance, it causes certain parts of the mind to become more quiet and other parts of the mind to become highlighted."[22]

As you have learned in this chapter, we are all connected to an invisible force that enables our existence, as well as that of the planet. Electromagnetic fields connect the micro and the macro realms: the human body, the earth, and the cosmos. Crystals, too, are connected to this force. Crystals are tools that can help us to systematically explore our unconscious because they allow us to tap into the deep inner layers of the mind, which are normally obscured and resonate with our transparent nature. Our consciousness is literally linked to crystals—from the biocrystalline microtubules of the brain that make consciousness possible to the transparency associated with the authentic self.

The release of false information is what allows us to connect with who we really are and to regain our crystal blueprint. Suffering provides an opportunity for this reconnection, as it is very much connected to the life-generating processes of the earth. It offers us a chance to break the structures and patterns of our minds' learned information so that we can experience new expansion and be who we truly are.

In the next chapter, you will wed your understanding of the deep unconscious with a thorough set of practical methods for working with crystals. You will learn about the importance of choosing the option that most resonates with you, from working by yourself or with a crystal healer, to choosing your crystal technique, to releasing unconscious learned patterns, to how to care for and cleanse your crystals. You will also learn how to choose specific crystals so that you can put all the information you've learned into practice and begin your healing process, which will eventually lead you to the illuminating authentic self of your crystal blueprint.

CHAPTER 8

Choosing an Authentic Way to Work with Quartz Crystals

"One of the functions of healing is to restore the original, orderly energy field of the person by the use of a strong harmonic vibration that disengages the interference pattern and momentarily brings into balance the person's own energy field."

— LEONARD LASKOW, M.D.[1]

Crystal healing is a technique with as many facets as crystals themselves. It is an art that, with the assistance of your deep inner work, can connect you with your well-being.

Since we are in search of our authentic selves, it's important to find resonance among the different approaches for working with crystals—from choosing to work individually or with a crystal healer to selecting different techniques that include working with crystal grids and meditation.

From this moment forward, I invite you to focus on what most resonates with your true essence—and from that place, you can choose your best path to healing with crystals.

Working by Ourselves vs. Working with a Crystal Healer

With so many books out there that offer us prescriptive ways of working with crystals, why should we bother to schedule a session with a crystal healer? Both options have many implications when it comes to reconnecting with your authentic self. As we discussed in Chapter 1, whether working by ourselves or with a crystal healer, it is important to recognize whether the information we are receiving originates from the false programming of the mind or the authentic, intuitive information of the deeper self.

As my teacher JaneAnn Dow wrote: "Bear in mind—should you decide to visit a psychic or a healer, you will be listening to someone else's viewpoint of who you are, why you are here, and how you are expressing yourself. If these ideas feel right to you, you may want to explore them further. If they do not feel right, if they do not resonate with your own inner knowing, you should reject them without hesitation. The information might be colored by the bias of the channel."[2]

The real problem here is that we are dealing with the unconscious, which is vast and often unknowable. If not handled properly, any information received during our healing sessions will be directed toward our unconscious and become another command that can activate more behaviors and beliefs in our daily life.

"When my clients are lying in front of me, covered with stones and ready to review their lives with soul-searching honesty, they are vulnerable energetically to everything that is happening around them and aware, on a superconscious level, of everything I am saying. It is as if they have a built-in recorder that encapsulates the entire session and plays it back into their conscious awareness whenever these memories resurface. With this in mind, I choose my words carefully. I have had clients return to me years later and repeat verbatim everything I said to them in sessions that are no longer a part of my own conscious awareness," JaneAnn wrote.[3]

That is why it is so important to choose the best channel to provide the information that you are receiving. Whether you choose to work with a crystal healer, read a book by an author, or depend on your own knowledge and intuition to select stones with which to work, you must consider that the information provided could be mixed with the contents of your own inner mind programming.

Quartz crystals themselves have special energetic properties that we can attune to, which have healing effects whether we decide to work on our own or with a crystal healer. If we work with a crystal healer, crystals can do their work by magnifying the healer's intentions. The crystal healers, through their experience and wisdom, can facilitate the process of recognizing the core wound or original source of our suffering and guide us toward the best choices to transcend and transform unconscious learned information and to reconnect with the original version of ourselves.

This can also be achieved by working individually with our commitment and discipline. Whichever way we choose, crystal healing occurs when the crystals are simply allowed to do their work without the interference of our minds' programming.

We know that crystals work through resonance, but as an individual who is seeking to connect with crystals, you must address some arguments around crystals.

The saying "As you believe, so they behave" is not necessarily true for crystals. Although crystals are highly sensitive to our conscious mind-set, it's also true that they resonate with the unconscious, which is invisible to us. Crystals are in service to helping us evolve and will balance anything known or unknown within us. Therefore, crystals are always open to working with you. Even if we believe that crystals are inanimate, they will have some effect on us, either conscious or unconscious.

At the same time, it would be irresponsible of me to tell you that the healing quality of working with a book about crystals will be *equivalent* to the experience of working with a healer. Crystal healing involves the unconscious, which entails handling energy and symbolic interpretation; without proper training and experience, we can either produce counteractive effects or lose important clues and links in our journey of reconnection with our authentic selves. If you want to deepen your energy work, it is better to seek skilled counsel or do it with an expert in the crystal energy field. Likewise, if you choose to work intuitively on your own, first it is necessary to discern between original and false learned information. To become the best version of yourself, I suggest you do it with the help of a crystal healer until you have begun to clear your mind and understand the process of reconnecting with your authentic self.

I would also suggest that you work with a crystal healer if you identify with your beliefs and haven't undertaken any personal work. Crystal healers are a wonderful first step. They can guide you initially, until you feel ready to work with crystals by yourself. They are like a crutch that you can drop whenever you are ready to walk your authentic story. When you have worked diligently on yourself, you learn to distinguish false information from authentic information and make the right choices in your path of self-awareness.

Authentic crystal healers are unconditionally connected to serving others. Their source of wisdom is life, and their knowledge is borne of navigating experiences through the adversities of life. Each experience that is overcome means that they have graduated from one specific area of life (e.g., divorce, bankruptcy, illness, etc.), and are ready to pass this wisdom on to others because they have been able to heal and integrate those experiences in themselves. For me, this is the true credential of a healer—the true awareness and wisdom gained from overcoming painful life experiences.

My title is merely a symbol that acknowledges that, through difficult life experiences, crystals guided me to recognize and reconnect with the real essence of who I am; from this place, I can help others to achieve the same. I can guide them through similar life processes that enable them to become whole and authentic again.

JaneAnn Dow has written that, while there is a bond between the crystal healer and the client, the healer is only the bridge.[4]

I myself am a specialist in divorce and parental alienation, matriarchal/patriarchal/cultural wounds, relationships, depression, and cancer, as well as self-empowerment and reconnection to the authentic. The solutions to my life experiences are already encoded within my energy field in such a way that contact with the client's energy field can bring resonance to solve the same issues in their lives.

Crystal energy catalyzes the process of healing, amplifying the energy in me to bring transformation and balance to the client's life.

Crystal resonance therapist Naisha Ahsian says, "When I talk about working with a crystal, I don't mean just sticking [a crystal] in your bra or in your pillow or nightstand, or sleeping with your stones or throwing them in your bathtub. I mean meditation with the stone, opening yourself to receive both the energy and whatever that energy brings up . . . and doing that as a disciplined practice in order to develop connection with the stones."[5]

For Ahsian, people's relationships with crystals can verge on the exploitative, so we must be cautious of not using crystals to further our own selfish agendas. "This is unbalanced, and it's not an ethical or a powerful way to connect with crystals and stones. It is the magic pill paradigm . . . people assume you can just pick up a stone and say, 'Hey, come here and do this for me,' and the stone is somehow going to fix something for them. The way that true healing works is that we must identify where we are out of balance within ourselves and reconnect to our higher spiritual power through the medium of an ally, which in this case would be a crystal that acts as both the source of energy but also as a teacher, a mentor, a support that can give us guidance or assistance."

Ahsian also acknowledges that crystal healers, as facilitators, can offer more insight on what might be happening energetically and vibrationally to cause a client's imbalance in the first place, and can provide greater objectivity to someone who might be caught in an unconscious pattern. However, "working with crystals and stones on your own first will give you an understanding of what they are bringing up, how they feel, how they move you. That will give you . . . discernment when engaging someone to facilitate you in a healing situation."

Consulting with a crystal healer involves working with someone who is committed to his or her internal process. The crystal healer is constantly filtering information, discerning between authentic and inauthentic sources of information, and thus working to recognize true intuition rather than mind-filtered information.

So, how does one go about choosing a crystal healer? First, the story of the crystal healer must resonate with your story—even better if the healer has overcome the problem you are facing and you are able to resonate with the healer's solution to the problem, as well. Second, the healer must be continuously engaged with his or her personal inner work and not assume that he or she has "arrived" at a permanent enlightened or "know-it-all" state! As the universe's evolution never stops, neither does our learning process.

Aside from selecting the right healer, I also recommend a non-prescriptive and resonant way of selecting the crystal(s) you work with: the one(s) that make you feel at ease. You can absolutely heal yourself and reconnect with the authentic self through crystals, and I encourage you to work with any of the techniques detailed below, especially meditation and thought management. I present several references and techniques that you can use to work with crystals on your own. The purpose of this information is not to feed your mind programming but to invite resonance so that you vibrate with the technique that is most inviting.

Questioning Old Crystal Techniques—Beginning with Chakras

We cannot discuss crystal healing without addressing the ancient Hindu concept of chakras, which are energy centers in the human biofield that influence our physical, emotional, and spiritual lives. Hinduism teaches that the human body contains seven energy centers and that each of these contains a symbolic lesson in our path of self-discovery. The ancient Vedic system of the seven chakras is an archetypal description of human self-awareness, as well as the evolution from being identified with false information to merging with one's authentic self.

Chakras, or "wheels" in Sanskrit, are vertically aligned, running from the base of the spine to the crown of the head; this suggests, in a way, that reconnection is a process of ascension. Each chakra represents something to release and integrate, to unlearn and reconnect within us. The idea is to upgrade our archetypes, to transform the meaning of any dysfunctional or negative archetype, and to keep evolving. As a person masters each chakra, he or she gains a new inner meaning and awareness, advancing the person closer to who he or she really is.

Chakras have made a huge impact on the Western imagination with respect to our understanding of the energetic body. However, our understanding of chakras is compromised by information filtered by and through the mind. With the exception of a few Sanskrit scholars, the original context of chakras has been almost entirely lost. This is due to many factors. For one, early works by Western scholars of Sanskrit have translated and deciphered terms on the basis of their own cultural biases and faulty understanding. As this information was filtered through the "spiritual" teachings of modern scholars and teachers, it strayed even further from the source.

According to Sanskrit scholar Christopher Wallis, our information on chakras is greatly flawed. Instead of there being seven agreed-upon chakras in the ancient yogic systems, many different branches of yoga described various chakra systems ranging from 5 chakras to 28 and even more! In fact, the seven-chakra system only came into popularity in the 16th century. [6]

Also, while contemporary Western sources describe the chakras as being a matter of "fact," ancient Sanskrit sources did not ascribe qualitative descriptions to each chakra. Rather, they gave us specific practices for visualizing and working with chakras. For example, the root chakra isn't the four-petaled lotus at the base of the body that many Western scholars have suggested it is; this visualization was posited by ancient scholars as a way of working with this energy center, not identifying it.

Wallis also notes that the chakras as we describe them emerge from a contemporary Western understanding of psychology, which would have been inconceivable to the ancient Indians who developed these systems. Sanskrit sources don't associate individual chakras with emotions and psychological states. This is truly a modern invention.

It is important to consider that false information that gets concretized in the mind as fact impacts the ways in which we approach ancient information such as the chakra system. What we have taken as authoritative information is severely compromised. Because so many crystal healers work with chakras, it is vital to recognize that much of the information we have today has been removed from its original context—not merely because of reinterpretation for a modern context or mind-set bias but also because of misinformation and mistranslation that has entered mainstream thinking. In most cases, people repeat information or assume it without knowing or even questioning the true origin.

I recommend that people proceed with caution when connecting crystals with ideas about chakras and what they represent. I also recommend that crystal healers break free from the assumption that they have absolute knowledge about the chakras, as every source of knowledge that we tend to refer to presents limited models, and there is no authoritative Western text on the subject.

I usually do not designate the use of certain gem colors to specific chakras or conditions but, rather, allow the frequency required by the patient to be selected through resonance. There are too many variables. Each client is an individual with specific mind patterns according to his or her own personal experiences and beliefs. If what causes our imbalance is particular to us, we cannot generalize their treatment. It follows that one gem might suit a certain individual but not another. Likewise, one's personal connection to one's body and mind's energy fields cannot be generalized to fit everyone else. For me, it is about recognizing one's individual inner patterns and wounds through crystals. Then, we can make the choice to release them, to transform ourselves and reconnect with who we really are. We can choose which techniques to work with based on whether or not they are authentic for us. The following is a very brief summary of our symbolic path of reconnection through chakras and crystals:

The Symbolism of Chakras and Stones		
Chakra	Associated Stone and Benefits	Symbolism
1st chakra	Smoky Quartz	Society, culture, and environment; false information that, when recognized, helps us begin our journey of inner transformation
2nd chakra	Carnelian Agate	Releasing the wounds of our parents and learned feminine and masculine models to create a new reality

3rd chakra	Citrine	Releasing negative bias to integrate personal power and abundance
4th chakra	Rose Quartz	Releasing the wounds of the heart to reconnect with all expressions of love
5th chakra	Blue Quartz	Releasing the false voice to reconnect with true self-expression
6th chakra	Amethyst	Releasing separation to amplify the mind
7th chakra	Clear Quartz	Living one's whole authentic self

We cannot rely on the theories we have learned without questioning or knowing the real source. However, we *can* connect with our authentic energy through resonance. Instead of relying on the chakras as a guiding paradigm, we will use questions and resonance to select crystals and place them over our bodies. In this way, we'll avoid the manipulation of the mind and direct the energy to where it needs to go.

Choosing Your Crystal Technique

Crystals are tools that enable us to tune into our bodies with a high degree of sensitivity. According to Gregg Braden, "Crystal is made of the earth, and different crystals have very specific properties. [Our ancestors] would use crystals of the Earth as a point of reference to help tune the body to the Earth, and Earth frequencies, in various specific ways to harmonize the human body with our natural environment. [For the ancients], the crystals were a temporary tool, a point of reference to help bring the body into alignment. And once that alignment was in place, it created a feeling in the body. If we can have the feeling, if we can preserve it, we can align the body and the emotions, and not use the external tools. But the external tools are powerful catalysts to get us into that place."[7]

The following exercise helps us to recognize false information inside our unconscious in order to begin a process of self-exploration to recognize our authentic self.

You can work either in the presence of real crystals or by seeing the crystals in the chart provided on www.beatrizsinger.com/p/crystalresonance.

First, it's important to create the "crystal connection" by tuning in to the crystal, as explained below, through breathing and grounding. This establishes resonance between you and the stone.

After formulating each question, you will approach the first crystal to which you feel attracted "without mind."

With each question, you might feel an impulse to immediately grab the crystal. Sometimes, you will feel resistance to certain stones. For example, you might avoid choosing black or small stones. If this happens to you, include in your stone selection the crystal that you are avoiding. Remember that the unconscious rejects what is not in its programming. The crystals that you resist will surely provide an important clue in the path of transformation.

You might also feel no particular attraction for any crystal when the question is framed. This could mean that the topic related to this specific question does not resonate with you, and so you can move on to the following one.

After choosing a crystal, you can practice this exercise either by sitting on a chair or by lying faceup with your back straight, being sure that your arms and legs are uncrossed.

Simply place the crystal or visualize the crystal where you sense it should go over or around your body, without thinking about it too much.

Here are the questions you should ask yourself:

1. Do I need to work on wounds that are associated with my lack of boundaries now?

2. Do I need to work on wounds that are associated with my excess of boundaries now?

3. Do I need to work on my mother wounds now?

4. Do I need to work on my father wounds now?

5. Do I need to work on my relationship wounds now?

6. Do I need to work on any wounds connected to prejudice and discrimination due to differences in gender, race, religion, culture, age, etc., now?

7. Do I need to work on the wounds originated in the information provided by the media, education, religion, politics, or other unconscious learned paradigms now?

8. Do I need to work on the wounds originated in the mental rigidity of my false mind programming now?

9. Do I need to work on the wounds originated in my negative bias now?

10. Do I need to work on my wounds originated in my attachment to my false reality now?

If you answered "yes" to any of the above questions, address these wounds by focusing on the part of the body you need to work on. Through resonance, you will know which areas of your body to place the crystals on. That means that after you choose the stones, you will place them on the first parts of your body that you visualize or that come to your awareness without the intervention of your mind.

I also encourage you to formulate more questions—as many as you feel are necessary. If you wish to dig further into the origin of your wound, keep doing so until you feel you have tapped into it. One of the most effective ways of directing energy is by asking questions. When working with stones, such questions can include: When did this wound originate? What was the information or experience that caused it? What is the best way to heal it? Who am I, beyond my learned beliefs and experiences? Is this information true for me?

The answers can come in the shape of a faint voice within us that becomes stronger as we engage in our inner work with crystals. For others, it can come as synchronicity or a deep confirmation that emerges from within or in any other way that is authentic to us. What is relevant here is to discover the authentic expression of our inner voice.

For each of us, crystals will reflect a different experience. An open attitude is all it takes to adopt an observer's eye that allows you to disidentify from the process and outcome. Remember that this is a process, and as such, it doesn't happen overnight. It requires our commitment and perseverance. Journaling about our experiences is a good way to keep track of our evolving process.

Thought Management to Reconnect with the Authentic within Us

The paradigms learned throughout Western cultures teach us to hold things outside of ourselves as responsible for our sorrows and problems. But the "enemy" is not necessarily on the outside; the enemy can also come in the form of the internalized voices of others that continue to speak through us.

For example, the problem of an alcoholic is not the bottle of alcohol but the mismanagement of the person's thoughts. In the same way, the problem of depression is not the sadness we fall prey to—it is our inability to understand the real nature and origin of our thoughts.

It is important to become aware of this and make a commitment to ourselves to exorcise all the torments of our minds.

The following two exercises are ones I have applied and continue applying in my life to filter thoughts and beliefs that I have learned unconsciously from third parties. The first exercise will help you recognize and get closer to your true essence.

Recognizing Your Authentic Truth

I suggest doing this exercise every time you recognize a thought that overwhelms you or with which you do not feel at ease, using any quartz you resonate with as a tool.

1. Recognize the thought.
2. Tune in.

3. Ask yourself where that information comes from.

4. Ask yourself if that belief is actually true for you.

5. Mind-travel to the place and time where you first learned this belief. Breathe in crystalline energy to amplify it and recognize the real source of that belief. When we breathe crystalline energy, we are opening ourselves to consciously receive and feel the crystal's waves. Crystalline energy may be experienced differently, depending on the frequency and amplitude of each crystal. For example, when some clients begin to breathe, they perceive and experience colors and temperature changes. The resonance between the crystal and our own energy in that moment will determine our unique crystalline energy experience.

6. Exhale and release the belief, allowing yourself to feel at peace. Allow the crystalline energy to transform your belief. Feel the balance and transformation that the crystal's inner geometric structure brings.

7. Go to a previous moment in life when you didn't have that belief. Wherever it takes you, ask yourself what your authentic belief is in this space. Breathe in the crystalline energy and amplify your authentic belief. Breathe out and feel how the crystalline energy grounds this authentic belief more deeply within you.

8. With the help of crystals, visualize yourself putting this belief into practice in your life right now. You can even add to this visualization sensory qualities and images, such as the specific colors you see, sounds, sensations in your body, etc. The more real the scene, the better. Experience the well-being that comes from living your authentic truth and all the amazing feelings and sensations of fulfillment.

9. Act on the authentic beliefs you just integrated and repeat them as a daily routine.

Releasing Negativity

This second exercise helps us to befriend our negativity rather than fighting against it or denying its existence. This means that we do not avoid it, argue with it, or pretend that it isn't affecting us.

Negativity multiplies just like the mythical hydra; every time you cut one of its heads off, other heads will crop up in their place—and instead of improving the situation, you will make it worse. Wherever you place your attention, energy grows. Let's use it in a positive instead of a negative way. By learning the original source of your negativity and judgment, you can discover patterns that trigger these behaviors and become aware of how to deactivate them. Don't forget to do this exercise with the help of a crystal placed inside your energy field so that you can experience its resonance more deeply.

1. Tune in.

2. Ask yourself where that negative belief or thought first originated.

3. Ask yourself if you want to change that negative thought or belief.

4. If the answer is yes, imagine that your negative belief is written on a piece of paper, and as you breathe in the crystalline energy, the words are slowly deleted until they completely disappear from the paper so that you can see the blank piece of paper.

5. Feel the crystalline energy balancing your mind and body with all the sensations that come from it.

6. Focus on the positive now, and on the blank space of the paper, write down a positive belief. For example, you might choose a belief like "All is well," or "I am harmony," or "I am love." Breathe in the crystalline energy and amplify your positive belief. Breathe out and feel how the crystalline energy grounds this authentic belief more deeply within you.

7. Take your attention to the frontal cortex, located at the top front area of your head, and visualize that crystalline energy as light spreading roots and creating new neural pathways that will enable you to experience this positive new belief as part of the authentic reality you are building with your daily habits.

Author Lisa Wimberger, founder of the Neurosculpting Institute, says that recent data shows that the frontal cortex is the section of the brain that correlates with active states of compassion, empathy, and joy.[8] Neuroscientists have also discovered that when the frontal cortex is electrically stimulated, this has the power to retrieve long-term memories. Quartz crystals, through their unique properties, can access and transform beliefs that are stored as memories, amplifying the positive effects of the frontal cortex. Moreover, we know that inside our brains, there are pyramidal neurons—including those that can be found in the cerebral cortex and also the amygdala, the area where negative bias originates—that resonate with quartz crystals' tetrahedral inner structure, thereby bringing balance. Just as crystals stabilize frequencies in electronic devices, they can stabilize inharmonious frequencies such as anger, which originates in the amygdala of the brain. With time and repetition, a new positive habit can be activated within our minds' programming, bringing healing, new possibilities, and the hope of a new life free of negativity.

The Power of Meditating with Crystals

Taking into account the sheer quantity of information we receive, imagine all the stories we could rewrite if we could filter false information and focus on amplifying our authentic information.

Geometry and physics help us understand how, on an energetic level, we create our reality. Our individual electromagnetic fields work like a torus. The energy enters our heads, circulates within our bodies and hearts at the center, then leaves the base of the perineum and loops around our body to enter our heads again. The structure of the torus allows feedback between what is coming from the outside and what is going into our internal environment. In other words, the vacuum of space informs us, and we inform the vacuum. Because of this continuous feedback, if you send negative thoughts out into the world, they most likely will create your reality. Meditation with quartz crystal can help you balance the energy of the torus and resonate with your infinite nature to co-create the best possible reality.[9]

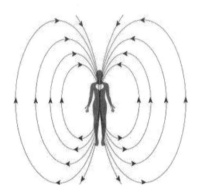

This is the torus-shaped human electromagnetic field. When our energy repeatedly turns inside-out, this creates self-awareness. Quartz crystals can help amplify this. The toroidal geometry of our electromagnetic field is also what allows our energy to have a direct influence on our environment. When we use a quartz crystal, we can balance not only ourselves but also our surroundings. Courtesy of Andrea Gatti

Recent neuroscientific studies have discovered that the brain can be changed and rewired through the act of meditation. In studies that included people who meditated, researchers discovered that meditation could reduce wandering thoughts and also reduce the size and activity of the amygdala, the part of the brain that processes fear and anxiety.[10]

Contemporary psychology has also reaped the benefits of meditation. With regular insight, you can recognize that your thoughts are not real or static. Cognitive behavioral therapy uses this practice. The subject learns to see the falseness of repetitive thinking as an interpretation that arises from learned beliefs—not reality. Meditation can help us to detach from intense emotional states, related to our thoughts, that bring suffering. It can also show us that our interpretations are nothing more than learned stories of the mind. As we practice meditation, which enables us to come into contact with reality as it is, those old unconscious learned stories stop being propagated—but it takes commitment and practice.

The amazing properties of quartz crystal can amplify the effects of meditation. According to Dr. Joe Dispenza, the brain processes 400 billion bits of information per second from our surroundings but we only perceive 2,000 due to our brain and mind processing.[11] When you sit in meditation with a crystal, you are able to amplify energy and receive more information, which otherwise goes unperceived.

For me, the main purpose of meditation with crystals is to recognize the nature of our thoughts. When we meditate with crystals, we are imbued with their resonance. During meditation, we process the information we receive with greater clarity and are able to recognize our thoughts, as well as their origins. This enables us to transcend them. As we deepen our meditation process, we can dissolve the learned information in the deeper layers of our unconscious until we reach a place where information is authentic. We recognize this when we begin to receive new information previously unknown to us. This information arises spontaneously without the resistance of the mind. At this point, we begin to flow with the whole and with the source of universal information.

Meditation also allows you to distinguish between thoughts that originate in the mind and those that truly originate in your authentic source. Although it's hard to accept for many of you, your thoughts are mostly learned. If you had a depressive mother, your thoughts are most likely going to be of a sad nature. In the same way, if your father was in fear and didn't trust anyone, the nature of your thoughts will be negative and mistrusting. In effect, the real problem we have isn't about not getting that job, or living with unmet needs, or being alcoholic and depressed. The true unease comes from the nature of our thinking and our ingrained tendency to buy into these thoughts and beliefs.

Knowing the nature of our thoughts can be a huge clue in our self-exploration journey. When we recognize the thoughts and beliefs that do not belong to us, we can recognize those that are authentic to us. We can recognize our own voice—and that voice includes our intuition. When you de-clutter your mind of other voices, you can even hear vibrations and the voice of crystals, as I did. Since all is energy, crystals will communicate with everything that is related to vibration, such as light, sound, thoughts, and memories. In addition, transformation is also part of a crystal's vibration. Being mindful and attentive of what the vibration of a crystal is bringing up in your mind, you can understand what the crystal is bringing to your awareness that needs to be healed within you.

For example, during one of my meditations, I received an image of myself enclosed in a square shape. I had no idea what the crystal was trying to tell me through the meditation. However, one day I realized that my limitations came not from others, but from me. I was blocking myself because I didn't feel good enough. I worked with the exercise on releasing negativity to address this belief. After some time, in another meditation, I saw myself enclosed again, but this time inside a circle. The circle represented the infinite, the unbound. The crystals not only showed me what I had to transform inside of me but also revealed when my energy shifted. Meditating with crystals certainly allows us to experience the authentic.

There are many different types of meditations that you can choose to practice with crystals. Guided meditations are the best place for beginners to start because they keep the egoic mind occupied with words and visions so that the deeper work can be done. You can also use mantra meditation, where you repeat a specific mantra to yourself.

A mantra is a word or sound that has a symbolic meaning that we repeat while touching the crystal beads. For example, the Hindu mantra *Om Namah Shivaya* is used in spiritual practice to transcend the mind. Tibetan Buddhists believe that by repeating the mantra *Om Mani Padme Hum*, you can connect with infinite compassion. In the same way, we can repeat our own authentic mantra, such as "I am unconditional love," "I am peace," "I am acceptance," and so on.

This form of sound vibration meditation is very useful, especially since it can move into the deeper layers of the unconscious mind. You can hold a quartz crystal bead mala during such a meditation.

Sound and quartz crystals are a powerful combination, as both work through vibrations. As we read in Chapter 6, sound is created when atoms bounce into each other and produce vibration and energy. Interestingly, a recent study demonstrated that sound can transform into light through piezoelectricity. According to Evan Reed, one of the authors of the study, "converting sound to light itself is novel, because there is only a very narrow frequency range—around 100 GHz to THz—where sound and light overlap." [12] Sound activates crystals' transformation properties. The light that passes through the crystal amplifies the energy. So when you work with a crystal bead mala and a mantra whose repetition releases the old and activates the formation of an authentic belief, you are amplifying, transforming, and repatterning your mind—and changing your reality, as well.

Mindful meditation described in the section below is another way to reconnect with the authentic within us; as a practice, it requires discipline, commitment, perseverance, and presence.

Guided Meditation

Sit with your back straight, or lie down so that you are comfortable. Work with the crystal you most resonate with, either by holding it or by placing it over some part of the body. I personally prefer to place crystals over the frontal cortex of the brain, between the eyebrows, or over the heart—which encompasses the largest energy field of the body. I like to work with clear quartz, which resonates with the liquid crystals within our brains and hearts.

Be sure to do this meditation in a quiet place where you will not be interrupted. Breathe deeply through your nose, from head to toe, consciously relaxing each part of your body. Let go of all the tension until your breathing becomes very subtle. As relaxation occurs, the mind becomes resonant and receptive, and the subtle vibration of the crystal can be felt. Allow yourself to be filled by the color, texture, shape, and size of the stone— by its energy, waves, and frequency. Hear the sound of your breath. Notice your identification with the stone. Allow yourself to become one with the crystal. Open yourself and surrender to this process. Let yourself see, hear, and feel the world through the quartz crystal's perspective.

Now you can ask the crystal what aspect of your life you need to work on, whether it is your relationships, your emotions, limiting thoughts, etc. In which area of your life do you have unconscious information that is preventing you from living a balanced life, to your fullest potential and sustained well-being? And what is really deep inside you that is separating you from the whole, from expressing who you authentically are in the world?

The energy of the crystal will express itself in many ways: through images, body sensations, colors, sounds, etc. Stay open and in this healing place as long as you need, and allow the information to naturally come to you. When you feel you are ready, connect with your conscious breathing again and open your eyes.

After meditating with a crystal for 15 to 30 minutes and clearing the mind, it's a good idea to pay attention over the next few hours and days to whatever pops up in your reality—because the meditation is just the opening of the door. As the energy of the crystal integrates within your body, your energy systems, and your life—which you are co-creating at every moment—certain situations will arise. Generally, you can expect synchronicities. A message related to your meditation might arrive in the form of a meaningful conversation with someone, a quote in a book, a song, a call or message from someone with whom you haven't had contact in a long time, etc.

These messages will be authentic to you and will clarify whatever it is the crystal is communicating to you.

Even though the meditation itself is a core point of interaction with the stone, it can take 24 to 48 hours for that experience to fully integrate so that you can understand whatever it is you need to know in order to come into a state of balance and reconnection with your authentic self. This might include information about further personal growth work that you need to do.

The Placement of Stones

As we explored in Part II, the idea of arranging stones into symbolic geometric patterns has been used since prehistoric times. Stonehenge, Göbekli Tepe, Nabta Playa, and many megalithic geometric configurations demonstrate that grids and mandalas were part of the ancients' language to communicate and integrate the invisible forces of the cosmos.

Crystal grids, which are often used in crystal healing, likely originated in these ancient configurations. It is believed that these crystal grids act as a technology that works in a way similar to electrical circuits. Each crystal generates energy waves and constructive interference with the electromagnetic waves of our organs and thoughts. This brings transformation and healing.

During a crystal healing session, the energy of each quartz crystal placed over the body intersects and begins to interact with the body and mind's energy on a subatomic level, creating an expansive ripple effect conducive to releasing stagnant energies. Photography: Stacey J. Byers, www.capturedspirit.net

Building a crystal grid is a very powerful way to build a strong energy field that can help repattern unhealthy energy fields in our bodies and their surrounding energy. They are especially effective when working with patterns of suffering.

In a crystal grid, crystals are arranged in patterns that resonate with the geometric structure of quartz but also with the patterns of our bodies and the universe. When we place crystals in geometric configurations over our bodies, we bring ourselves into resonance with the natural flow of universal energies, which leads to healing. In the same way, if we place geometric crystal configurations within our environments, we can turn them into sacred spaces where universal harmony and well-being reign and permeate.

I highly recommend using sacred geometric patterns present within nature, such as concentric circles, ovals, and spirals, while working with the principles of numerology (see Chapter 3). For anyone building a crystal grid, I suggest the following:

1. Think about your intention in creating your crystal grid— be it individual or collective healing, harmonizing a space, protection, recharging, etc.

2. Tune in.

3. Choose the crystals with which you resonate and that feel aligned with your purpose.

4. Decide on the geometric pattern you resonate with (you can also choose to work with numerology based on the chart in Chapter 3).

5. "Connect all the dots"—and by this, I mean stones. In your mind, visualize how the energy flows between all crystals. Trace the geometric pattern of the grid in the same way that electricity would flow in an electric circuit. This is what it means to activate the crystal grid. You can go through the same process by connecting the stones and tracing over them with a quartz crystal point.

Over the Heart

The popular adage "Listen to your heart" is a reminder to listen to the deepest core of our being, which transcends both thought and emotion and takes us into the terrain of the authentic self.

While the brain is considered the master organ of the human body, new science has revealed that the brain receives many of its instructions from the heart. According to Gregg Braden, "The heart and the brain work together. So this is a partnership: two different organs working in harmony as a single system to regulate the human body. There is a conversation that is happening between the heart and the brain, and the quality of that conversation is determined by the quality of the emotions that we hold in the heart."[13]

Braden goes on to explain that many of the emotions that we classify as "negative" are not simply anger, hate, jealousy, or rage—but rather, unresolved anger, hate, jealousy, rage, and so on. "The emotions themselves aren't the problem. It's when the emotions continue with no resolution that they can become a problem to the body. So those kinds of negative emotions send a signal to the brain, a very chaotic kind of signal. And the brain releases the chemistry that matches the stress chemistry, such as high levels of adrenaline and cortisol. When the conversation between the heart and the brain changes to what we call a positive emotion—gratitude, or appreciation, or compassion—then the signal changes to a more balanced, coherent signal, and that changes the chemistry that the brain releases into the body."

Braden notes that there are specialized cells in the human heart known as sensory neurites, which operate in much the same way as neurons in the brain. There are about 40,000 or so neurites in the heart. They make up what is known as "the little brain in the heart."

Ancient traditions didn't understand the science behind the little brain in the heart, but they understood the relationship. "Ancient traditions have always said that the heart is the seat of the soul . . . the doorway, or the pathway to deep human wisdom, and understanding, and intuition, and compassion. [Ancients tried to] enhance the power of the human heart to have this relationship with the brain. So there were ceremonies that were used in the past—including plant medicine, and altered states of consciousness that are induced. One of the ways that those altered states were induced was through the use of crystals," says Braden.

We store the chemistry of our hurt, as well as the chemistry of our joy, in different organs. The heart is one of the organs in which both men and women store the chemistry of our emotions.

We know that quartz crystals resonate with the crystalline structures of the heart to help balance and transform unresolved emotions. So when we work with the heart, we bring the body back into harmony, and we begin to resolve our body's chemistry and energetic patterns. The following exercise can help you reconnect with your authentic self through the heart.

Reconnecting with the Authentic Self through the Heart

1. Find a silent and comfortable place where you can lie down.

2. Make sure that your arms are at your sides and your palms are facing up. Also make sure that your back is straight and that you are not crossing your legs.

3. Place a clear quartz crystal over your physical heart and tune in.

4. Close your eyes and connect with your breathing as you deeply inhale and exhale through your nose.

5. Allow your awareness to move from your mind to your heart.

6. Breathe slowly from your heart.

7. Listen to your heartbeat until you become one with it.

8. Go deeper until you find the deepest current, as powerful as a slow but mighty river.

9. Locate your inner wisdom and flow.

10. Simply remain within this flow as long as it feels good to you.

11. When you are ready, come back to your conscious breathing and open your eyes.

Creating Crystal Connections

Before you work on your own or with a crystal healer with any of the techniques that are described above, it's important to create the proper space for healing. I suggest a quiet, uninterrupted space where all electronic devices are turned off, which will enable you to concentrate on your inner work.

Everything is energy, including empty spaces, and energy tends to behave like a fluid. If you throw anything inside that fluid, it creates waves that interact with each other. In the same way, we can bring crystals into our spaces to create harmony prior to a crystal healing session. Amethyst helps to clear energy. Clear quartz and rose quartz in any form are great for energizing the room in a positive way. You can place the crystals on your altar, or you can create a crystal grid around the room, using the different corners of the room as demarcation points.

Since crystals work with energy, it is important to favor the direction that runs the energy of our planet. The crystal core of the planet generates electric currents. The rotation of the earth on its axis causes these electric currents to form a magnetic field around the planet. The earth behaves as a dipole magnetic bar, meaning that electric currents move from south to north.

The best way to work with crystal healing is by lying on the earth or the floor, face up. This might be on a natural fiber mat with your head pointing toward the north, or where the natural current of the earth is heading. If you are not able to lie on the floor, you can sit on a chair with your back straight and your head pointing toward the north. Healing requires removing all metals unless they are gold, silver, or copper. The electric field inside a metal is zero. When an electromagnetic wave strikes a metal, there is no electromagnetic radiation and energy cannot be transmitted.

Crystals must be in direct contact with the skin if possible; if this isn't possible, be sure that they are in contact with clothing made from cotton, as it has better energetic absorbency than synthetic fibers. Clothing color does not matter as long you resonate with it and can enrich the crystal session with its frequencies.

Cleaning and Clearing Crystals

Crystals can be programmed thanks to their ability to store information and resonate with it. There are many ways to clear and cleanse crystals to remove previous energies from the crystals. You do not want anyone else's energy in the crystal that you use for healing, including all those who handled or worked with the crystal prior to you. Crystals have a very extensive memory. They remember everything: the places where they have been and the people who touched them—from miners to sellers. The crystals also store the thoughts and emotions that were in these people's energy fields. The crystal is an information system that interacts with our energy field, contaminating the field with information provided by others when it has not been cleared. If we are working to reconnect with our authentic information, we must be sure that our crystals are free from other people's information.

Clearing in energetic terms can be understood as recharging. Recharging happens when the electrons reset the system back to its original state. When the crystal is in touch with the energy field of a particular person, the flow of electrons runs in one direction (in this case, from inside to the outside, as we saw in Chapter 6). When we cleanse or clear a crystal, an external source of direct electrical current can supply electrons, forcing them into reverse or back to the original placement—until the crystal is recharged.[14]

Negative ions (also known as anions) are molecules charged with extra electrons, and they are perfect for recharging and clearing crystalline energy. Nobel Prize–winning scientist Philipp Eduard Anton von Lenard confirmed that negative ions are found in high concentrations at the seashore and in the basins of waterfalls. Negative ions can be generated by moving water. When the water droplets collide with one another while moving through the air, they become negative ions. The U.S. Department of Agriculture discovered that when we ionize a room, this can decrease dust by 52 percent and reduce bacteria by up to 95 percent.[15]

Running water that comes from such sources as oceans, rivers, water faucets, or showers can help recharge crystals. So can the smoke or oil from white sage, as many Native American tribes have witnessed. Being exposed to the sun can also help recharge crystals; so can placing them over crystal clusters—especially those of amethyst and clear quartz—and burying them inside the earth.

Like any object in nature, crystals have a natural frequency at which they prefer to resonate. Jonathan Goldman, author of *Shifting Frequencies*, Grammy nominee, and director of the Sound Healers Association, says that sound has the ability to rearrange molecular structure and that frequencies can be shifted through sound to rearrange vibratory patterns.[16] Through sound, crystals can restore their balance. Special instruments such as tuning forks help align quartz with its original resonant frequency, clearing all that is out of tune with it.

Visualization is particularly useful when you cannot use other cleansing techniques. For example, when you are about to touch a stranger's crystal in a shop, picture in your mind an energy meter with a dial that goes from 0 to 100. Wherever you see the indicator needle, move it left to 0, imagining that the crystal is being cleared of other people's energies.

Here is a graphic that summarizes the different ways to clean crystals.

Here are some other considerations to take into account with respect to quartz crystal care:

- Do not allow anyone, including a crystal healer, to handle your personal crystals. The vibrations have been specifically tuned to those of your own body, mind, and energy field. Your crystals represent your energy; as such, only you can be responsible for maintaining your energy.

- Do not touch other people's crystals unless invited to do so. They may not wish for your vibrations to be incorporated into them.

- Subjecting crystals to thermal stress (such as freezing temperatures or hot water) may cause cracking and, thus, compromise the properties of the crystal.

- Never leave colored quartz crystals such as amethyst in the sun for prolonged periods of time, as they may lose color, also compromising the flow, accuracy, and, stability of the crystal's frequency. When transporting crystals, wrap each one separately in a soft, natural material. Avoid wrapping them in plastic or synthetic material.Never leave clear crystals in the sun without monitoring them. They are prone to concentrating sunlight and can run the risk of producing fires.

Tuning In

As we know, it is important to choose crystals through our resonance with the stone and to keep our intellect out of the selection process so that we can become sensitive to a crystal's energy without the interference of our unconscious programming.

When we tune in, we release the resistance of the mind and sync back with the original information of our authentic selves—that which is genuine to us. We allow the energy of crystals to intersect with our own so that our resonances become sympathetic. A bond then can take place, and information can be transferred between the crystal and us.

Good listening is mindful listening. Like mindfulness itself, listening requires a combination of intention and attention. We set our intention when we identify our purpose for working with a crystal. We use our attention to simply stay present, open, and unbiased as we receive information that includes that of our own resonant frequency and authentic inner voice. We open to the crystal healing process and the information that arises from tuning in to the crystal's frequency and experiencing the interaction of our energy field with that of the crystal's.

The foundation for tuning in is self-awareness. Here are some tips that will help you to better listen to your authentic voice prior to choosing your crystals and receiving information during the session itself:

1. **Check inside**: Ask yourself: *How am I feeling now? Is there anything getting in the way of my being present?* If something is in the way, use slow and mindful breathing to gently release it. Breathe in and out deeply a couple times and visualize whatever energy isn't allowing you to be present simply dissolving through your exhalations.

2. **Feel your own sense of presence and direct it accordingly**: Allow yourself to be open to healing and to resonate with and attract that which is best for you in this exact moment. You can also allow the area of concern

that you want to change to come into your mind. If this is a physical symptom, direct your attention toward that place on your body. If, for whatever reason, you are directed toward a different area of your body or your life, focus your attention there without resistance.

3. **Choose your crystal(s)**: As you focus on the sensations and images that come to your mind, draw a deep breath and choose, through resonance, the crystal(s) you want to work with. Do not think about this process too much. Allow it to flow from your intuitive, authentic awareness.

Just Breathe

The energy of breath has been a part of spiritual and healing traditions for millennia. *Prana, chi,* and *ruach* are some of the names by which it is known in different traditions. When you inhale, your body and energy field take on this charge of energy; holding your breath builds the charge, while exhaling releases it.

According to Dr. Richard Brown, an associate clinical professor of psychiatry at Columbia University and co-author of *The Healing Power of the Breath*, breathing can transform the response of the body's autonomic nervous system, which controls unconscious processes such as heart rate.[17]

Breathing can help us connect our conscious with our unconscious processes, and vice versa, as we undergo crystal healing. Breathing before a crystal healing session is a preliminary practice to release the distractions of the mind and to build resonance during the process of choosing the crystals. We sit with our eyes partially closed and turn our attention to our breathing. We breathe naturally, preferably through the nostrils, without attempting to control our breath. Breathing through the nose stimulates the parasympathetic nervous system. This reduces heart rate and lowers the frequency of our brain waves.

At first, our minds will be very busy, and we might even feel that we are failing, but in reality we are simply becoming aware of the processes of the mind—to which we are often oblivious. There will be a great temptation to follow the different thoughts as they arise, but we should resist this and remain focused on the sensation of the breath, continuing to bring our attention back to our breathing each time our minds wander.

We should repeat this as many times as necessary until the mind is clear and settles on the breath. After this, we are going to breathe in deeply to the count of four, until the air flows into all parts of the lungs. Then, we hold the breath to the count of four and breathe out slowly through the nose again to the count of four.

You are now ready to be attracted through resonance to the crystals you should work with at this time, which will help you to resolve the issues that most need your attention.

Grounding

Our body is an energetic circuit and, just as with electrical circuits, may need to be connected to the earth—either to absorb energy or to neutralize excess amounts of energy. This is known as grounding. Grounding connects us to the earth so that we can protect ourselves against energetic shorts, interference, or overcharge. Grounding protects the body's delicate bioelectrical circuitry against static charges and interference, but most importantly, it facilitates the reception of free electrons and the stabilizing electrical signals and energy of the earth.[18] From above to below, we are part of an energetic continuum that we become ever more attuned to when we consciously work with energy. Grounding balances our nervous systems and reduces our stress response.

In the same way, we need to be grounded when we work with the energy of quartz crystals.

We can ground ourselves before choosing stones by incorporating crystals into our breathing practice. For example, we can place smoky quartz at the level of the soles of our feet, whether we are sitting or lying on the floor. Due to its brown color, smoky quartz resonates with the energy of soil and roots, which can nurture and ground us.

As we breathe, we can visualize that from our feet emerge roots that go all the way into the center of the earth, keeping us energetically anchored and preparing the body so that it works as an energetic circuit that is capable of withstanding a greater amount of energy.

Remember that in crystal healing, the physical body and the energies of the mind may come into contact with stronger energies. The weaker body will adjust its energy to match that of the stronger body. In this case, your human bodies and biofield will "rise" to meet the frequency of the crystal and to resonate with it.

Living the Crystal Experience

A crystal takes millions of years to form—so just imagine all the wisdom it has accumulated over the eons that it is now sharing with you.

After choosing your stones, please remember to note your thoughts, feelings, judgments, and memories. This focus will take you even deeper in your crystal healing experience, which I strongly recommend journaling about.

What I want to convey to you goes beyond using the stones just for personal or spiritual benefit. It is about allowing ourselves to merge with crystalline energy, which expands beyond a stone's physical form and boundaries. The energy can be felt as the tingling that we sometimes experience when we hold crystals. It is important to remain open to the experience but also to become aware of when we resist, as both are part of the healing experience. If we inquire into what we resist, we will recognize old programming that we must let go of in our path to release suffering and reach our authenticity.

To work with crystals, it is important to understand that, beyond merely helping us reach our goal, crystals lead us on a journey inward—a journey that is more of a path than a destination. Crystals lead us to uncharted territories and unfamiliar experiences so that we can break with our learned mind patterns. They can help us release the controls of the mind and, with their crystalline energy, guide us toward the different worlds that live deep under the layers of false information. In this way, we tap into what is original and attract it through resonance to our reality.

In our crystal experience, transformation may also be understood as a shift in our perception. Things are happening for us, not to us, for our highest good.

It is important to trust in the process and enter in perfect communion with the crystal energies so that we can effectively reconnect with our true potential and gifts. As we enter into crystalline consciousness, we must take into consideration the following:

1. Being in front of a crystal is not the same as being inside a crystal. During our sessions, we can experience healing when we actually allow ourselves to become one with the crystal. We can imagine that the crystal with which we are working has a door through which we enter and become one with the stone. This image makes for an easier connection with the crystal's energy.

2. It is important to free ourselves from any learned beliefs or stereotypes, such as the notion that stones are inanimate objects.

3. We must surrender to what we do not know and trust that there is a universal blueprint beyond all the boundaries of the learned mind that will enable our healing in ways that the rational brain cannot calculate.

4. Through the transparency of the crystal, we can allow ourselves access to its crystalline power, which will shine through our unconscious and shed light on our learned beliefs and wounds to transform them.

5. Finally, we can recognize that by wanting to "program" a crystal with a prescribed function through our limited minds, we are limiting its potential. We are reducing its capacity, as well as losing the possibility of connecting to the infinite and to our whole, holographic selves through crystals.

Self-Empowering with Crystal Healing

Crystals are not coincidences but resonances. When you choose a crystal through resonance, you are choosing a particular part of your story that you need to recognize in order to transform it.

Go to www.beatrizsinger.com/p/crystalresonance to choose the crystal with which you most resonate now.

Taking into consideration all you have learned through this chapter, choose a crystal with the purpose of reconnecting to the authentic self, following the crystal connection protocol and choosing the technique with which you resonate most.

Through this chapter, we realized that if we want to reconnect to our true nature using crystal energy, our crystals must be cleared of other people's vibrations; resonating with our own preferred crystal practice is essential. Our practice will help us become aware of learned unconscious patterns and their origins but also of latent universal patterns and the natural flow of energy and wisdom within us. That is why I encourage you to work through resonance instead of prescription. As you learned, we cannot completely depend on theories that have been passed down through history, as the true sources may have been misinterpreted or diluted over time. Crystals work with and for us through resonance—and through diligent inquiry, we can partner with them and undergo profound healing.

The next chapter will pick up where we left off, in a thorough description of the stages of healing that crystals guide us through on our journey back to the authentic self. From a psychological, quantum, neurological, and crystal healing perspective, we will look at the process that begins from the moment a person chooses to undergo a crystal energy healing session to reconnect with the authentic self and re-establish themselves in their original crystal blueprint.

CHAPTER 9

Healing Chaos:
Crystal Healing and the
Process of Reconnecting
to the Authentic Self

"Do not try to transform yourself. Move into yourself."

— Marion Woodman[1]

OVER A LIFETIME, the people and places in our lives might change, but the same circumstances will tend to repeat because we haven't yet worked to transform ourselves. While the situations are completely new at the beginning, our experiences end up in the same painful repercussions because we haven't become aware of the root of the problem, of that which is creating our resonance with the situation at hand: the specific vibration of our unconscious learned information in our minds' energy fields, which equals the vibration of our surrounding energy—thus attracting our current reality.

I am reminded of the story of one of my clients. She continued repeating the same situation over and over in her life. No matter where she was or with whom she was interacting, she couldn't shake the sense that everyone seemed to reject her. Rejection was an experience that was deeply familiar and that she had come to expect.

We have learned from our environment that the source of our suffering and any potential solutions are outside of us. My client believed that the problem originated in her physical appearance, in what she said or had not said, did or failed to do. She even thought this pattern was related to her financial and social status.

In crystal healing, we understand that the origin and solutions of our problems are within us. We constantly draw these circumstances into our lives because they resonate with the unconscious contents inside us. Until we become aware of these contents and consciously work on them to free ourselves, we will not be able to change the resonance. Without changing our resonance, we will magnetize the same situations over and over again and experience a very limited version of our lives.

The mixture of ancestral wisdom and the properties of crystals discovered by science make crystal healing an excellent holistic method for changing our inner resonance. We just have to dig inside and find the pathway through crystals' symbols, energy, and resonance. The unique properties of crystals guide our consciousness throughout the different layers of our inner universe to the first piece of our psychological puzzle. In my client's case, this was the piece that generated the rejection pattern.

During a crystal session, once we recognize the origin of the pattern, we can choose to take conscious action in order to deactivate the learned pattern and generate new resonance. First, I take my clients through an intake process in order to get a sense of what is going on with them unconsciously and energetically, and to also begin creating energetic resonance with their personal healing process and stones during that session. Before the first session, I have the clients fill out a form to inquire about their upbringing and childhood, relationships, beliefs, and mind-set. Then, during this first session, the information is complemented by an astrology reading. For me, the astrological chart resembles a clinical history through which I can review the unconscious origin of obstacles that disable the full expression of the authentic self. The chart also helps me identify the client's authentic gifts. Sometimes, when extra guidance is needed, I have the client choose one or two crystals that I symbolically read using my intuition and experience. The crystals chosen are symbols that mirror unconscious patterns or the parts of yourself that need healing.

I then encourage the clients to tune in to their authentic energy—that which is without mind—before selecting the stones to work with. I ask them to focus on the present, and I invite them to draw a deep breath and choose different crystals—the ones to which they feel most connected in the moment.

Resonance drags us to our most sympathetic vibration. While our rational minds cannot discern the exact frequency of a given quartz crystal, we are naturally drawn to the crystal with the particular frequency and characteristics that are necessary to balance our own frequency so that it resonates with our authentic selves. Through resonance, the energetic exchange between the client and crystals is initiated.

My client Lisa chose those crystals that energetically and symbolically resonated with her unconscious. Among many crystals, she chose tangerine quartz, amethyst, rose quartz, and citrine. She arranged the stones in a chaotic pattern on the floor. Then she placed the rose quartz over her heart, the tangerine quartz and citrine on her head, and amethyst under her feet. The rose quartz was larger than the other stones; the amethyst was the thinnest and smallest.

From a symbolic perspective, this crystal selection can have multiple meanings. Amethyst is purple (the combination of red and blue), rose quartz is pink (the combination of red and white), tangerine is orange (the combination of yellow and red), and citrine is yellow. There was an excess of yellow and red in Lisa's selections, as well as a lack of brown, blue, and white. For the ancients, red symbolized suffering. From the neuroscience perspective, red can stimulate the amygdala response. From a physics perspective, red is the color with the longest wavelength and least energy on the spectrum of visible light.

This stone selection reflected that Lisa was ready to change her world.

The first crystal usually tells me about the purpose of the healing. On other occasions, the repetition of a certain crystal, color, size, or shape can also show me the purpose. In her case, her first selection and largest crystal was rose quartz. To me, this indicated the need to connect with unconditional love, but it also revealed her lack of self-esteem and that her wound was related to her relationships.

The tangerine quartz and citrine revealed the source of the original wound: her mother and father. But they also showed me her dominant emotions and mind-set: fear and anger.

Amethyst at her feet was indicating the path and outcome: transforming her world by transforming her mind-set.

Lisa needed to heal and transcend the unconscious learned models acquired from her mother and father in order to transform her world and connect with unconditional love.

The way crystals are arranged during a crystal energy session also has a symbolic meaning. For me, my client's chaotic placement of stones over the floor reflected the pattern of her inner chaos.

Although I am observing all these facets during a session, I never share what I feel is the true purpose of a client's healing until the end of the crystal session, so as to avoid manipulating the crystal healing process or predisposing the client to specific ideas.

At this stage of the healing, I complement the crystals chosen by my clients with others that I intuitively sense are appropriate. I usually create crystal grids on and around the client, as circuits through which the energy can flow. We are parts of a greater whole, so crystal grids can help us to reestablish resonance with the energy of the whole.

I compare working with crystals to throwing stones in a pond. When you throw different stones, each one will generate waves of different sizes. Some will also move faster, while others will move more slowly. The crystals my client selected were producing multiple wave patterns at an energetic level without her conscious awareness. The atoms of each crystal placed on and around her body were interacting with the atoms in the energy fields of her body and mind. The energy corresponding to the crystals vibrated with the maximum amplitude, while the energy corresponding to the mind vibrated with the lowest. As her atoms were absorbing the crystals' energy, her energy began to amplify and counteract the destructive interference originated in the energy of her unconscious learned information. Her mind's frequency slowly began to shift to a higher vibration, generating an expansive field that balanced her unconscious information. All of this created constructive interference, which reactivated the flow of energy within her energy system. Crystal resonance to those spaces where there is similar information—such as the pyramidal neurons in our brains that are related to our minds, but also the crystalline structures within our bodies—enables the interaction of energy fields and, thus, healing. For example, the rose quartz over Lisa's heart was resonating with the crystalline structures of her heart.

Crystal energy can also resonate with the pigments within our bodies, as well as their associated processes. The purple color of the amethyst, for example, is associated with melanopsin, a pigment sensitive to short wavelengths such as violet. This pigment plays a major role in synchronizing circadian rhythms and restoring the natural flow of energy within us. Red resonates with hemoglobin's physical energy, while yellow resonates with the kidneys and the liver, which are related to the detoxification of the body. Crystal energy also resonates with the highly stable tetrahedral structure of the vacuum of space—a resonance that works to restore our geometry and our balance and connection to the universal flow of energy.

Quartz crystal's inner structure resonates with the tetrahedron grid in the vacuum of space, helping to restore our mental and physical energetic field to its original blueprint. Photography: Stacey J. Byers, www.capturedspirit.net

As the energy of the client's body and mind, the energy of the healer's mind, and the light in the environment all strike the surface of the quartz crystals, the energy of both client and healer is amplified.

The rhythm of Lisa's breathing began to alter during this process, and she started to share what appeared to be memories from her past: "I feel nervous . . . but I don't know why . . . I am feeling stressed, not loved, as if someone is rejecting me . . ." As the session progressed, she realized that she was experiencing the toxic and complex thoughts and emotions her mother had experienced while my client was still in her womb.

Although Lisa was aware of her parents' struggles, she only discovered in this session that her mother had unexpectedly become pregnant with her and was upset because she was not happy in her relationship with Lisa's father. As a result, Lisa felt more rejected than welcomed by the world. What she didn't know was that everything that she had experienced inside her mother's womb would become a pattern that she would attract through resonance and relive through all her relationships.

Quartz crystals can bring all these memories to the surface during a crystal energy session by virtue of the property of nonlocality, which renders the presence of an event in a specific space or time illusory. Thus, although Lisa might not have been physically near her mother and not literally inside her mother's womb, crystal healing altered this perception of separation so that the experience felt as if it were happening in real time. In this way, crystal healing enables the traumatic experiences of our past to be resolved in the present moment. That is why, during your healing, you can access the past but also create your future. You can make a choice in the present that sends ripple effects into the past and future.

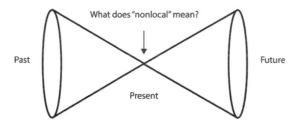

During a crystal healing, nonlocal energy properties can heal the past—repatterning all that is off balance to create the future in the present.

Becoming aware of the source of her problem brought great sadness and tears to Lisa. But the inner vibratory oscillations of crystals are regular and precise. They organize the discordant vibrations and feelings that arise during the crystal session—restoring balance to everything that is off balance. At a quantum level, the crystal's electrical charges are passed on to neighboring atoms through the inner structure of the quartz's tetrahedral grid, and energy is transmitted through expansive waves from the quartz into her energy field. This is what unblocks stagnant energy and brings about transformation.

While this is happening, it is sending literal chain reactions to all the energy fields, reorganizing the information on an atomic level. Lisa told me that she felt warmth in her heart. She had the experience of her heart becoming lighter and more transparent. Then, suddenly, she felt energy entering her feet, as if she were connecting with the earth and, thus, more deeply with herself.

Her transformation included a shift in her perception. Over the session, Lisa's sadness dissipated and was replaced by a deep sense of peace and clarity. She came to the realization that her relationships in one way or another were reflections of her original wound. Since coming into this world, she had been viewing her life through a perspective of rejection. Not only had she rejected herself, but this was also reflected in her self-esteem problems and her perception of being rejected by those around her. She felt rejected by her mother but also by men, in the same way that her mother had rejected her father while Lisa was still in the womb.

Our energetic resonance unconsciously attracts to our lives both events and people. This means that when we relate to other people, we're not merely selecting who we think they are on a conscious level; we are also attracting them unconsciously through resonance with the inner contents of our minds. The same goes for them; they are attracted to us because they also resonate with our inner programming. Thus, our partners could be the unconscious models of our mothers or fathers—and thus, they might resonate with our deepest wounds. Unfortunately, when we are not conscious, we can re-create this again and again until we consciously work on and transcend it.

I ended the crystal session by removing the stones, guiding Lisa to ground, and going through the takeaways before closing the session. We discussed the breakthroughs and messages from the crystal healing session. I asked her a number of questions: What did she become aware of during her session? What patterns did she recognize she was repeating from others? What patterns had she chosen to consciously change? Next, we created a follow-up plan to initiate a self-awareness and exploration process working with crystals, crystal water, affirmations, meditation, breathing, and awareness practices, among many others. Finally, we scheduled the next crystal healing session based on her desire to move forward with me.

After the session, Lisa felt a deep connection with the rose quartz and decided that she wanted to keep working with it to develop the habit of self-love. If she could love herself, she knew she could attract people who would also love her instead of rejecting her.

This was merely one of many crystal energy sessions in her process of self-discovery and transformation to become her authentic self. During this process, she eventually shared her healing story with her mother, at which point her mother revealed something to her that she hadn't previously known.

Lisa's grandmother, Martha, had adopted her mother early in her life. Lisa's mother's biological parents were both college students who had been renting a room at Martha's house; one day, they asked Martha to take care of their baby until they were able to make some money. They never returned. Lisa came to realize that her mother had similarly been rejected by her own parents and was unconsciously repeating the same pattern with her. This breakthrough led to other breakthroughs and a broader understanding along the path of finding her true self. Through the compassion she felt for her mother, she ended up healing her own wounds. This allowed her to find love in her heart for her mother, for men, for people in general—and ultimately for her true self. Rejection and judgment had transformed into compassion and love.

To this day, Lisa credits the quartz crystals for helping her see and embrace the information that had triggered her current situation. The crystals allowed her to better understand her true self, move toward transformation, and bring stability into her life.

With each healing, a client is no longer resonating with patterns that don't serve them. They are coming closer to releasing themselves from the core beliefs that established the original unbalanced pattern.

Our beliefs and attitudes are distributed as layers within our unconscious minds. Through our personal development and crystal healing, we work through each layer so we can heal it and get to our core. Some of us have already been doing our internal work before coming to crystal healing, so we don't have as many layers to peel away—but others are just beginning.

During the process of peeling back the layers, you will be able to recognize others' beliefs and where they originated, and if you choose, you will release them. Eventually, this process will lead you to the deepest part of the self—your authentic self.

What You Might Experience during a Crystal Healing Session

We cannot generalize the effects of each crystal because each human being is different and reacts differently. What you experience could be similar but never the same as what someone else might experience, as crystals honor your authentic energy.

Every client's experience during a crystal healing session is unique and singular. Some relate the experience of floating; others travel to distant places in space, as well as to periods of their distant past; others experience energy as colorful patterns and shapes; still others might experience energy circulating throughout the body.

Crystals communicate through vibrations and symbols. It is common for clients to see these vibrations and symbols as colors, visions, or sounds. They might remember painful experiences with clarity—or experience physical pain where their specific energy blockage is, followed by ease. A host of physical sensations might ensue—ranging from the feeling of warmth and tingling throughout the body to a feeling of becoming very light. People might also experience fluctuations in temperature. Heat indicates that energy is entering the body, and cold means that energy is being released. Some might also experience dizziness or weakness. Some people may feel very energized, and some may feel very tired, as if they have been running for hours. When working with crystals, we are literally mobilizing energy. It is important to understand that the sensation is temporary while our bodies adjust to the new frequency.

Also remember that working with crystals facilitates the process of releasing strong or repressed emotions. Emotional catharsis can be expected during a crystal session, as crystals' properties allow emotions associated with old traumatic events to come to the surface. Clients can experience both extremes during a crystal healing session: a great deal of emotional pain, followed by peace. Many people even fall asleep during a session, and still others think that they haven't experienced anything at all. But what most people feel is that something has changed, although they may not know what. During a session, healing is always experienced on some level, either conscious or unconscious.

Our tangible experience doesn't matter, though, as crystals respond to resonance—and their energy will go wherever we need healing. For this reason, people who aren't open to crystal healing can still experience its multiple benefits. This is because, beyond our mind-sets, crystal works with authentic energy. Unconsciously, we are all authentic on some level.

By resonance, crystal's energy can reach the most unlikely places. Fundamentally, we are all pure energy. Although our learned beliefs may cause us to perceive crystals as mere inanimate objects, the universe runs through all of us without exception. Crystals can awaken that resonance within each of us, regardless of what we consciously believe.

How Crystals Can Heal and Prevent Disease

Ancients believed that all diseases could be prevented and healed from within, by removing the original wound from which suffering and disease stem. When we are healthy, all our body parts and associated fields are in tune and vibrating in harmony with our authentic nature. When we are ill, our bodies are communicating that we are out of sync through the language of their frequency. When we are off balance, this requires our immediate attention. We have to work it out and heal it before it develops into a major disease.

For example, sometimes people come to heal a stomachache, but this is actually related to the anger they have toward their fathers. We are not often consciously aware of the root cause, which is what we really need to heal.

The kidneys are organs that filter waste from our blood, balance our body fluids, and aid in other crucial functions. In the emotional dimension, the kidneys are in a state of harmony when we don't react to the world with fear. However, when we do not trust others and are continually stressed—a behavior that might have originated in one of our parents—this disharmony can be reflected in the kidney's energy field and later as a disease in this organ when not worked on internally.

According to Chinese medicine, the kidneys are especially vulnerable to damage from excessive stress. Emotional disharmony creates a contractive vibrational state that tangles and eventually decreases the flow of the energy field, gradually affecting the physical health of the body. Since everything is in continuous connection and movement, this disharmonious condition permeates the entire being. Some energy backs up, some energy stagnates, and other energy heats up, creating all sorts of imbalances.

Fears that establish themselves in youth may not manifest as a specific physical condition until later in life. Yet, during the span of life, the health issues that arise will have some connection to this ongoing internal disharmony.

If illness is a manifestation of suffering, then naturally, crystals can help bring stability to those struggling with chronic or acute disease. Energy can be measured in frequencies, and our bodies have a certain frequency when healthy (typically, 62 to 72 MHz) and a different frequency when sick (58 MHz and lower).[2] Through resonance, we choose crystals with the exact frequency we need to heal symptoms in our bodies. Crystal energy behaves in a similar way as sonar, naturally directing its balancing vibrations toward the organ or part of the body that requires healing—raising or reducing its frequency until the body has reached equilibrium.

It may seem strange to think about health in terms of symbols and frequencies. But it is a very useful tool, both for determining the degree of one's health or illness and also for knowing how we can encourage particular responses in the body.

Two of my clients were siblings who both had thyroid problems. They came to me requesting a crystal energy healing session, but neither of them was aware that I was treating the other brother. One needed thyroid surgery, while the other had just been diagnosed with the disease. During their crystal energy sessions, both chose different stones and arrived separately at the root cause of their illness. The root cause for both siblings, who were adults and lived in different places at the time, was the same: the murder of their mother and their inability to deal with and express their feelings about it when they were still young. After a few crystal energy sessions, both experienced complete remission.

While quartz crystals should never be used in place of medicine or other prescribed remedies, they can contribute enormously to our ongoing health and wellness. Crystals are effective ways of shifting our flow of energy, as well as raising or lowering our frequencies to an optimal level so that our entire system can be brought into balance.

What to Expect after Working with Crystals

Archaic rites of initiation were known to be part of ancient cultures. According to scholar and anthropologist Mircea Eliade, symbolic death represents change for the entire psyche and life of a person.[3] It signals both internal and external change, not a simple adaptation or switch in lifestyle. Initiation includes death and rebirth, a radical altering of a person's "mode of being," a shattering and shaking all the way to the core of the soul. The initiate becomes a brand-new person: more emotionally mature and spiritually aware than before.

Crystals can similarly invoke initiation into new ways of life. Remember that our reality is the repetition of the contents of our unconscious minds. Through crystal healing, we use crystals as tools for emptying these contents.

Typically, our minds are set in a fixed mode that doesn't respond or allow new information in. Our minds will reject anything that differs from their original contents through different protective mechanisms—the first one being resistance. When we resist information, it is surely counteracting some content in our minds' programming.

Fear is another resource that uses the mind to keep us stuck in our old programming. Who has not experienced fear of new experiences? In reality, we do not experience fear of the unknown but rather fear of releasing the old learned information from our minds.

Sadness is another mind-gripping psychological device. Sadness is the preparation of the mind to release the old and accept the new. If you realize that you are sad, you refer to a past situation with nostalgia. But what sadness is really announcing to us is the transition between the old and the new.

With commitment and continued inner work, we can use crystals as tools to free our minds from their contents—which is seldom a comfortable process.

One way to recognize that our unconscious has moved through some major shifts is by noticing sudden changes in our reality. When the mind—the storage center of all the contents of our learned programming—is emptied, our lives go into a kind of reset mode. The new void that has opened in our minds is reflected in our exterior circumstances. It literally feels like being suspended in space—between past and future, between our false selves and our authentic being. This void is what saints and scholars have referred to as the "dark night of the soul," a period of personal paralysis in which nothing seems to work and the old structures of one's life have died. Eckhart Tolle refers to this as the collapse of a perceived meaning.[4] Nothing makes sense anymore because we no longer resonate with the contents of our minds.

As painful as it can be, loss of identity is essential to rites of passage and our evolution as human beings. People and situations leave our lives because they don't resonate with us anymore. In this process, everything might feel as if it is falling apart; we can lose our partners, our jobs, our children, our health, and even our culture and nationality. This is what happened to me.

Interestingly, from the perspective of physics, suffering can also be seen as the vacuum of space—energy without movement, which corresponds to the state of suspension we may experience. Our society teaches us to evade suffering at all costs, but the transition provided by suffering might be serving another purpose: co-creating our new authentic reality.

Suffering can be seen as a process of transition between old and new. Crystals may ease and catalyze that transition process, releasing blocks in our minds so that we can reconnect with the authentic self and resonate with new, healthier experiences.

Many years ago, when I began this journey, I took my commitment to working with crystals seriously. Having released my learned unconscious information, my life literally disappeared in front of my eyes. Everything that happened after losing my life in Colombia reflected in one way or another what was going on inside of me. There were many attempts, without success, to continue the regular course of my life. I eventually had to surrender and realize that this was a time to simply be with myself. Today I can recognize that something was gestating inside of me. It was certainly a moment of transition between what was and what would be my life from this moment forward.

Co-Creating Our Authentic Reality

If we think of our lives as a car, most of us don't know who's driving the car or where we're being taken. How can we expect to arrive at our ideal destination if many faceless drivers have assumed control of the car without even asking us where we want to go? Even worse, if we had to decide where to go, most of us wouldn't even be able to identify our desired destination.

Inner work enables us to recognize who is driving our car. It helps us to take the driver's seat, set our own course, and take responsibility for our own lives.

Whether conscious or unconscious, the observer effect (which we covered in Chapter 5) converts waveforms to matter and plays an important role in the process of co-creating our authentic reality. The more authentic the content of our unconscious, the more it will resonate and become our reality; thus the importance of releasing the false contents of the mind.

During a crystal energy session, we are working at a quantum level, and our conscious actions are needed in order to support and materialize the process we've experienced during the healing. The crystal healing process is continuous work that does not end with the crystal session. It is necessary to reinforce the process of healing after the session in order to integrate the new information in the unconscious mind, which helps us build resonance with a new reality.

Many people report that writing has an impact on their thought processes and even how they view their situation. Writing about what you experienced, as well as your feelings and thoughts about it, can help you gain clarity and evolve. Write just for yourself. Simply go wherever your mind takes you without judgment. By doing this, you begin the process of stepping out of the old you.

When you write routinely, you are firing your neurons and helping to change learned habits. Writing requires processing in the higher brain, which is in the left hemisphere of the brain, an area where many of our verbal, sequential, and symbolic processes take place. When we write about our experiences with crystals, we become more conscious in our healing process; we're actually bringing the unconscious to our conscious reality. Journaling also tracks our evolution as we move toward our authentic selves.

In order to change our resonance, aside from emptying the contents of our minds, we have to ensure that the old mind programming is completely disabled and does not recur. We also have to neutralize the negative bias of our minds so that we are not polluted again with false information. We must work to reinforce the activation and installation of the new authentic programming. This process doesn't occur overnight and requires our commitment, consistency, and relentless discipline.

Live Fully Conscious

Both the conscious and unconscious minds have critical roles to play in the equilibrium of the total self. Our lives and all their strains are the result of the stress between the lives we live outwardly and our authentic selves—which remain unconscious to us.

Most of us are so preoccupied in our lives that we don't approach our unconscious voluntarily, only when we are in distress. When we approach the unconscious through *fully conscious* choice, however, we begin to live in partnership with the unconscious rather than at its mercy or in constant warfare with it. We learn to abide by our authentic blueprint.

When we address where we are getting hooked through conscious awareness, we can unlock hidden unconscious realities that have the potential to lead us from unhappiness to healing and sustained well-being.

If we compare our lives with a mathematical equation, we will recognize that the "I am" is missing. We resonate with collective learning, paradigms, and beliefs—everything we unconsciously learned from everything and everyone else except our true selves.

The first change necessary to begin our path of self-discovery is to learn to live fully *conscious*. This means that we are living in the present and choosing to be fully conscious of each of our thoughts, and of each of our responses to these thoughts. We are aware of our actions—as well as their true origin, source, and intentions.

From this state of consciousness, we are able to make responsible choices that bring us closer to who we really are. We are able to discern false information, which is really about learning how to manage information in order to include ourselves in our life equation.

It's important to be conscious and track down all that is inauthentic in our lives. One of the ways of doing so is by consciously questioning everything that we come across. Questioning is an art that can be developed over time and that can help us discern and choose which information we will allow inside our unconscious minds—that is, the information with which we will consciously resonate.

Ask yourself: *Who am I beyond my learned beliefs? At what point in my life's story did I stop being myself in order to adopt the interests and beliefs of others? Am I this information? Is this information true to me? Who am I, really?*

During this process, it is important to become aware of where your answers come from: your learned false programming or your authentic self.

The second way of discerning your false self from your authentic self is by filtering information. This is about being constantly vigilant and recognizing the true sources of our current thoughts or of the information we receive so that we are consciously choosing what we allow into our unconscious.

Here, I share an exercise that will help you recognize the patterns you have learned from others. I call it the "drawer exercise." Imagine that you are in front of a cabinet with many drawers and that you can assign to each drawer a label—one that says "Mom," another that says "Dad," and another specifying your gender. One will bear the name of the philosophy or religion you practice: Christianity, Judaism, Islam, Buddhism, and so on. To another, you'll assign the name of the country where you were raised—the United States, India, Colombia, or Saudi Arabia, for example. You will label another drawer "environment," and it will include all those who have influenced you in your immediate environment (aunts and uncles, cousins, neighbors, teachers, bosses or co-workers, and so many more). Still another will say "media," and this is where you'll place all the information you received from the Internet, social media, television, magazines, and news outlets. And finally, you'll have a label that bears your name.

The idea is to bring that imaginary set of drawers with you during your day and bring to your awareness the source from which your thoughts and actions arise. You will also become aware of how many thoughts and beliefs are authentically *yours*. When you recognize who you aren't, you can recognize who you really are. Wearing crystals while doing this can magnify your ability to discern information.

In this way, when I see myself being prompted to do something that doesn't feel authentic, I can recognize that it doesn't belong to me, that I learned it from another person. Finally, I can release it. I can reconfigure the contents of my mind to open to the path of who I truly am.

We need an empty canvas to resonate with the best version of ourselves and our reality. In order to understand the way resonance works, we must understand that everything is a pattern. Moreover, we are pattern-recognizing and pattern-forming creatures. By unconsciously succumbing to the habits, beliefs, and thoughts of others, we set a repeating response pattern that, over time, becomes a rigid habit that does not support answers or points of views different from those that already known to us. We can spot these because they are predictable behaviors that are generated by specific experiences and stimuli.

Did you know that by transcending the limitations of your false programming repeatedly, you can deactivate old programs but also incorporate new ones in your unconscious mind? Information repetition is required to codify any pattern, and we can influence our unconscious in positive ways by consciously choosing to repeat specific patterns. The unconscious repetition of behaviors and routines strengthens neural pathways in our brains. When we are able to recognize our unconscious behaviors and consciously choose to change a learned pattern on a regular basis through conscious actions, we are able to debilitate this neural pathway and deactivate this pattern in our unconscious minds.

Alcoholism is a mind pattern that originates in the repetition of treating alcohol as a solution for anxiety. Depression arises from repetitive thoughts of sadness; obesity, from repetitive thoughts of food; and obsession, from repetitive thoughts on specific topics.

When we are aware of our internal patterns, where they originate, and what triggers them, we can consciously seek an antidote. And by antidote, I refer to something that only *you* know will disassemble the pattern—a piece of knowledge that inquiry with the use of crystals can uncover. It is important to repeat the antidote each time we identify the pattern.

Another client, Dan, came to me to work on his anger. During the crystal healing session, he realized that he had unconsciously learned to overreact in the same way his father did when things didn't go his way, as a mechanism to perpetuate control. He recognized that, just like his father's, his own episodes of anger were associated with power games. At this point, he could take conscious action to disassemble the pattern. Because he associated the healing process with crystals—specifically, clear quartz—crystal became an anchor for him. In neuro-linguistic programming (NLP), an anchor helps us to connect an inner response to either an external or internal trigger. When we experience the trigger, we can quickly access the desired response. In the same way, crystals during a healing session can become a link or antidote that disconnects us from old, unconscious programs and responses and activates new, conscious ones.

The general consensus of how long it takes the unconscious mind to integrate new thoughts or beliefs is around 21 days. After which, the information that is repeated continuously is integrated into our unconscious mind programming. We can replace negative habits with positive ones, such as music, writing, painting, spirituality, etc. The negative bias of our brains can also be neutralized with conscious actions such as positive affirmations and visualizations.

Of course, crystals can reinforce this entire process. Whenever you want to reinforce a positive behavior, you can visualize quartz energy in the frontal cortex of your brain or lie down and place a crystal on top of your forehead.

Given the deeply unconscious nature of many of our minds' patterns, JaneAnn Dow offers the following caveat about positive thinking: "I realized that if you can change your thought or image of an issue, you can change the issue itself. The problem with positive thinking, however, is that we rarely know what the issue really is. It is one thing to sit around and think beautiful thoughts but quite another to seek out the thoughtforms in the mental body [a.k.a the unconscious mind] that are manifesting as what I like to call challenges. Positive thinking, in the way most people practice it today, is a form of denial that can actually do more harm than good, because the source of the initial problem is still registered in the light system that constantly feeds into our consciousness."[5]

Thus, positive affirmations are simply not sufficient. In order to rewire ourselves and extricate ourselves from the unconscious mind patterns that have taken hold in our lives, we must make small but consistent changes to our daily patterns and routines. This can include taking a different route on the drive home, placing ourselves in other people's shoes, and rethinking our accepted paradigms altogether. This can prevent our minds from becoming fixed and help incorporate new information that will eventually change our resonance and reality.

Crystal Water, Essences, and Jewelry

Crystal water, essences, and jewelry are other ways to continue the healing process after a crystal session and incorporate information to change our resonance.

Quartz (SiO_2) and water (H_2O) have similar tetrahedral geometries that resonate with the energies of our minds and bodies. Due to the molecular structure and geometric resonance it shares with quartz, water has the capacity to store and transfer the information held in a quartz crystal.

Alkaline water together with quartz crystal works like a battery charging the water with equal number of protons and neutrons. This balanced charge translates within us as body and mind balance.

The process of creating crystal water is simple:

1. Wash the crystal with alkaline water.
2. Place the crystal inside a glass container with alkaline water.
3. Tune in.
4. With your eyes closed, imagine the water being dyed by the crystal coloration. Hold that vision for one minute.
5. Place the glass container in a quiet place where it can receive some natural sunlight. Allow it to settle for 12 hours.
6. You can now drink the water.
7. Repeat this procedure every time you need more crystal water.

If you are new to crystal healing, I recommend working with a single crystal in the water. Each crystal represents a different energy pattern and frequency. Among all the patterns, choose the one that you want to work through the most. In order for the water to have an effect, you should drink it for at least 21 days.

You can also prepare crystal essences. Crystal water and essences are basically the same, as crystals share their energy field of information with water. The difference is in the process of preparation. Crystal essences include alcohol, which help to preserve the properties and essence of the stone. The preparation of essences requires a specialized protocol performed by an expert.

According to Leo McFee, an expert in crystal essences, when creating an essence, it's not necessary to physically crush the stone. The frequency of the stone, when placed in water, is transmitted to the water. You then simply use the water.

Quartz crystals are nontoxic materials with no known adverse health effects from drinking water in which they've been infused. Nevertheless, it is important to take into consideration that some crystals may contain poisonous mineral traces, so we must always do our own meticulous research into the crystals' contents to avoid any harm. For example, blue quartz (dumortierite) contains aluminum. Additionally, some crystals have been exposed to radiation—including certain forms of smoky quartz and citrine. Please make sure that the crystals used in your crystal water or essence have not been exposed to any type of radiation.

Crystal water and essences are great aids to reinforce our crystal healing, as they can incorporate the frequencies of the crystals used during a session. We can also achieve this same resonance by wearing the stones that were used during a session. Crystals will amplify and continue transforming your energy when worn directly over the skin. The crystal receives a continuous charge from the heat expelled by the body. This keeps its electrons in an endless state of excitement— amplifying, transforming, and balancing energy within and outside us.

The recommended place to wear crystals is over the physical heart, as science has shown that the heart possesses not only the largest electromagnetic field in the body but also crystalline structures that resonate with crystals. A tetrahedron-shaped crystal will also increase its resonance.

But remember, this is about *you*. Tune in and feel what shape you resonate with to continue your healing process. And no matter what, remember that the crystal clearing we talked about in Chapter 8 (page 191) is necessary before wearing any stone—even in jewelry.

It's important to pursue the experience of working with crystals: meditating with crystals, holding a crystal, drinking crystal water, wearing crystals . . . whatever feels authentic to you. As you work on yourself and you start to peel away your unconscious layers, you will feel the change.

The beauty of all that we are learning is that we can choose to change our patterns consciously. We can prevent them from repeating in our lives by working on ourselves on an ongoing basis.

The Power of Crystal Healing

Ancient wisdom tells us that true healing doesn't come from rejecting or fighting with our thoughts and emotions—rather, it comes from acknowledging and learning from our experiences, and embracing them.

Crystals provide the energetic support necessary for the full healing process. Over time, as you clear your learned patterns and heal by working with the stones, you receive a less personal and more macrocosmic understanding of your relationships—with others, the world, and yourself.

Katrina Raphaell has said, "This conscious reprogramming process is one of the most powerful tools towards self-change and personal empowerment."[6]

While working with crystals, you may experience "aha" moments and many synchronicities that will lead toward your true path. The advantage of working internally with these tools is that they can magnify and accelerate processes that would normally only occur over long periods of time. This is because we are working with root causes. In crystal work, a bridge is formed between the problem and the source of the problem. When this bridge is identified, it is then the responsibility of the individual receiving the healing to let go of the old and receive the new energy, using it to re-create their authentic identity.

JaneAnn Dow has written: "By using crystals to access the initial trauma, we can alter the perspective of the thoughtform and the problem is then transformed from a shadow or glitch in the system into a point of light. When I watch the light body of a client at the moment of transformation, all of the patterning shifts as if to indicate that the entire light body has been altered by the resolution of this one thoughtform. The more shadows that we can transform in ourselves, the more we can let go of our density and become light."[7]

Crystal healing begins in your mind and ends in your manifest reality. You need to commit on a daily basis to making this change in yourself over time.

As this final chapter of the book has shown you, in choosing to heal your patterns and reconnect with your authentic self, you are not only able to see the great picture of your personal story and the part that each piece played on your path to reconnection; you also recognize that you have the power to transform the meaning of these pieces.

As we change the meaning of our learned models and place our experiences of suffering in the context of our growth and healing, we are able to exchange those paradigms for authentic ones. At a subatomic level, our crystal blueprint creates a chain reaction not only in our own energy field but also in our surrounding energy fields, taking our transformation into our world. In the words of the Indian sage Jiddu Krishnamurti, "What you are, the world is. And without your transformation, there can be no transformation of the world."[8]

CONCLUSION

Creating a Crystalline World

"Forming in perfect geometric shapes, crystals remind us that our earth demonstrates the laws of unity. And so, like the atoms of a crystal, we can all align and work together to create a unified humanity."

— KATRINA RAPHAELL[1]

WE ARE A LARGE COMMUNITY of boundless energetic beings that are all connected. Science has shown that the world we perceive with our five senses is an illusion created by our brains and that, in fact, we are all interconnected energy fields. These include the physically measurable electromagnetic fields generated by all living cells, tissues, and organs; our minds' unconscious contents; and apparently inert objects like crystals.

In this invisible world of energy, we are continuously affecting the whole and the whole is affecting us, even if we are not aware of it.

But if we all are interconnected, why we are not reflecting this in our common reality and world?

As you have learned throughout this book, the thing that prevents us from experiencing our connection is our identification with our learned beliefs. Additionally, to make sense of all the data we receive from the world, the mind has the tendency to automatically define, classify, divide, and separate according to our unconscious learned beliefs and paradigms. From this perspective, I am a human being, that is a dog, and that is a crystal. This is the United States, and that is Russia. They are Muslims, and they are Christians. They are white, and they are black, and so on.

We have learned to identify with the world of matter instead of energy, and discard everything invisible to the human eye. But our times are changing and, with them, our paradigms.

When we are unaware of the invisible, interconnected world and we identify with matter and our mind programming, it is natural for us to *think* that we live in a disconnected world where everything is separate. When we set our inner dial to separation by the law of resonance, this is what we will attract—not only individually but also collectively. The mind's inner contents reflect our reality, and our reality mirrors not merely the contents of our individual minds but also those of the collective mind. Wars, conflicts, and segregation are examples of this.

Our lives expose us to a broad scope of experiences that act as mirrors, helping us to gain feedback and become aware of what lies hidden within us so that we can heal ourselves, recognize our true potential, and create our best reality. But individual experiences are not the only ones that help us reflect and integrate learning; collective experiences also help raise awareness, as they are the aggregate of all individual learned unconscious beliefs. Just like personal crises, global crises are a call to all of us to heal our unconscious on a collective level.

Often, when people are drawn to destructive behaviors, they are acting from the learned belief in separation that is taken in habitually from their surroundings without full awareness or consent—and they then operate automatically on this belief. The problem with situations of conflict that we encounter both within and without is that we are constantly re-creating them because they remain in the learned mind programming of the collective unconscious; in this way, they create an endless cycle of conflict.

So, how can we end this cycle and bring lasting peace and well-being to humanity?

The answer lies in each of us.

Are you aware that others have created the reality you are living? Are you aware of your own unconscious conditioning? That you unconsciously follow, copy, and repeat the beliefs and behaviors of others without questioning if they are true or resonate with your authentic self?

Indian philosopher Jiddu Krishnamurti points out that "the primary cause of disorder in ourselves is the seeking of reality promised by another."[2] By unconsciously allowing others' contents into your mind, you are allowing others to create not only your reality but also the conflicts in your life.

From our leaders to each one of us, our planet is driven by the unconscious programming learned from our predecessors in family, community, culture, citizenry, politics, religion, health, work, and so on. We keep accepting, imitating, and repeating the old, where violence and conflict are solutions to change our reality. However, real change is generated not from the outside but from the inside. Imagine, if we all could live our authentic truth, how the world would benefit from each one of us committing to developing a crystalline world.

Instead of our limited learned beliefs, our choices must come from our wholeness and deepest truths in the light of who we really are. Crystals' transparent nature can help us reconnect and resonate with the transparency of our boundless, invisible, energetic world. They can awake us from the separation mind-set, numbness, and oblivious state in which our unconscious mind programming has kept us. They can usher us into a recognition of our greater reality, where we are all interconnected and make conscious and responsible choices in the best interests of the whole.

Creating a Crystalline World

Currently, 7.5 billion people inhabit our planet, and by the time you read these lines, there will be even more. How can we pretend that we all see the world in the same way if each of us, through our unconscious learning, naturally sees it differently? Our reality is shaped according to the lens of the nuclear families in which we were born or raised, our cultures or countries of origin, our religions or philosophies of life, our genders, the people we spend time with, our teachers or learning models, the media, and now the Internet, which allows us to access information instantly from anywhere in the world—and thus transform the very borders of our minds.

Crystals remind us that although we can be different on the outside, and come in different forms and shapes, our essence remains untouchable.

Working with crystals, we can consciously transcend the beliefs and borders of our minds to reconnect with the crystalline within us and gain a more integrated vision of the world. Crystals are the archetype of the crystalline parts inside us. They are "transparent" and symbolize the emptiness of learned false information in our minds. They symbolize the purity of our authentic selves. Working with crystals as tools of transformation can help us resonate with the crystalline and release false information. When you are crystalline from the inside out, you are able to see and connect with your true potential and gifts and share them with the world.

Evolution doesn't stop with our genetic codes; we can upgrade ourselves through new perceptions. Working with crystals continuously, we can create new positive habits that will lead to lasting changes and well-being.

We have all inherited the stories of our ancestors and our family lineage. Now, I invite you to revise the story of your mother and the story of your father, as well as the ones who came before them. You will come to recognize that you are unconsciously repeating parts of their story and maybe parts of your ancestors' stories. With crystals, we can break the chain of information that has been unconsciously transmitted from generation to generation. We can finally clear out information from past generations, and also from future ones.

When quartz's amplifying properties are used over the physical heart, the organ with the largest electromagnetic field, crystal energy can generate constructive interference in one's energy field that can be detected several feet away from one's body and transferred to people that are in proximity. When we release false learned information, we generate resonance and constructive interference. War, suffering, and conflicts are originated in false beliefs and create destructive interference. Peace in the world is the sum of all energy fields generating constructive interference.

While working with crystals, we are balancing and transforming energy. Just as sound waves from the strings of an acoustic guitar

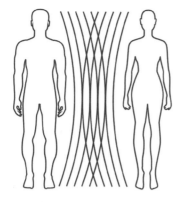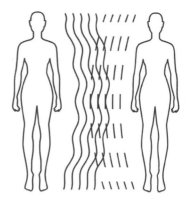

When two people are in harmony
they exhibit similar frequency pattern

When two people are in disharmony
they exhibit different frequency pattern

Energy resonance between people. Learned unconscious beliefs create destructive interference, while living in your authentic self creates constructive interference.

set surrounding energy into vibrational motion and create sound waves in other guitars, by working with crystals over our physical hearts, we can expand and share our balanced vibrations and bring transformation to our individual and collective surroundings.

Crystals work deep within us and reveal other alternatives for solving conflicts, or any other hostility that originates in the mind. It is no coincidence that crystals are being reintroduced to the mainstream; they are here to remind us of who we really are and to reconnect us with our wholeness.

We are crystals, but we have forgotten to shine. We have the same abilities that crystals have. We are light; we only have to remember it.

Becoming Crystalline

It is thought that the first human beings started to realize that they were fundamentally energy and that everything was interconnected about 2,500 years ago. This realization is what the ancients believed would lead to the end of suffering.

From here, we can understand how all suffering is based on the illusion of separation. Today, we know that we are trillions of self-contained atoms and interlocked energy fields. When separation occurs, we disconnect from the truth of who we are and from the crystalline part of the self—that original information that others have not influenced.

Our lack of transparency creates a world without true and authentic values; instead, we are ruled and limited by the sum of beliefs of the majority and are subsequently subjected to their chaos.

It may be hard to face, but we are each responsible for every war and conflict in our world until we commit to working internally on ourselves and de-cluttering all unconscious information that is not originally ours.

But what can a human being do to create a completely different world? First, we have to bring to our awareness that we are more than our limited individual and collective experiences and beliefs. We are more than our political, cultural, racial, religious, and gender differences.

It's important to become aware of our individual and collective unconscious. When we are able to transcend our false information, we become crystalline and come into resonance with our wholeness rather than our divided parts. In the words of Krishnamurti, "Forget all you know about yourself; forget all you have ever thought about yourself; we are going to start as if we knew nothing."[3]

Crystals help us to transform and to remember that we are energy. In order for the mind to become free, we must first realize that we have been conditioned and second commit to and take conscious action toward continuous inner work.

By studying our relationship to external things, situations, and people, as well as to our inner world, we are able to understand that which we are co-creating and attracting into our lives. External circumstances can mirror and offer feedback about our inner contents, and vice versa.

The inner self must be kept not in a static state but in a continuous flow. Spanish author Jaime Rodríguez Arana refers to this as "open, dynamic, and consistent thinking in an intellectual style that responds to the reality of things . . . opening on the horizon a space of thought that breaks left-right polarization and is characterized by its nature as open, critical, diversified, and anti-dogmatic, just the opposite, for example, of that civic education literally tailored to provide citizens cut from the pattern of submission, manipulation, and the fear of liberty."[4]

Questioning our beliefs and that which we've previously perceived as the foundation of our lives can feel like an earthquake; everything that once provided us with a semblance of stability begins to shake and crumble. Although this might feel chaotic, chaos is what can help us see the world from a new perspective, allow the flow of new ideas, expand our limited perception of the world, and create new resonance.

Nature is in constant flow and change. It follows that our thoughts, like everything in the universe, must evolve constantly. Spring gives way to summer, summer in turn to autumn, and autumn to winter. Day turns into night and night into day. Flowers become fruit and seed and then a new tree. The path is continuous, infinite, and constant—contrary to limiting beliefs, which are mostly finite and offer resistance to change.

When we offer resistance and keep ourselves closed, negative, unresponsive, distant, and intolerant of any new information, we will resonate with and attract closed systems that prevent us from progressing, transforming, and inducing a better reality.

When we change the way we observe and encode our reality, we are, in effect, changing it.

What would it be like for us to perceive a situation without the distortions of our minds? It can seem almost incomprehensible. Krishnamurti wrote, "For centuries we have been conditioned by nationality, caste, class, tradition, religion, language, education, literature, art, custom, convention, propaganda of all kinds, economic pressure, the food we eat, the climate we live in, our family, our friends, our experiences—every influence you can think of—and therefore our responses to every problem are conditioned . . . . We are disturbed about life, politics, the economic situation, the horror, the brutality, the sorrow in the world as well as in ourselves, and from that we realize how terribly narrowly conditioned we are."[5]

With so many contaminations, we have lost our capacity to see life as it is. Because of this, it is important to continuously remember to see the world as if we were seeing it for the first time—free of mental contents. In this way, we will be able to watch phenomena as they are without trying to shape them—never taking sides, never opposing or agreeing, never judging.

We live in an era of self-victimization. We prefer to point fingers at others and blame our life circumstances for our uncomfortable situations instead of taking responsibility. But when we are blaming others, we are projecting onto them what we need to work on in ourselves. It's time to take responsibility for our inner personal and collective work. By clearing the toxic contents of our minds, we are building the blocks of a crystalline world in which wholeness and lasting peace are possible.

It's important to remember that we remain connected to our true blueprint beyond our false learned information—even when it feels elusive. The authentic remains in us as an underlying force, which is why the "crack" generated by suffering can release it. When we release the mind's false programming, we awaken to who we really are—our crystalline selves. While the false programming creates a sense of being incomplete, the authentic self inspires, motivates, and brings about a sense of wholeness.

When we are complete within, this is also reflected without. The mind that has emptied itself of unwanted contents is like a crystal that can shine with its own light. Such a mind is in flow and no longer limited by beliefs. It is also in constant movement. There are times we stand still and times we move, times we hold on and times we let go, times we know and times we don't know. There is no right or wrong, just gateways we pass through as we grow and expand.

Awakening is a natural process of evolutionary growth. There is a feeling that we are being guided from within by our authentic voice. Through this awakening process, we will live through numerous experiences and transformations, and many of our realizations will be consolidated. During this process, we evolve from a state of dependency on external factors to a sense of fundamental responsibility for ourselves. We leave all we have learned behind to build meaning, fulfillment, and a sense of accomplishment and mastery.

This sense of awakening is not the same as enlightenment. It is an initial realization of a higher purpose that requires continual direction, support, and commitment.

We are moving from ignorance and confusion to a new reality where everything has a purpose for us. We might feel as if we are coming back to something that was already there, something that feels like home. In the same way the whole tree is inside a seed, our whole path—that which is authentic to us—is inside us. Awakening allows us to identify our authentic pattern or frequency, and how each of us plays our own unique melody and role as part of the collective and universal harmony.

Crystals: Frequency-Shifters

According to Jonathan Goldman, author of *Shifting Frequencies: Sounds for Vibratory Activation*, "A primary purpose for frequency-shifting involves expanding consciousness. We acknowledge the importance of aligning and balancing that which is out of alignment, but the frequency shift does not end there. It continues with the activation and expansion of the Individual's consciousness, which then often prompts him to alter his lifestyle and life's work. As the person's awareness is expanded he begins to understand his connection to others, to the planet and to all."[6]

The conditions that are present in our lives remain until we learn the lesson that is necessary to expand our consciousness and to transform our deeply encoded beliefs and patterns. The process of what Goldman calls "frequency-shifting" actually alters our internal vibrational pattern so that we can become more awakened, conscious, and authentic. This is precisely the kind of shift that crystals can effect within us—on a quantum level.

Shifting frequencies means being able to encode more light, being in balance with the implicate and explicate orders within us, and seeing ourselves as not only separate individuals but also entangled parts of the whole and co-creators of a new authentic reality. Such a life project can support us and promote our evolution and a process of self-expansion toward our true selves.

When we identify with the mind and stay asleep within our unconscious, life itself leads us down the path of pain. This is so that we can be re-sensitized to and eventually recognize our unconscious patterns, release them, and reconnect with our true selves.

But you also have the option to work internally—without pain as a prompt—to change your world into a more crystalline one.

When we willingly break through established structures and habitual ways of thinking, we can reach a higher level of consciousness. This means that we perceive everything differently, including whatever we experienced in the past. When our unconscious is crystalline, we are able to see and connect with the world in a different way. This creates the most ideal context to support and sustain any situation we are in.

Our crystallinity will express itself in many ways. The first, and perhaps most dramatic, is freedom from control and manipulation. When we become free of the mind and the illusion of separation, and begin to see the world completely from our authentic nature, our true essence will come to the surface. From this place, we will experience a sense of kinship with all beings on the planet; we will finally understand that our environment is not separate from us but is an extension of ourselves. Our priorities change because we actually see the entire world as our own self. We see the suffering of others as our own suffering. We come to recognize our essential interconnectedness, rather than differentiating or setting unconscious learned boundaries among ourselves on the basis of family, culture, geography, race, religion, or any other learned belief.

Thus, it is important to build a life project that is consistent with our authentic selves and designed to connect us with our true path rather than to take us away from it. We must shift our frequencies so that we can disassemble the conditions and beliefs that promote separation and seek instead all that integrates and unifies us as citizens of this planet.

This is the story of the Eleven Tears Memorial that resides in the American Express Building, across the street from Ground Zero. Following the tragedy of 9/11, the memorial was created to honor the American Express family members who died on that day. The centerpiece of the memorial is a giant crystal, serving as a resonance-shifter that is felt on many levels.

Crystal artist Lawrence Stoller created the crystal centerpiece of the sculpture. "Shortly after the tragedy of September 11, 2001, my wife, Sunni, and I pictured a giant crystal installed at 'Ground Zero.' We shared a vision of a monument that would bring badly needed light and healing to our country's collective wound."[7]

Two years later, in 2003, their vision was realized as the memorial was unveiled. The memorial consists of an 11-sided pool of water whose shape is mirrored 35 feet above by an 11-sided canopy in the ceiling. A sculpted, 11-sided, 600-pound crystal suspended by 11 cables hovers two inches above the water, with the crystal's image mirrored in the reflecting pool. Drops of water intermittently fall from 11 small holes in the ceiling, symbolizing tears for those lost; thus the name Eleven Tears. Those who visit cannot help but feel the magnitude of its presence.

Since 2003, this quartz crystal has been doing its collective work—healing and transforming the environment and bringing light to hearts and minds, as well as to the souls of all the victims and those who still mourn their loss.

When crystals are impacted and excited by sound or other forms of electromagnetism, their resonance becomes stronger. The scale of the Eleven Tears Memorial ignites in us the power of collective healing and how shared intentions can catalyze transformation. In the presence of the memorial, one is reminded that we can be united in bringing peace to our world in consort with crystals.

Making Room for the New: My Story

The universe has a way of informing you that you are on the right path and in sync with your authentic story. After the pain of losing my children and the life I had known in Colombia, it was clear that the old was dying inside of me to let in the new.

While I still mourned my separation from my children and the dissolution of my previous life, I decided to write newsletters to heal myself. Every time I experienced some unpleasant feeling inside me, I imagined that a client was asking me how to handle that situation; the answers were reflected in my newsletters. I was attempting to pull myself out from the dark place I was in. Crystals were always by my side. Each newsletter was dissipating the darkness, breaking apart the old, and letting the light shine again in my life. The name of my newsletter, "Cohesion Culture," reflected the process of integration that was occurring within. Each newsletter was one piece that was connecting my life to the whole to create something new. All of the research I undertook when I put my newsletters together helped me to understand that my suffering wasn't entirely mine; it was the suffering of my mother and father, and also of my ex-husband's mother and father. I learned a great deal about myself, and I reconnected again with who I really am.

I began to apply what I was learning in my life. At the same time, I did my best to build bridges to get closer to my children. Little by little, I began the process of healing my relationship with them.

My life began to reflect my crystalline self.

I didn't realize that through my newsletters, I was also helping others to heal themselves. I received a great deal of praise for the newsletters; many of the comments included the suggestion to write a book.

I am a faithful believer that everything is information and a reflection of our unconscious world. The book was a sign of the authentic within my unconscious, so I decided to flow with this idea. At that time, I was on Hay House's mailing list. One day, I received an e-mail announcing their writer's workshop. This was an opportunity I was not going to miss. I signed up immediately. Although the workshop also included the possibility of competing to become a published author with Hay House, I entered the contest without ever expecting to win. Imagine my surprise when I received a phone call from Reid Tracy, Hay House's CEO, announcing that I had won first prize and that my book on crystals was going to be published!

For me, this book is a symbol of my authentic self. It reflects that I have freed myself from my mind's contents and all that did not belong to me. My inner work using crystals as tools has given me tangible results.

Over the years, because of my journey through suffering, I transformed. I became more connected to the whole, which includes the entire world. I integrated additional information and expanded my life in such a way that I began to feel compassion for everyone and everything on this planet. I reconnected with my authentic self, which alone influenced all my relationships and opened new possibilities that were potentially there for me, waiting to be seen.

I attribute my transformation to my inner work and crystals, which have connected me to my authentic self and my true path: teaching and sharing this information to create a crystalline world.

Suffering is no longer the villain of my story. I have learned to see it as a guide, as it has helped to dismantle the obsolete structures of my mind so that I can reconnect with who I really am.

It is never too late to make the choice to reconnect with our authentic, crystalline selves. Through exploration of ancient cultures and modern science, we are rediscovering the capacity of crystals to transform the inner contents of our minds and our world.

Despite the plethora of historic and scientific evidence on the healing powers of quartz crystals, the debate continues over whether crystals actually have any real healing power. Throughout this book, I have exposed you to a number of different studies and points of view that will help you to answer the question for yourself: Are crystals merely a placebo, or do they have the capacity to effect real transformation through their unique properties?

It is your choice what to believe. Allow your response to come from the authentic self within you.

The world in which we live has made us believe that the only way to be happy is to pursue the truth and dreams of others. It's time to identify and become aware of all the false filters that prevent you from seeing who you really are—and take deliberate action to change your current situation to walk your own path and live your own dreams.

I like to see the world as a clear quartz cluster, in which we are all transparent and shine and share our light with one another.

There is a pathway inside each of us that will lead us back to our crystal blueprint, which is our true nature. As they did with me, crystals will take you on this journey within yourself to discover that which has always been there, hidden from view.

You can absolutely change your story by working with crystals. I am a testament to all the benefits that they can bring into your life. I know firsthand that engaging with crystals in a conscious way is opening one more door to help humanity reconnect with our authentic story. But this requires a great deal of personal commitment and responsibility.

The crystal blueprint is a universal path to collective healing for both the planet and ourselves, and it runs through each and every of us. If everybody chooses to heal themselves, this chain reaction—which can be accelerated and amplified with crystals as a guide and ally—will have an astounding impact.

Our crystal blueprint is an intrinsic part of the unseen implicate order that binds together everything in existence. We know that the world is a reflection of our inner world and can change by changing our beliefs, so it follows that our consciousness is more than our brains and the known mechanisms of the physical body. All is energy, and everything is connected . . . so why wait to shift our frequencies and discover who we really are?

The choice is ultimately yours, but remember, all stories have a beginning. To begin your process, tune in and ask yourself: "Where can I begin to reconnect with my crystalline story?" Then, simply choose a stone.

ENDNOTES

Introduction

1. Richard Gerber, M.D., *Vibrational Medicine: The #1 Handbook of Subtle-Energy Therapies* (Rochester, VT: Bear & Company, 2001), 364.

2. Thomas P. Dolley, "Silica," *2012 Mineral Yearbook,* United States Geological Survey, August 2016, https://minerals.usgs.gov/minerals/pubs/commodity/silica/myb1-2012-silic.pdf.

Chapter 1

1. Lawrence Stoller, in discussion with the author.

2. Dan Willis, Dreamhill Research Facility, http://www.marcelvogel.org. [June 2017.]

3. Rollin McCraty, Ph.D., "Energetic Communication," *Science of the Heart: Exploring the Role of the Heart in Human Performance*, HeartMath Institute, accessed June 17, 2018, https://www.heartmath.org/research/science-of-the-heart/energetic-communication/.

4. Naisha Ahsian, in discussion with the author.

5. Ibid.

6. R. Buckminster Fuller, *Synergetics: Explorations in the Geometry of Thinking* (New York: Macmillan Publishing Company, 1982), sec. 503.03.

7. Resonance Science Foundation (@TheResonanceProject), "A 64 tetrahedron geometry like the one pictured here is Nassim Haramein's theorized foundational geometric structure of the vacuum of space," *Facebook,* October 23, 2013, https://www.facebook.com/TheResonanceProject/photos/a.224460250920411.60587.216281778404925/660219904011108/?type=1&theater.

8. Nassim Haramein, "Quantum Gravity and the Holographic Mass," *Physical Review & Research International* 3, no. 4 (October–December 2013): 270–92, http://www.journalrepository.org/media/journals/PRRI_4/2013/Apr/1367405491-Haramein342013PRRI3363.pdf.

9. Nassim Haramein, *Black Whole: Scientific Evidence That Everything Is One* (Conscious Media Productions, 2011), https://www.gaia.com/video/black-whole?fullplayer=feature.

10. Ibid.

11. Roy Melvyn, ed., *The Essential Nisargadatta* (Boulder, CO: Summa Iru Publishing, 2013), 171.

12. Eckhart Tolle, *Stillness Speaks* (Novato, CA: New World Library, 2003), 1.

13. Nelson Spruston, "Pyramidal Neurons: Dendritic Structure and Synaptic Integration," *Nature Reviews Neuroscience* 9, (March 2013): 206–11, https://www.nature.com/articles/nrn2286.

14. Raj Raghunathan, Ph.D., "How Negative Is Your Mental Chatter?," *Psychology Today*, October 10, 2013, https://www.psychologytoday.com/blog/sapient -nature/201310/how-negative-is-your-mental-chatter?amp.

15. Candace Pert, Ph.D., *The Healing Field: Exploring Energy and Consciousness*, directed by Penny Price (Lagrangeville, NY: Penny Price Media, 2016), DVD.

16. Gregg Braden, in discussion with the author.

Chapter 2

1. James Allen, *As a Man Thinketh* (New York, 1903), paraphrased in Penney Peirce, *Frequency: The Power of Personal Vibration* (New York: Atria Paperbacks, 2009), 160.

2. Gil Fronsdal, *The Dhammapada: Teachings of the Buddha* (Boston, MA: Shambhala Publications, Inc., 2005), 3.

3. Dr. Joe Dispenza, *Breaking the Habit of Being Yourself: How to Lose Your Mind and Create a New One* (Carlsbad, CA: Hay House, 2012), 45.

4. Robert A. Johnson, *Transformation: Understanding The Three Levels of Masculine Consciousness* (New York: HarperCollins Publishers, 1991), 4.

5. Carl G. Jung, *Man and His Symbols,* eds. M. L. von Franz et al. (London, UK: Dell Publishing, 1964), 257.

6. U.S. Bureau of Labor Statistics, Current Population Survey, accessed November 9, 2017, https://www.dol.gov/wb/media/gender_wage_gap.pdf.

7. Marion Woodman and Jill Mellick, *Coming Home to Myself* (San Francisco, CA: Conari Press, 2000), 221.

8. R. G. Collingwood, *The Idea of History,* ed. Jan Van Der Nussen (UK: Endeavour Ltd., 2015), 181.

9. Jiddu Krishnamurti, *The Impossible Question* (Hampshire, UK: Phoenix Books, 2003), 118.

10. Marshall McLuhan and Lewis H. Lapham, *Understanding Media: The Extensions of Man* (Boston, MA: MIT Press, 1994).

11. Salman Aslam, "Facebook by the Numbers: Stats, Demographics & Fun Facts," Omnicore Agency, August 11, 2017, https://www.omnicoreagency.com /facebook-statistics/.

12. Internet Live Stats, accessed November 9, 2017, http://www.internetlivestats. com/google-search-statistics/.

13. Internet Live Stats, accessed November 15, 2017, http://www.internetlivestats. com/twitter-statistics/.

14. Salman Aslam, "Instagram by the Numbers: Stats, Demographics & Fun Facts," Omnicore Agency, August 10, 2017, https://www.omnicoreagency.com/ instagram-statistics/.

Chapter 3

1. Randall N. Baer and Vicki V. Baer, *Windows of Light: Quartz Crystals and Self-Transformation* (San Francisco, CA: Harper & Row, 1984), 1.

2. W. C. Pei, "Notice of the Discovery of Quartz and Other Stone Artifacts in the Lower Pleistocene Hominid-Bearing Sediments of the Choukoutien Cave Deposit," *Bulletin of the Geological Society of China* 11, no. 2 (1931), 120.

3. Bruce G. Knuth, *Gems in Myth, Legend, and Lore* (Colorado: Jewelers Press, 2007), 1.

4. Freddy Silva, "They're Alive! Megalithic Sites Are More than Just Stone," *Ancient Origins*, May 5, 2016, http://www.ancient-origins.net/opinion-guest-authors /they-re-alive-megalithic-sites-are-more-just-stone-005827; and Pierre Méreaux, *Carnac: Des Pierres pour les Vivants* (Kerwangwenn, Nature & Bretagne, 1992).

5. Carl G. Jung, *Man and His Symbols*, eds. M. L. von Franz et al. (London, UK: Dell Publishing, 1964), 257.

6. George Frederick Kunz, A.M., Ph.D., *The Curious Lore of Precious Stones* (New York: Dover Publications, 1941), 22.

7. Sheila Paine, *Amulets: A World of Secret Powers, Charms and Magic* (London, UK: Thames & Hudson, 2004), 23.

8. David Hatcher Childress, *Technology of the Gods: The Incredible Sciences of the Ancients* (Kempton, IL: Adventures Unlimited Press, 2000).

9. Andreas Guhr and Jörg Nagler, *Crystal Power: Mythology and History* (Findhorn, UK: Earthdancer Books, 2006), 17.

10. Ibid, 21.

11. D. J. Conway, *Crystal Enchantments: A Complete Guide to Stones and Their Magical Properties* (Watsonville, CA: Crossing Press, 1999), 8.

12. B. G. Aston, J. A. Harrell, and I. Shaw, "Stones," *Ancient Egyptian Materials and Technology*, eds. P. T. Nicholson and I. Shaw (Cambridge: University of Cambridge Press, 2000), 5–77; and J. Baines, "Stone and Other Materials in Ancient Egypt: Usages and Values," *Pierres Égyptiennes: Chefs-d'Oeuvre pour l'Éternité*, eds. C. Karlshausen and T. DePutter (Mons, Belgium: Faculté Polytechnique de Mons, 2000), 29–41.

13. Stephen Mehler, in discussion with the author.

14. "The Great Pyramid of Giza: A Tesla-like Power Plant Built Thousands of Years Ago?," *Ancient Code Blog*, accessed November 9, 2017, https://www.ancient -code.com/great-pyramid-giza-tesla-like-powerplant-created-thousands-years -ago/.

15. Morris Jastrow, *Die Religion Babyloniens und Assyriens*, vol. 1 (Giessen, 1905), 374.

16. Andreas Guhr and Jörg Nagler, *Crystal Power: Mythology and History* (Findhorn, UK: Earthdancer Books, 2006), 14.

17. JoAnn Scurlock, *Magico-Medical Means of Treating Ghost-Induced Illnesses in Ancient Mesopotamia* (Leiden, Netherlands: Brill/Styx, 2006), 140.

18. R. Tripp Evans, *Romancing the Maya: Mexican Antiquity in the American Imagination 1820–1915* (Austin, TX: University of Texas Press, 2004), 114.

19. Keith M. Prufer, "Caves and Crystalmancy: Evidence for the Use of Crystals in Ancient Maya Religion," *Journal of Anthropological Research*, March 1999, 131.

20. Ibid, 132.

21. Jaap van Etten, Ph.D., *Crystal Skulls: Interacting with a Phenomenon* (Flagstaff, AZ: Light Technology Publishing, 2007), 13.

22. Ibid, 13–15.

23. Nichola Erin Harris, *The Idea of Lapidary Medicine: Its Circulation and Practical Applications in Medieval and Early Modern England: 1000–1750* (dissertation, Rutgers University, May 2009).

24. Ibid.

25. Plato, *Phaedo,* trans. Edward Meredith Cope (Cambridge, UK: C. J. Clay, M.A. at the University Press, 1875), 96–97.

26. Theophrastus, *De lapidibus*, ed. and trans. D. E. Eichholz (Oxford, UK: Clarendon Press, 1965), 2–4.

27. Pedanius Dioscorides, *The Greek Herbal of Dioscorides*, trans. John Goodyer, ed. Robert Gunther (London: Hafner Publishing Company, 1968).

28. Nichola Erin Harris, *The Idea of Lapidary Medicine: Its Circulation and Practical Applications in Medieval and Early Modern England: 1000–1750* (dissertation, Rutgers University, May 2009).

29. Ibid.

30. Ibid.

31. Harriet Keith Fobes, *Mystic Gems* (Gorham Press, 1924), 58–59.

32. W. T. Fernie, M.D., *Precious Stones: For Curative Wear; and Other Remedial Uses: Likewise the Nobler Metals* (Bristol, UK: John Wright and Co, 1907), 312.

33. Isaac del Sotto, *Le Lapidaire du Quatorzième Siècle*, trans. Kate Blanas (Geneva, Switzerland: 1862, Slatkine Reprints, 1974), 23.

34. D. J. Conway, *Crystal Enchantments: A Complete Guide to Stones and Their Magical Properties* (Freedom, CA: The Crossing Press, 1999), 41.

35. Claude Lecouteux, *A Lapidary of Sacred Stones: Their Magical and Medicinal Powers Based on the Earliest Sources*, trans. Jon E. Graham (Rochester, VT: Inner Tradition, 2011), 47.

36. A. Hyatt Verrill, *Precious Stones and Their Stories: An Article on the History of Gemstones and Their Use* (Red Books Ltd., 2013).

37. Bruce G. Knuth, *Gems in Myth, Legend, and Lore* (Colorado: Jewelers Press, 2007), 59.

38. Ibid, 60.

39. A. Hyatt Verrill, *Precious Stones and Their Stories: An Article on the History of Gemstones and Their Use* (Red Books Ltd., 2013).

40. D. J. Conway, *Crystal Enchantments: A Complete Guide to Stones and Their Magical Properties* (Freedom, CA: The Crossing Press, 1999), 78.

41. Isaac del Sotto, *Le Lapidaire du Quatorzième Siècle*, trans. Kate Blanas (Geneva, Switzerland: 1862, Slatkine Reprints, 1974), 53.

42. D. J. Conway, *Crystal Enchantments: A Complete Guide to Stones and Their Magical Properties* (Freedom, CA: The Crossing Press, 1999), 70.

43. Ibid, 72.

44. William Jones, F.S.A., *History and Mystery of Precious Stones* (London, UK: Richard Bentley and Son, 1880), 31.

45. D. J. Conway, *Crystal Enchantments: A Complete Guide to Stones and Their Magical Properties* (Freedom, CA: The Crossing Press, 1999), 169.

46. James Remington McCarthy, *Rings through the Ages: An Informal History* (New York: Harper & Brothers, 1945), 35.

47. George Frederick Kunz, A.M., Ph.D., *The Curious Lore of Precious Stones* (New York: Dover Publications, 1941), 38.

48. W. T. Fernie, M.D., *Precious Stones: For Curative Wear; and Other Remedial Uses: Likewise the Nobler Metals* (Bristol, UK: John Wright and Co, 1907), 163.

49. Camillus Leonardus, *Speculum Lapidum (The Mirror of Stones)* (Venice, Italy: 1502), 229.

50. Bruce G. Knuth, *Gems in Myth, Legend, and Lore* (Colorado: Jewelers Press, 2007), 200.

51. D. J. Conway, *Crystal Enchantments: A Complete Guide to Stones and Their Magical Properties* (Freedom, CA: The Crossing Press, 1999), 178.

52. S. R. N. Murthy, "Vāgbhaṭa on medicinal uses of gems," *Indian Journal of History of Science* 14, 1979, 134.

53. Leslie J. Franks, *Stone Medicine: A Chinese Medical Guide to Healing with Gems and Minerals* (Rochester, VT: Healing Art Press, 2016), 140.

54. C. W. King, M.A., *The Natural History of Gems or Decorative Stones* (Cambridge, UK: Deighton, Bell, & Co, 1867), 285–86.

55. W. T. Fernie, M.D., *Precious Stones: For Curative Wear; and Other Remedial Uses: Likewise the Nobler Metals* (Bristol, UK: John Wright and Co, 1907), 180.

56. "Similia similibus curantur," Drugs.com, accessed November 10, 2017, https://www.drugs.com/dict/similia-similibus-curantur.html.

57. Ibid.

58. Isaac del Sotto, *Le Lapidaire du Quatorzième Siècle*, trans. Kate Blanas (Geneva, Switzerland: 1862, Slatkine Reprints, 1974), 59.

59. W. T. Fernie, M.D., *Precious Stones: For Curative Wear; and Other Remedial Uses: Likewise the Nobler Metals* (Bristol, UK: John Wright and Co, 1907), 174.

60. William Jones, F.S.A., *History and Mystery of Precious Stones* (London, UK: Richard Bentley and Son, 1880), 35.

61. Claude Lecouteux, *A Lapidary of Sacred Stones: Their Magical and Medicinal Powers Based on the Earliest Sources*, trans. Jon E. Graham (Rochester, VT: Inner Tradition, 2011), 47.

62. Bruce G. Knuth, *Gems in Myth, Legend, and Lore* (Colorado: Jewelers Press, 2007), 173–74.

63. George Frederick Kunz, A.M., Ph.D., *The Curious Lore of Precious Stones* (New York: Dover Publications, 1941), 154–55.

64. Ibid, 273–74.

65. Mircea Eliade, *The Sacred and the Profane: The Nature of Religion*, trans. Willard R. Trask (New York: Houghton Mifflin Harcourt, 1959), 116.

66. Andreas Guhr and Jörg Nagler, *Crystal Power: Mythology and History* (Findhorn, UK: Earthdancer Books, 2006), 25.

67. "Ezekiel 28:13," *The Complete Jewish Bible with Rashi Commentary*, accessed November 9, 2017, https://www.chabad.org/library/bible_cdo/aid/16126.

68. Bruce G. Knuth, *Gems in Myth, Legend, and Lore* (Colorado: Jewelers Press, 2007), 13.

69. John Sinkankas, *Emerald and Other Beryls* (Prescott, AZ: Geoscience Press, 1989), 24.

70. Claude Lecouteux, *A Lapidary of Sacred Stones: Their Magical and Medicinal Powers Based on the Earliest Sources*, trans. Jon E. Graham (Rochester, VT: Inner Tradition, 2011), 7.

71. John Sinkankas, *Emerald and Other Beryls* (Prescott, AZ: Geoscience Press, 1989), 24.

72. Andreas Guhr and Jörg Nagler, *Crystal Power: Mythology and History* (Findhorn, UK: Earthdancer Books, 2006), 135.

73. *A History of Geology and Medicine*, eds. C. J. Duffin, R.T.J., and C. Gardner-Thorpe (London, UK: The Geological Society, 2013).

74. "Sphatika Mala," The Hinduism Forum, IndiaDivine.org, accessed November 9, 2017, http://www.indiadivine.org/content/topic/1161309-sphatika-mala/.

75. Stephen Skinner, *Sacred Geometry: Deciphering the Code* (New York: Sterling Publishing, 2006), 54–55, 79.

76. Laurence Hecht, "The Geometric Basis for the Periodicity of the Elements," *21st Century*, May–June 1988, 18–30, accessed March 3, http://21sci-tech.com /Articles%202004/Spring2004/Periodicity.pdf.

77. Nassim Haramein, *Black Whole: Scientific Evidence That Everything Is One* (Conscious Media Productions, 2011), https://www.gaia.com/video/black -whole?fullplayer=feature.

78. George Frederick Kunz, A.M., Ph.D., *The Curious Lore of Precious Stones* (New York: Dover Publications, 1941), 338.

79. Jacobi Gaffarelli, "Curiositates Inauditæ" (Hamburg, 1706), 146, 147; and George Frederick Kunz, A.M., Ph.D., *The Curious Lore of Precious Stones* (New York: Dover Publications, 1941), 340.

80. Marcilio Ficino, *De vita coelitùs comparanda*, cap. 13, quoted in Julius Reichelt, *De*

Amuletis (Argentorati, 1676), 45; and George Frederick Kunz, A.M., Ph.D., *The Curious Lore of Precious Stones* (New York: Dover Publications, 1941), 341.

81. Rupert Gleadow, *The Origin of the Zodiac* (New York: Dover Publications, 1968), 136.

82. Ibid.

83. George Frederick Kunz, A.M., Ph.D., *The Curious Lore of Precious Stones* (New York: Dover Publications, 1941).

84. Rupert Gleadow, *The Origin of the Zodiac* (New York: Dover Publications, 1968), 136.

85. *Catalogus Codium Astrologorum Graecorum*, vol. 12, *Greek Astrology*; and Rupert Gleadow, *The Origin of the Zodiac* (New York: Dover Publications, 1968), 136.

86. Rupert Gleadow, *The Origin of the Zodiac* (New York: Dover Publications, 1968), 136.

87. George Frederick Kunz, A.M., Ph.D., *The Curious Lore of Precious Stones* (New York: Dover Publications, 1941), 343.

88. Ibid, 18.

89. Ibid, 19.

90. Ibid, 19–20.

91. David Bressan, "A Tribute to the Year of Crystallography: Haüy's Models," *History of Geology*, December 30, 2014, http://historyofgeology.fieldofscience. com/2014/12/a-tribute-to-year-of-crystallography.html?m=1.

Chapter 4

1. John Vincent Milewski and Virginia L. Harford, eds., *The Crystal Sourcebook: From Science to Metaphysics* (Sedona, AZ: Mystic Crystal Publications, 1987), 5.

2. Mircea Eliade, *Shamanism: Archaic Techniques of Ecstasy*, trans. Willard R. Trask (Princeton, NJ: Princeton University Press, 1992), 350.

3. Llewellyn Editorial Staff, *Llewellyn Educational Guide to the Truth About Crystal Healing* (St. Paul, MN: Llewellyn Publications, 1986), 5.

4. Ibid, 3.

5. John Vincent Milewski and Virginia L. Harford, eds., *The Crystal Sourcebook: From Science to Metaphysics* (Sedona, AZ: Mystic Crystal Publications, 1987), 7.

6. Jerome Meyer Levi, "Wii'ipay: The Living Rocks—Ethnographic Notes of Crystal Magic among Some California Yumans," *Journal of California Anthropology* 5, no. 1 (Summer 1978), 43, https://escholarship.org/content/qt5092355x /qt5092355x.pdf.

7. Keith M. Prufer, "Caves and Crystalmancy: Evidence for the Use of Crystals in Ancient Maya Religion," *Journal of Anthropological Research*, March 1999, 131.

8. Stephen C. Finley and Torin Alexander, eds., *African American Religious Cultures* (Santa Barbara, CA: ABC-CLIO, 2009), 670.

9. Gerardo Reichel-Dolmatoff, *The Sacred Mountain of Colombia's Kogi Indians* (Netherlands: Leiden-Brill, 1990).

10. Malidoma Patrice Somé, *The Healing Wisdom of Africa: Finding Life Purpose through Nature, Ritual, and Community* (New York: Penguin Putnam, 1998), 244–45.

11. Mircea Eliade, *Shamanism: Archaic Techniques of Ecstasy*, trans. Willard R. Trask (Princeton, NJ: Princeton University Press, 1992), 349.

12. Robert E. Ryan, Ph.D., *The Strong Eye of Shamanism: A Journey into the Caves of Consciousness* (Rochester, VT: Inner Traditions Bear Company, 1999), 109.

13. *The Birth of a New Humanity* (Drunvalo Melchizedek, 2010), DVD.

14. Eric Hand, "Maverick Scientist Thinks He Has Discovered a Magnetic Sense in Humans," *Science Magazine*, June 23, 2016, http://www.sciencemag.org/news/2016/06/maverick-scientist-thinks-he-has-discovered-magnetic-sixth-sense-humans.

15. *Solar Revolution* (Scottsdale, AZ: Screen Addiction, 2012), DVD.

16. Ibid.

17. Leo McFee, in discussion with the author.

18. Stephen Mehler, in discussion with the author.

19. JaneAnn Dow, *Crystal Journey: Travel Guide for the New Shaman* (Santa Fe, NM: Journey Books, 1994), 39.

Chapter 5

1. Ra Bonewitz, *Cosmic Crystals: Crystal Consciousness and the New Age* (UK: Turnstone Press Limited, 1984), 9.

2. Gregg Braden, *The Divine Matrix: Bridging Time, Space, Miracles, and Belief* (Carlsbad, CA: Hay House, Inc., 2007), 3.

3. Nassim Haramein, *Black Whole: Scientific Evidence That Everything Is One* (Conscious Media Productions, 2011), https://www.gaia.com/video/black-whole?fullplayer=feature.

4. *The Connected Universe*, directed by Malcom Carter (Chronos Global Media Inc, 2016), http://www.the connecteduniversefilm.com.

5. Dean Radin, "Physics and the Nonlocal Mind," conference speech, Institute of Noetic Sciences, June 2017, https://www.facebook.com/Mr.Gamma/posts/10210977056836619.

6. Gregg Braden, *The Divine Matrix: Bridging Time, Space, Miracles, and Belief* (Carlsbad, CA: Hay House, Inc., 2007), 27.

7. David Bohm, *Wholeness and the Implicate Order* (London, UK: Routledge & Kegan Paul, 1980), 62.

8. Michael Talbot, *The Holographic Universe* (New York: Harper Perennial, 2011), 50.

9. "Hindu Scriptures," *Surya's Tapestry: Ancient Rishis' Pathways to Hinduism, Hindu Wisdom*, October 28, 2008, http://www.hinduwisdom.info/Hindu_Scriptures.htm.

10. Michael Talbot, *The Holographic Universe* (New York: Harper Perennial, 2011), 179.

11. Gregg Braden, *The Divine Matrix: Bridging Time, Space, Miracles, and Belief* (Carlsbad, CA: Hay House, Inc., 2007), 9.

12. Olivia Lee Shuk-Ming, "Radiation Emitted by Human Body: Thermal Radiation," Hong Kong Observatory, September 2010, http://www.hko.gov.hk/education /edu02rga/radiation/radiation_02-e.htm.

13. Richard Gerber, M.D., *Vibrational Medicine: The #1 Handbook of Subtle-Energy Therapies* (Rochester, VT: Bear & Company, 2001), 338.

14. Jane Solomon and Grant Solomon, *Harry Oldfield's Invisible Universe* (London, UK: Harper Collins, 1998), 14.

15. Sara Childre, "Raising Our Vibration through Compassion and Unconditional Love," HeartMath Institute, April 4, 2017, https://www.heartmath.org/articles-of-the-heart/raising-vibration-compassion-unconditional-love.

16. *The Healing Field: Exploring Energy and Consciousness* (Lagrangeville, NY: Penny Price Media, 2016), DVD.

17. Ibid.

18. Ibid.

19. Glen Rein, Ph.D., "Biological Effects of Quantum Fields and Their Role in the Natural Healing Process," *Frontier Perspectives* 7 (1988) 16–23.

20. *The Healing Field: Exploring Energy and Consciousness* (Lagrangeville, NY: Penny Price Media, 2016), DVD.

21. Cyndi Dale, "Energetic Anatomy: A Complete Guide to the Human Energy Fields and Etheric Bodies," *Conscious Lifestyle Magazine*, September 11, 2017, https://www.consciouslifestylemag.com/human-energy-field-aura/.

22. Ibid.

23. Ibid.

24. Ibid.

25. Richard Gerber, M.D., *Vibrational Medicine: The #1 Handbook of Subtle-Energy Therapies* (Rochester, VT: Bear & Company, 2001), 60.

26. Michael Talbot, *The Holographic Universe* (New York: HarperCollins, 1991), 175–76.

27. Jon Whale, Ph.D., *Naked Spirit: The Supernatural Odyssey* (Long Beach, CA: Clear Lotus Publishing, 2008), 17.

28. Helmholtz-Zentrum Dresden-Rossendorf, "Pulsating Dissolution Found in Crystals: Pulsing Rings Are Found in Surface Reaction Rate Maps of Dissolving Crystals," *Science Daily* 16 (January 2018), accessed March 5, 2018, http://www.sciencedaily.com/releases/2018/01/180116111102.htm.

29. Michael Talbot, *The Holographic Universe* (New York: Harper Perennial, 2011), 14–15.

30. Michael Talbot, *The Holographic Universe* (New York: Harper Perennial, 2011), 31.

31. Dr. Joe Dispenza, *Breaking the Habit of Being Yourself: How to Lose Your Mind and Create a New One* (Carlsbad, CA: Hay House, 2012), 4.

32. Michael Talbot, *The Holographic Universe* (New York: Harper Perennial, 2011), 34.

33. Nick Herbert, "How Large Is Starlight? A Brief Look at Quantum Reality," *Revision* 10, no. 1 (Summer 1987) 31–35; and Michael Talbot, *The Holographic Universe* (New York: Harper Perennial, 2011), 34.

34. David J. Bohm, "A New Theory of the Relationship of Mind and Matter," *Journal of the American Society for Physical Research* 80, no. 2 (April 1986), 128; and Michael Talbot, *The Holographic Universe* (New York: Harper Perennial, 2011), 121.

35. Michael Talbot, *The Holographic Universe* (New York: Harper Perennial, 2011), 84.

36. William A. Tiller, "Consciousness, Radiation, and the Developing Sensory System," quoted in Bill Schul, ed., *The Psychic Frontiers of Medicine*, (New York: Ballantine Books, 1977), 95; and Michael Talbot, *The Holographic Universe* (New York: Harper Perennial, 2011), 189.

37. Gregg Braden, conference speech, Self-Empowered Wisdom, Stellar Productions Live, 2017; and "Study: Pulsating Dissolution Found in Crystals," *Scienmag Science Magazine*, accessed February 20, 2018, https://scienmag.com/study -pulsating-dissolution-found-in-crystals/.

38. Galina Merline, "The Human Body Frequency," Healtone, Healing Sounds Laboratories LLC, accessed November 17, 2017, http://www.healtone.com /pages/the-human-body-frequency.html.

39. Ibid.

40. Sara Childre, "Raising Our Vibration through Compassion and Unconditional Love," HeartMath Institute, April 4, 2017, https://www.heartmath.org/articles-of -the-heart/raising-vibration-compassion-unconditional-love/.

41. "The Energetic Heart Is Unfolding," HeartMath Institute, July 22, 2010, https:// www.heartmath.org/articles-of-the-heart/science-of-the-heart/the-energetic -heart-is-unfolding/.

42. Sara Childre, "Raising Our Vibration through Compassion and Unconditional Love," HeartMath Institute, April 4, 2017, https://www.heartmath.org/articles-of -the-heart/raising-vibration-compassion-unconditional-love/.

43. Ryan Jones, "Brain Battery," *Knowing Neurons*, December 14, 2012, http:// knowingneurons.com/2012/12/14/brain-battery/.

44. Ned Hermann, "What Is the Function of the Various Brainwaves?," *Scientific American*, December 22, 1997, https://www.scientificamerican.com/article/what -is-the-function-of-t-1997-12-22/; and Jeffrey L. Fannin, Ph.D., "Understanding Your Brainwaves," white paper, accessed November 17, 2017, http:// drjoedispenza.com/files/understanding-brainwaves_white_paper.pdf.

45. Plato, *Timaeus and Critias*, 6th ed., trans. Desmond Lee (Middlesex, UK: Penguin Books, 1979), 119.

46. Harry Oldfield and Roger Coghill, *The Dark Side of the Brain: Major Discoveries in the Use of Kirlian Photography and Electrocrystal Therapy* (UK: Element Books Limited, 1988), 123–24.

47. Jon Whale, Ph.D., *The Catalyst of Power: The Assemblage Point of Man* (Scotland: Findhorn Press, 2001), 7–8.

48. Ron Turmel, "Resonant Frequencies and the Human Brain," *The Resonance Project*

1 (Summer 1997), The Vaults of Erowid, https://erowid.org/culture/references /other/1997_turmel_resproject_1.shtml.

Chapter 6

1. R. Miller, "The Healing Magic of Crystals: An Interview with Marcel Vogel," *Science of Mind*, August 1984.

2. Jane Solomon and Grant Solomon, *Harry Oldfield's Invisible Universe* (London, UK: Harper Collins, 1998), 99.

3. Ibid, 99.

4. Sid Perkins, "Quartz Fingers Weak Spots in Earth's Crust," *Science*, March 16, 2011, http://www.sciencemag.org/news/2011/03/quartz-fingers-weak-spots-earths-crust.

5. Richard Gerber, M.D., *Vibrational Medicine: The #1 Handbook of Subtle-Energy Therapies* (Rochester, VT: Bear & Company, 2001), 388.

6. "Crystals: Basic Terms," The Quartz Page, last modified May 21, 2010, http://www .quartzpage.de/crs_terms.html.

7. Lauren Murray, "Science Summary on Light," Michigan State University, accessed November 10, 2017, https://msu.edu/~murrayl3/Coursework/LightPaper.pdf.

8. Ra Bonewitz, *Cosmic Crystals: Crystal Consciousness and the New Age* (UK: Turnstone Press Limited, 1984), 106–7.

9. "Introduction," The Quartz Page, last modified May 24, 2011, http://www .quartzpage.de/intro.html.

10. Ra Bonewitz, *Cosmic Crystals: Crystal Consciousness and the New Age* (UK: Turnstone Press Limited, 1984), 28–29.

11. Plato, *Timaeus and Critias* (New York: Oxford University Press, 2008), 50.

12. "Quartz Structure," The Quartz Page, last modified January 6, 2017, http://www .quartzpage.de/gen_struct.html.

13. Stephen Skinner, *Sacred Geometry: Deciphering the Code* (New York: Sterling Publishing, 2006), 48.

14. Demonstration of Quartz Crystals Energy video, https://www.youtube.com /watch?v=2onEsj7MtPc&feature=youtu.be.

15. Michael Rice, "The Science of Seeing," Academy of Sacred Geometry, accessed November 17, 2017, http://academysacredgeometry.com/articles/science -seeing.

16. Ra Bonewitz, *Cosmic Crystals: Crystal Consciousness and the New Age* (UK: Turnstone Press Limited, 1984), 104.

17. Benjamin Radford, "Why Is Quartz Used in Watches?," *Live Science*, February 21, 2013, https://www.livescience.com/32509-why-is-quartz-used-in-watches.html.

18. Ra Bonewitz, *Cosmic Crystals: Crystal Consciousness and the New Age* (UK: Turnstone Press Limited, 1984), 104.

19. Chris Woodford, "Piezoelectricity," *Explain That Stuff!*, last modified August 11, 2017, http://www.explainthatstuff.com/piezoelectricity.html.

20. Ra Bonewitz, *Cosmic Crystals: Crystal Consciousness and the New Age* (UK: Turnstone Press Limited, 1984), 104.

21. Michael Gienger, *Crystal Power, Crystal Healing: The Complete Handbook*, trans. Astrid Mick (UK: Cassell & Co, 1998), 185.

22. Harry Oldfield and Roger Coghill, *The Dark Side of the Brain: Major Discoveries in the Use of Kirlian Photography and Electrocrystal Therapy* (UK: Element Books Limited, 1988), 153.

23. Jon Whale, Ph.D., *Naked Spirit: The Supernatural Odyssey* (Long Beach, CA: Clear Lotus Publishing, 2008), 301.

24. Harry Oldfield and Roger Coghill, *The Dark Side of the Brain: Major Discoveries in the Use of Kirlian Photography and Electrocrystal Therapy* (UK: Element Books Limited, 1988), 149.

25. Randall N. Baer and Vicki V. Baer, *Windows of Light: Quartz Crystals and Self-Transformation* (San Francisco, CA: Harper & Row, 1984), 55.

26. Rupert Sheldrake, *A New Science of Life: The Hypothesis of Formative Causation* (Los Angeles: J. P. Tarcher, Inc., 1981); and Harry Oldfield and Roger Coghill, *The Dark Side of the Brain: Major Discoveries in the Use of Kirlian Photography and Electrocrystal Therapy* (UK: Element Books Limited, 1988), 158–59.

27. Randall N. Baer and Vicki V. Baer, *Windows of Light: Quartz Crystals and Self-Transformation* (San Francisco, CA: Harper & Row, 1984), 14.

28. Semyon D. Kirlian and Valentina H. Kirlian, *Photography and Visual Observations by Means of High-Frequency Current*, trans. Foreign Techn. Divn., U.S. Air Force Systems Command (1963).

29. Semyon D. Kirlian and Valentina H. Kirlian, *Investigation of Biological Objects in High-Frequency Electrical Fields—Bioenergetic Questions—and Some Answers* (USSR: Alma Ata USSR, 1968).

30. Harry Oldfield and Roger Coghill, *The Dark Side of the Brain: Major Discoveries in the Use of Kirlian Photography and Electrocrystal Therapy* (UK: Element Books Limited, 1988), 64.

31. Ibid, 144.

32. Ibid, 101–2.

33. Ibid, 102.

34. Ibid, 102–3.

35. Ibid, 102

36. Ibid, 153.

37. Craig Freudenrich, Ph.D., "How Ultrasound Works," *How Stuff Works*, accessed November 17, 2017, http://science.howstuffworks.com/ultrasound2.htm.

38. *Minerals Yearbook: Metals and Minerals 2008*, vol. 1, U.S. Department of the Interior/U.S. Geological Survey, 66-4.

39. Tarun Agarwal, "What Is Crystal Oscillator Circuit and Its Working?" Edgefx Kits and Solutions, accessed November 17, 2017, https://www.edgefx.in/crystal

-oscillator-circuit-workingapplications/?sa=X&ved=0ahUKEwiXg4uC3JPVAhUj5YM
KHXDaB9YQ9QEIDjAA.

40. "Quartz Crystal Resonator Timeline and History," Electronics Notes, accessed November 17, 2017, https://www.electronics-notes.com/articles/electronic _components/quartz-crystal-xtal/timeline-history-development.php.

41. Tarun Agarwal, "What Is Crystal Oscillator Circuit and Its Working?" Edgefx Kits and Solutions, accessed November 17, 2017, https://www.edgefx.in/crystal -oscillator-circuit-working-applications/?sa=X&ved=0ahUKEwiXg4uC3JPVAhUj5YM KHXDaB9YQ9QEIDjAA.

42. Sebastian Anthony, "Will Your Body Be the Battery of the Future?" *Extreme Tech*, September 5, 2012, https://www.extremetech.com/extreme/135481-will-your -body-be-the-battery-of-the-future.

43. "Piezoelectric Transducer," *Instrumentation Today*, July 27, 2011, http://www .instrumentationtoday.com/piezoelectric.transducer/2011/07/.

44. Jane Solomon and Grant Solomon, *Harry Oldfield's Invisible Universe* (London, UK: HarperCollins, 1998), 67.

45. Boguslaw Lipinski, *Biological Significance of Piezoelectricity in Relation to Acupuncture, Hatha Yoga, Osteopathic Medicine and Action of Air Ions* (Boston, MA: Vascular Laboratory, Lemuel Shattuck Hospital, Tufts University School of Medicine, 1977).

46. Ibid.

47. Ibid.

48. "Manganese," University of Maryland Medical Center, accessed November 17, 2017, http://www.umm.edu/health/medical/altmed/supplement/manganese (article removed from the website by June 22, 2018); and Andrew Weil, "Chromium," Healthy Lifestyle Brands, LLC, accessed November 17, 2017, https://www.drweil.com/vitamins-supplements-herbs/supplements-remedies /chromium/.

49. David H. Nguyen, "What Colors Are the Cells in Your Body?" seattlepi.com, Heart Seattle Media, LLC, accessed November 17, 2017, http://education.seattlepi. com/colors-cells-body-5632.htm.

50. Linda Crampton, "Pigments in the Human Body: Functions and Health Effects," Owlcation, June 26, 2017, https://owlcation.com/stem/Pigments-in-the-Human -Body-Functions-and-Health-Effects.

51. Ibid.

52. J. Nissilä et al., "P-780—The Abundance and Distribution of Melanopsin (OPN4) Protein in Human Brain," *European Psychiatry* 27 (2012), 1–8.

53. Boguslaw Lipinski, *Biological Significance of Piezoelectricity in Relation to Acupuncture, Hatha Yoga, Osteopathic Medicine and Action of Air Ions* (Boston, MA: Vascular Laboratory, Lemuel Shattuck Hospital, Tufts University School of Medicine, 1977).

54. Gabriel Cousens, M.D., *Spiritual Nutrition: Six Foundations for Spiritual Life and the Awakening of Kundalini* (Berkeley, CA: North Atlantic Books, 2005), 141.

55. S. Baconnier et al, "Calcite Microcrystals in the Pineal Gland of the Human Brain: First Physical and Chemical Studies," *Bioelectromagnetics* 23, no. 7 (October 2002), 488–95, https://www.ncbi.nlm.nih.gov/m /pubmed/12224052/.

56. Tao Babe [pseud.], "The Body (Piezo) Electric," *Thoughts of a Taoist Babe* (blog), accessed November 18, 2017, https://taobabe.wordpress.com/the -body-piezo-electric/.

57. John Vincent Milewski and Virginia L. Harford, eds., *The Crystal Sourcebook: From Science to Metaphysics* (Sedona, AZ: Mystic Crystal Publications, 1987), 78–79.

58. "The Water in You," U.S. Department of the Interior/U.S. Geological Survey, accessed November 18, 2017, https://water.usgs.gov/edu/propertyyou.html.

59. James L. Oschman, *Energy Medicine: The Scientific Basis* (New York: Churchill Livingston/Harcourt Publishers, 2000), 52–55; and Warren Hammer, "Piezoelectricity, a Healing Property of Soft Tissue," *Dynamic Chiropractic* 20, no. 25 (November 30, 2002), http://www.dcpracticeinsights.com/mpacms/dc /article.php?id=15481.

60. Glenn H. Brown and Jerome J. Wolken , *Liquid Crystals and Biological Structures* (New York: Academic Press Inc., 1979).

61. Glen Rein, Ph.D., "Biological Effects of Quantum Fields and Their Role in the Natural Healing Process," *Frontier Perspectives* 7 (1988) 16–23.

62. Bernal et al., "Liquid Crystals and Anisotropic Melts," *Trans Faraday Society* 29 (1933), 1082.

63. Jonathan B. Wittenberg and Beatrice A. Wittenberg, "Myoglobin Function Reassessed," *Journal of Experimental Biology* 206 (2003), 2011–20, http://jeb .biologists.org/content/206/12/2011.

64. "HADH Gene: Hydroxyacyl-CoA Dehydrogenase," National Institutes of Health/ U.S. National Library of Medicine, accessed November 18, 2017, https://ghr.nlm .nih.gov/gene/HADH.

65. P. A. Michels and D. J. Rigden, "Evolutionary Analysis of Fructose 2,6-Bisphosphate Metabolism," *IUBMB Life* 58, no. 3 (March 2006), 133–41, https://www.ncbi .nlm.nih.gov/m/pubmed/16766380/.

66. Glen Rein, Ph.D., "Biological Effects of Quantum Fields and Their Role in the Natural Healing Process," *Frontier Perspectives* 7 (1988) 16–23.

Chapter 7

1. Larry Chang, ed., "Oneness/Unity/Wholeness," *Wisdom for the Soul: Five Millennia of Prescriptions for Spiritual Healing*, (Washington, DC: Gnosophia Publishers, 2006), 521.

2. "The Big Bang," *Science Beta*, NASA, accessed November 18, 2017, https://science. nasa.gov/astrophysics/focus-areas/what-powered-the-big-bang.

3. David Whitehouse, *Journey to the Centre of the Earth: The Remarkable Voyage of Scientific Discovery into the Heart of Our World* (London, UK: Weidenfeld & Nicolson, 2012).

4. Ra Bonewitz, *The Cosmic Crystal Spiral: Crystals and the Evolution of Human Consciousness* (Great Britain: Element Books, 1986), 25–26.

5. "'Quartz' Crystals at the Earth's Core Power Its Magnetic Field," *Tokyo Tech News*, February 23, 2017, https://www.titech.ac.jp/english/news/2017/037545.html; and Kei Hirose et al., "Crystallization of Silicon Dioxide and Compositional Evolution of the Earth's Core," *Nature* 543 (March 2, 2017), 99–102, https:// www.nature.com/articles/nature21367.

6. Ra Bonewitz, *Cosmic Crystals: Crystal Consciousness and the New Age* (UK: Turnstone Press Limited, 1984), 16.

7. Ibid, 18.

8. A. G. Cairns-Smith, "The Origin of Life and the Nature of the Primitive Gene," *Journal of Theoretical Biology* 10 (1966), 53–58.

9. Martha Henriques, "The Idea That Life Began as Clay Crystals Is 50 Years Old," BBC.com, August 24, 2016, http://www.bbc.com/earth/story/20160823-the-idea-that-life-began-as-clay-crystals-is-50-years-old.

10. Rupert Sheldrake, *The Presence of the Past: Morphic Resonance and the Memory of Nature* (Rochester, VT: Park Street Press), 262.

11. William Brown, "The Light Encoded DNA Filament and Biomolecular Quantum Communication," accessed November 18, 2017, http://exopolitics.blogs.com/files/synopsis---the-light-encoded-dna-filament-and-biomolecular-quantum-communication.pdf.

12. Andreas Bjerve, "Consciousness and the Brain in a Fractal-Holographic Universe," Holofractal.net, accessed March 4, 2018, http://holofractal.net/2015/09/01/consciousness-and-the-brain-in-a-fractal-holographic-universe/.

13. Stuart Hameroff and Roger Penrose, "Consciousness in the Universe: A Review of the 'Orch OR' Theory," *Physics of Life Reviews* 11, no. 1 (March 2014), *Elsevier*, http://dx.doi.org/10.1016/j.plrev.2013.08.002.

14. National Institute on Aging, "What Happens to the Brain in Alzheimer's Disease?" accessed March 5, 2018, https://www.nia.nih.gov/health/what-happens-brain-alzheimers-disease.

15. Daphney C. Jean and Peter W. Baas, "It Cuts Two Ways: Microtubule Loss During Alzheimer Disease," *Embo Journal* 32, no. 22 (November 13, 2013), 2900–02.

16. Yale University, "Negative Beliefs About Aging Predict Alzheimer's Disease in Study," ScienceDaily, December 7, 2015, http://www.sciencedaily.com/releases/2015/12/151207145906.htm.

17. Bryant A. Meyers, *PEMF: The Fifth Element of Health* (Bloomington, IN: Balboa Press, 2014), 19, 21, 95–98.

18. Annette Deyhle, Ph.D., "Influence of Geomagnetism and Schumann Resonances on Human Health and Behavior," HeartMath Institute, July 15, 2009, https://www.heartmath.org/gci-commentaries/influence-of-geomagnetism-and-schumann-resonances-on-human-health-and-behavior/.

19. *Solar Revolution* (Scottsdale, AZ: Screen Addiction, 2012), DVD.

20. Lisa Zyga, "Entanglement Is an Inevitable Feature of Reality," Phys.org, September 1, 2017, https://phys.org/news/2017-09-entanglement-inevitable-feature-reality.html#jCp.

21. Bryant A. Meyers, *PEMF: The Fifth Element of Health* (Bloomington, IN: Balboa Press, 2014), 57.

22. Naisha Ahsian, in discussion with the author.

Chapter 8

1. John Vincent Milewski and Virginia L. Harford, eds., The Crystal Sourcebook: From Science to Metaphysics (Sedona, AZ: Mystic Crystal Publications, 1987), 124.

2. JaneAnn Dow, *Crystal Journey: Travel Guide for the New Shaman* (Santa Fe, NM: Journey Books, 1994), 29–30.

3. Ibid, 30.

4. Ibid.

5. Naisha Ahsian, in discussion with the author.

6. Christopher Wallis, "The Real Story on the Chakras," Tantrik Studies (blog), February 5, 2016, https://tantrikstudies.squarespace.com/blog/2016/2/5/the -real-story-on-the-chakras.

7. Gregg Braden, in discussion with the author.

8. Lisa Wimberger, "Using Neuroscience to Find Healing and Happiness: The Neuroscience Training Summit 2017," http://www.soundstrue.com.

9. N. Haramein and E. A. Rauscher, "The Origin of Spin: A Consideration of Torque and Coriolis Forces in Einstein's Field Equations and Grand Unification Theory," The Resonance Project Foundation, 2004; Richard L. Amoroso, Bo Lehnert, and J-P Vigier, eds., *Beyond the Standard Model: Searching for Unity in Physics* (The Noetic Press, 2005); and Nassim Haramein, *Black Whole: Scientific Evidence That Everything Is One* (Conscious Media Productions, 2011), https://www.gaia.com /video/black-whole?fullplayer=feature.

10. Brigid Schulte, "Harvard Neuroscientist: Meditation Not Only Reduces Stress, Here's How It Changes Your Brain," *The Washington Post*, May 26, 2015, https:// www.washingtonpost.com/news/inspired-life/wp/2015/05/26/harvard -neuroscientist-meditation-not-only-reduces-stress-it-literally-changes-your -brain/?utm_term=.f3ff6ad149ba.

11. "Human Brain—Neuroscience—Cognitive Science," Basic Knowledge 101, accessed November 17, 2017, http://www.basicknowledge101.com/subjects /brain.html.

12. Brooke Borel, "Sound Becomes Light: New Research Confirms a Theory: high-frequency acoustic waves can be converted to light," *Popular Science*, March 19, 2009.   https://www.popsci.com/scitech/article/2009-03/sound-becomes-light

13. Gregg Braden, in discussion with the author.

14. Kenneth Buckle, "How Do Batteries Store and Discharge Electricity?" *Scientific American*, accessed November 18, 2017, https://www.scientificamerican.com /article/how-do-batteries-store-an/.

15. Bailey Mitchell et al., "Reducing Airborne Pathogens, Dust and Salmonella Transmission in Experimental Hatching Cabinets Using an Electrostatic Space Charge System," United States Department of Agriculture Agricultural Research Service, #118844, last modified June 21, 2018, https://www.ars.usda.gov /research/publications/publication/?seqNo115=118844.

16. Jonathan Goldman, *Shifting Frequencies: Sounds for Vibratory Activation* (Flagstaff, AZ: Light Technology Publishing, 2010), 109–10.

17. Lesley Alderman, "Breathe. Exhale. Repeat: The Benefits of Controlled Breathing,"

New York Times, November 9, 2016, https://www.nytimes.com/2016/11/09/well/mind/breathe-exhale-repeat-the-benefits-of-controlled-breathing.html.

18. Clinton Ober, Stephen T. Sinatra, and Martin Zucker, *Earthing: The Most Important Health Discovery Ever?* (Basic Health Publications, 2014).

Chapter 9

1. Marion Woodman and Jill Mellick, *Coming Home to Myself: Reflections for Nurturing a Woman's Body and Soul* (San Francisco, CA: Conari Press, 1998), 65.

2. "Vibrational Frequency List," *Just a List . . .* (blog), accessed March 4, 2018, http://justalist.blogspot.com/2008/03/vibrational-frequency-list.html.

3. Mircea Eliade, *Rites and Symbols of Initiation: The Mysteries of Birth and Rebirth* (Thompson, CT: Spring Publications, 1984), 45.

4. Eckhart Tolle, "Eckhart on the Dark Night of the Soul," October 2011 newsletter, Eckhart Teachings, https://www.eckharttolle.com/newsletter/october-2011.

5. JaneAnn Dow, *Crystal Journey: Travel Guide for the New Shaman* (Santa Fe, NM: Journey Books, 1994), 34.

6. Katrina Raphaell, *Crystal Enlightenment: The Transforming Properties of Crystals and Healing Stones* (Santa Fe, NM: Aurora Press Inc., 1985), 34.

7. JaneAnn Dow, *Crystal Journey: Travel Guide for the New Shaman* (Santa Fe, NM: Journey Books, 1994), 34.

8. Larry Chang, ed., *Wisdom for the Soul: Five Millennia of Prescriptions for Spiritual Healing,* (Washington, DC: Gnosophia Publishers, 2006), 716.

Conclusion

1. Katrina Raphaell, *Crystalline Illumination: The Way of the Five Bodies* (Kapaa, HI: The Crystal Academy of Advanced Healing Arts, 2010), 179.

2. Jiddu Krishnamurti, *Freedom from the Known* (New York: HarperCollins, 1969), 11.

3. Ibid, 20.

4. Jaime Rodríguez Arana, "Pensamiento Abierto," trans. Holly Starley, *Syntagma: Centro de Estudios Estratégicos*, November 10, 2011, http://syntagma.org/wp_studio/2011/11/pensamiento-abierto-jaime-rodriguez-arana/.

5. Jiddu Krishnamurti, *Freedom from the Known* (New York: HarperCollins, 1969), 25.

6. Jonathan Goldman, *Shifting Frequencies: Sounds for Vibratory Activation* (Flagstaff, AZ: Light Technology, 2010), 139.

7. Lawrence Stoller, "Eleven Tears," *Lapidary Journal* (January 2004), 18–20.

ACKNOWLEDGMENTS

Dreams don't come true . . . they *are* true. They live within us, in the deepest parts of our crystal blueprint, waiting until we are clear enough to live them as reality.

I want to thank all the people whose efforts have contributed and aided in the research and preparation for *The Crystal Blueprint* to come to fruition.

First and foremost, I am very honored and grateful to Hay House for giving me a voice and platform to share my crystalline dreams with the world; to Louise Hay for being a constant inspiration on my journey to reconnect with the authentic; to Reid Tracy, president and CEO, for giving me the opportunity with the Writer's Workshop first prize to be published and belong to this respected circle of authors and light workers; to Sally Mason-Swaab, my Hay House editor, for her guidance during this process; to Anne Barthel, Hay House's Editorial Director; Marlene Robinson, Hay House's Editorial Assistant; Byron Campbell for his extraordinary copyedit and fact-checking work. Thanks to Jessica Kelley for also helping me with fact-checking.

This book also could not have been accomplished without the wisdom and knowledge of Kelly Notaras and her wonderful and dedicated team, who supported my work. Many thanks to Prem Chandika Devi, Matthew Klein, Mark Chait, Crystallin Dillon, Alice Sullivan, and especially Nirmala Nataraj for her editing skills and finding the right words and structure to clearly express my ideas. I want to add Holly Starley to this list. My first editor in the US who believed in my message and helped me manifest it through Cohesion Culture.

I also would like to thank my graphic designers, Arturo Ponce de Leon and Ninon Fregoso. I'm also thankful to Stacey Byers for the quartz crystals and crystal healing photographs, Jordan Hamilton for being our crystal healing model and Thornton Streeter for his wonderful advice during my research process.

The support and contributions to the research by several key people must be noted: Gregg Braden, scientist and five-time *New York Times* best-selling author (www.greggbraden.com); Judy Hall, international best-selling crystal author; Stephen Mehler, credentialed field archaeologist with over 40 years of experience, expert in ancient cultures and best-selling author; Lawrence Stoller, internationally recognized award-winning sculptor specializing in large crystals— among them, Eleven Tears 9/11 Memorial inside the American Express Building across from Ground Zero; Jorge Luis Delgado, Inca *chacaruna* and author of *Andean Awakening*; Julian Sasari, Inca *chacaruna*; Naisha Ahsian, crystal resonance therapist, teacher, and best-selling crystal author; Leo McFee, crystal healer and teacher; Suzan Moore; and Mohamed A. Fahmy.

I also want to thank my Hindu teachers, as well as my primary crystal teachers, Katrina Raphaell and JaneAnn Dow, and all indigenous and ancient wisdom that guided me through my path. Without them, my crystal journey would never have happened.

Thanks also go to my family, especially my father, David, who always believed in me—and in the writer within me. I am grateful to Consuelo Casilimas, my soul sister and guardian angel bringing light and inspiration in every step of this journey. To Nathalie Akinin, Fabian Hirose, Johanna Pieschacon, Kiko Kairuz, David Robertson, and Nancy Furman-Alex, thanks for your unconditional support and love.

To my children, Andrea and Mark, the loves of my life: thank you for being my teachers and inspiration to constantly improve myself to leave my best legacy and example to you. And my bonus kids, Nicki, Ili, and Karen, for being a loving mirror reflecting that we "all" are family beyond experiences, consanguinity, and learned limiting beliefs.

To David, my life companion, thank you for all your unconditional love, support, wise advice, and patience during this process. To Shanti and Merlin, my furry family, what a joy and blessing to share my life with you!

And finally, a very special thanks to all my clients, students, and supporters of my work and life path. To all of you, I remain very grateful.

ABOUT THE AUTHOR

BEATRIZ SINGER was initiated into the art of crystal healing by Hindu masters in India and world-renowned crystal masters JaneAnn Dow and Katrina Raphaell. She has been a holistic therapist and workshop leader with an expertise in crystals since 2001. Beatriz was first recognized as a crystal healer in Colombia, where she was a pioneer of crystal healing and became the founder and director of one of the first interfaith alternative-therapy centers, Centro de Integración Shambalah (Shambalah Integration Center). She was frequently interviewed for Colombian television news and magazine shows, as well as local print media. She has authored numerous articles about alternative therapies for Spanish-language magazines, led a variety of crystal workshops, and lectured about crystal healing in South America and the U.S.

Her background and personal story are what make her unique. She is a trained healer who has used crystals to heal and reconnect with her own authentic self. She has studied directly with South American shamans, Tibetan Buddhist monks, Indian gurus, and other masters—and has drawn great knowledge from these ancient cultures and traditions. As a university-trained journalist, Beatriz has the ability—and an inclination—to observe, question, and research. Besides delivering the sensitivity, awareness, and intuition of a healer, she also brings the information-gathering skills and mind-set of a journalist. Together, these attributes allow other people to resonate deeply with her message and find inspiration for their own healing journeys. Beatriz finds in crystals tools that help us build clarity and catalyze healing and transformation to create an authentic life. She draws on both her intuition and deep knowledge to help clients heal, transform, and reconnect.

Beatriz knows the power of crystals to alleviate real-world suffering. Twenty-five years ago, she embarked on a quest to heal herself. Ultimately, her quest for truth—and her far-reaching curiosity—led her to find in crystals new opportunities to bring balance and wellness to all. She continues to lead crystal workshops in person and online, and she also offers personal assessments and guided self-healing. To learn more about her work, go to: www.beatrizsinger.com

Free e-newsletters
from Hay House, the Ultimate
Resource for Inspiration

Be the first to know about Hay House's free downloads, special offers, giveaways, contests, and more!

 Get exclusive excerpts from our latest releases and videos from *Hay House Present Moments*.

 Our *Digital Products Newsletter* is the perfect way to stay up-to-date on our latest discounted eBooks, featured mobile apps, and Live Online and On Demand events.

 Learn with real benefits! *HayHouseU.com* is your source for the most innovative online courses from the world's leading personal growth experts. Be the first to know about new online courses and to receive exclusive discounts.

 Enjoy uplifting personal stories, how-to articles, and healing advice, along with videos and empowering quotes, within *Heal Your Life*.

 Have an inspirational story to tell and a passion for writing? Sharpen your writing skills with insider tips from *Your Writing Life*.

Sign Up Now!

Get inspired, educate yourself, get a complimentary gift, and share the wisdom!

Visit www.hayhouse.com/newsletters to sign up today!

 HAY HOUSE

 HAYHOUSE RADIO®
radio for your soul®

 HAYHOUSE online learning